GRUMBLE ™

VOLUME III
MEMPHIS & BEYOND
THE INFINITE

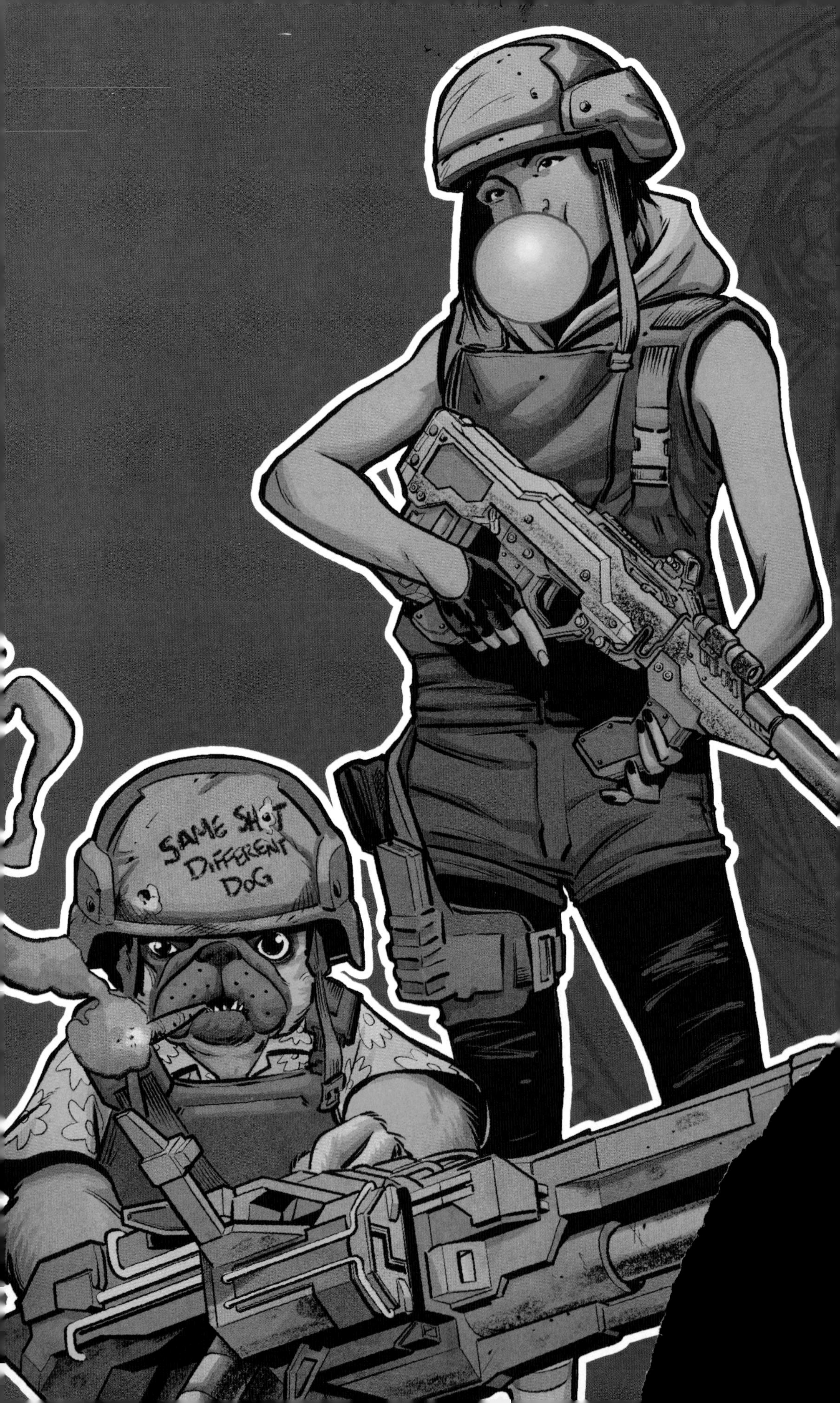
SAME SHIT
DIFFERENT
DOG

ALBATROSS FUNNYBOOKS PRESENTS

GRUMBLE™

VOLUME III
MEMPHIS & BEYOND
THE INFINTE

CREATED BY

RAFER ROBERTS - WRITER   **MIKE NORTON - ARTIST**

MARISSA LOUISE - COLOR ARTIST

CRANK! - LETTERER

ALEJANDRO ARBONA - EDITOR

SERIES COVERS BY
MIKE NORTON & ADDISON DUKE

VOLUME COVER BY
MIKE NORTON & LOOPY DAVE DUNSTAN

This volume collects issues 1-5 and of GRUMBLE: MEMPHIS AND & BEYOND THE INFINITE published by Albatross Funnybooks.

GRUMBLE: MEMPHIS & BEYOND THE INFINITE Published by Albatross Funnybooks, PO Box 60627, Nashville TN 37206. Grumble™&© 2021 Mike Norton and Rafer Roberts. All contents and related characters™&© Mike Norton and Rafer Roberts. All rights reserved. No portion of this product may be reproduced or transmitted, by any form or by any means, without express written permission of Mike Norton and Rafer Roberts. Albatross Funnybooks and the Albatross Funnybooks logo are registered trademarks of Eric Powell. Names, characters, places, and incidents featured in this publication are fictional. Any similarity to persons living or dead, places and incidents is unintended or for satirical purposes.   Printed in Canada.

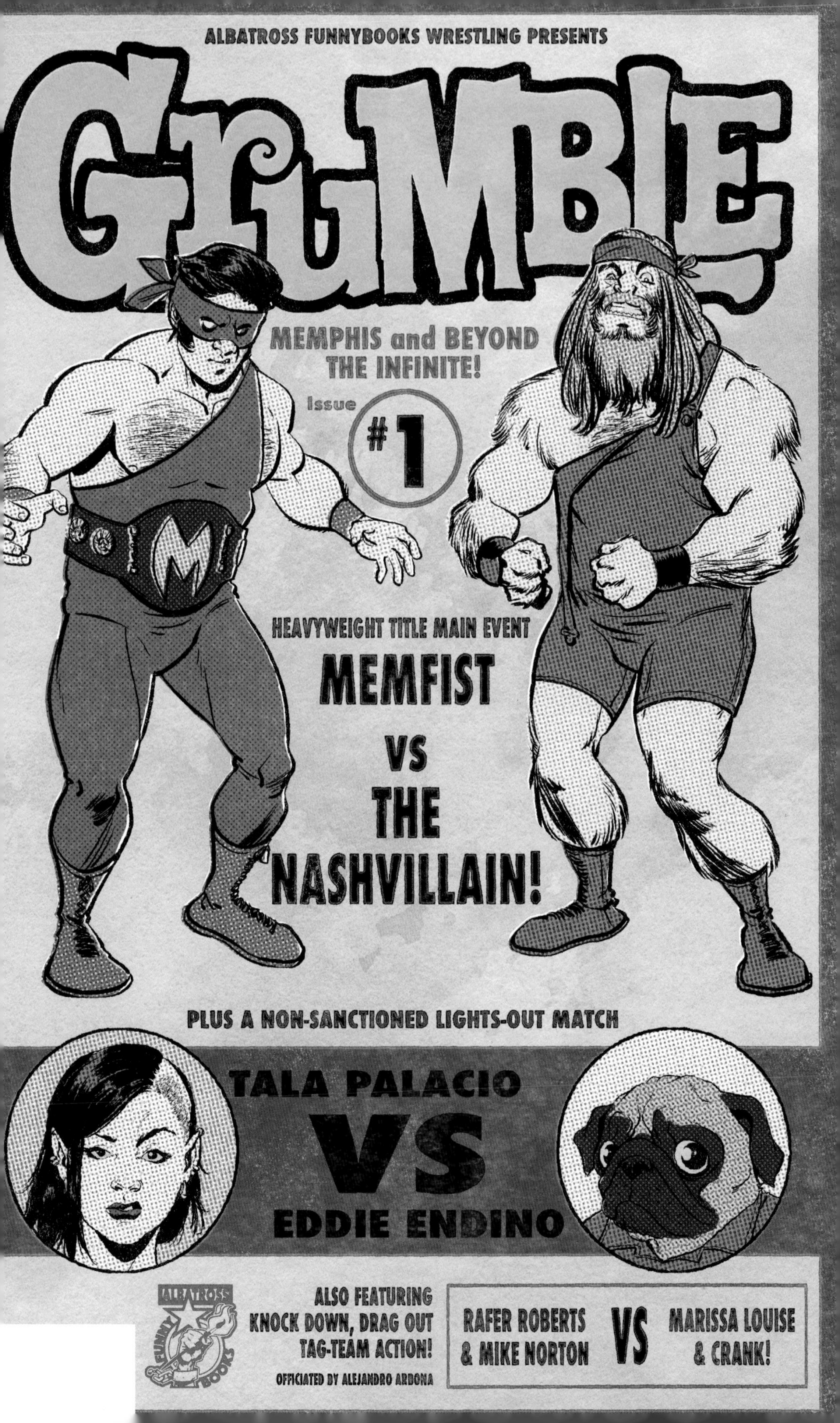
ALBATROSS FUNNYBOOKS WRESTLING PRESENTS
GRUMBLE
MEMPHIS and BEYOND THE INFINITE!
Issue #1
HEAVYWEIGHT TITLE MAIN EVENT
MEMFIST
VS
THE NASHVILLAIN!
PLUS A NON-SANCTIONED LIGHTS-OUT MATCH
TALA PALACIO
VS
EDDIE ENDINO
ALBATROSS FUNNYBOOKS
ALSO FEATURING
KNOCK DOWN, DRAG OUT
TAG-TEAM ACTION!
OFFICIATED BY ALEJANDRO ARDONA
RAFER ROBERTS & MIKE NORTON
VS
MARISSA LOUISE & CRANK!

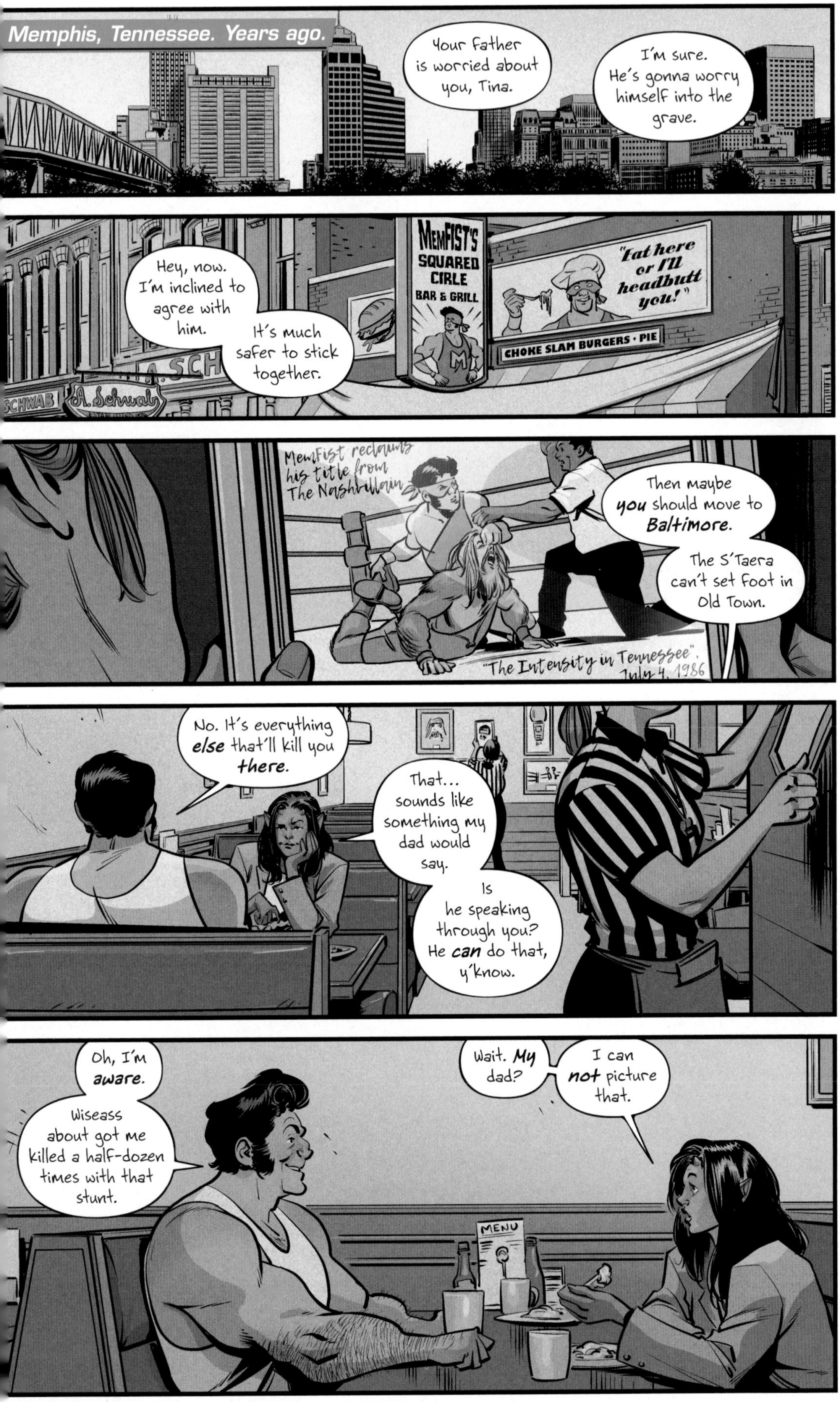
Memphis, Tennessee. Years ago.
Your father is worried about you, Tina.
I'm sure. He's gonna worry himself into the grave.
MEMFIST'S SQUARED CIRLE BAR & GRILL
"Eat here or I'll headbutt you!"
CHOKE SLAM BURGERS · PIE
A. Schwab
SCHWAB
Hey, now. I'm inclined to agree with him.
It's much safer to stick together.
MemFist reclaims his title from The Nashvillain
"The Intensity in Tennessee", July 4, 1986
Then maybe **you** should move to **Baltimore**.
The S'Taera can't set foot in Old Town.
No. It's everything ***else*** that'll kill you ***there***.
That... sounds like something my dad would say.
Is he speaking through you? He **can** do that, y'know.
Oh, I'm **aware**.
Wiseass about got me killed a half-dozen times with that stunt.
Wait. ***My*** dad?
I can ***not*** picture that.
MENU

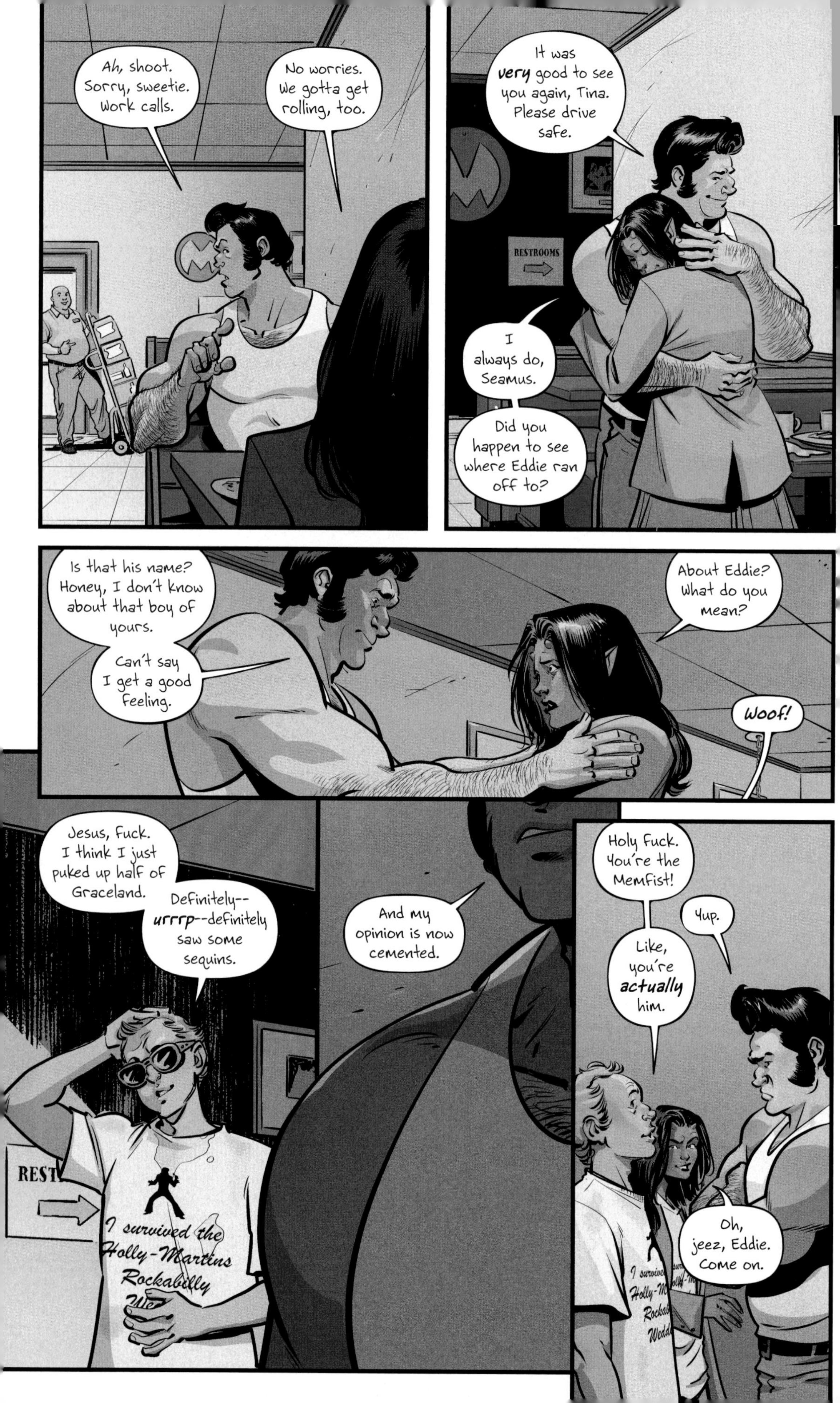

Ah, shoot. Sorry, sweetie. Work calls.
No worries. We gotta get rolling, too.
It was **very** good to see you again, Tina. Please drive safe.
RESTROOMS
I always do, Seamus.
Did you happen to see where Eddie ran off to?
Is that his name? Honey, I don't know about that boy of yours.
Can't say I get a good feeling.
About Eddie? What do you mean?
Woof!
Jesus, fuck. I think I just puked up half of Graceland.
Definitely-- **urrrp**--definitely saw some sequins.
And my opinion is now cemented.
I survived the Holly-Martins Rockabilly
Holy fuck. You're the Memfist!
Yup.
Like, you're **actually** him.
Oh, jeez, Eddie. Come on.

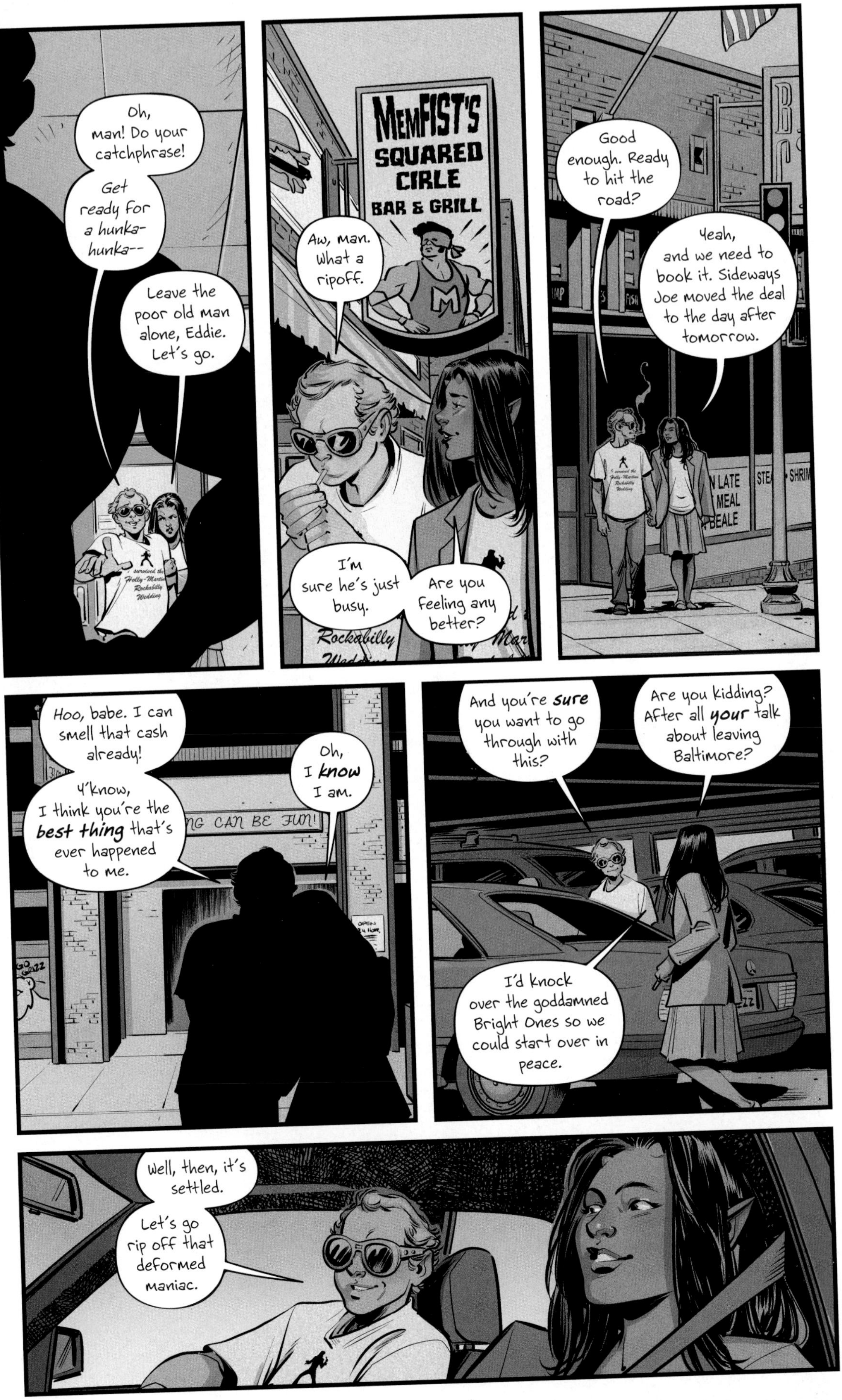
Oh, man! Do your catchphrase!
Get ready for a hunka-hunka--
Leave the poor old man alone, Eddie. Let's go.
I survived the Holly-Martin Rockabilly Wedding
MEMFIST'S SQUARED CIRLE BAR & GRILL
Aw, man. What a ripoff.
I'm sure he's just busy.
Are you feeling any better?
Rockabilly
Good enough. Ready to hit the road?
Yeah, and we need to book it. Sideways Joe moved the deal to the day after tomorrow.
Hoo, babe. I can smell that cash already!
Y'know, I think you're the **best thing** that's ever happened to me.
Oh, I **know** I am.
And you're **sure** you want to go through with this?
Are you kidding? After all **your** talk about leaving Baltimore?
I'd knock over the goddamned Bright Ones so we could start over in peace.
Well, then, it's settled.
Let's go rip off that deformed maniac.

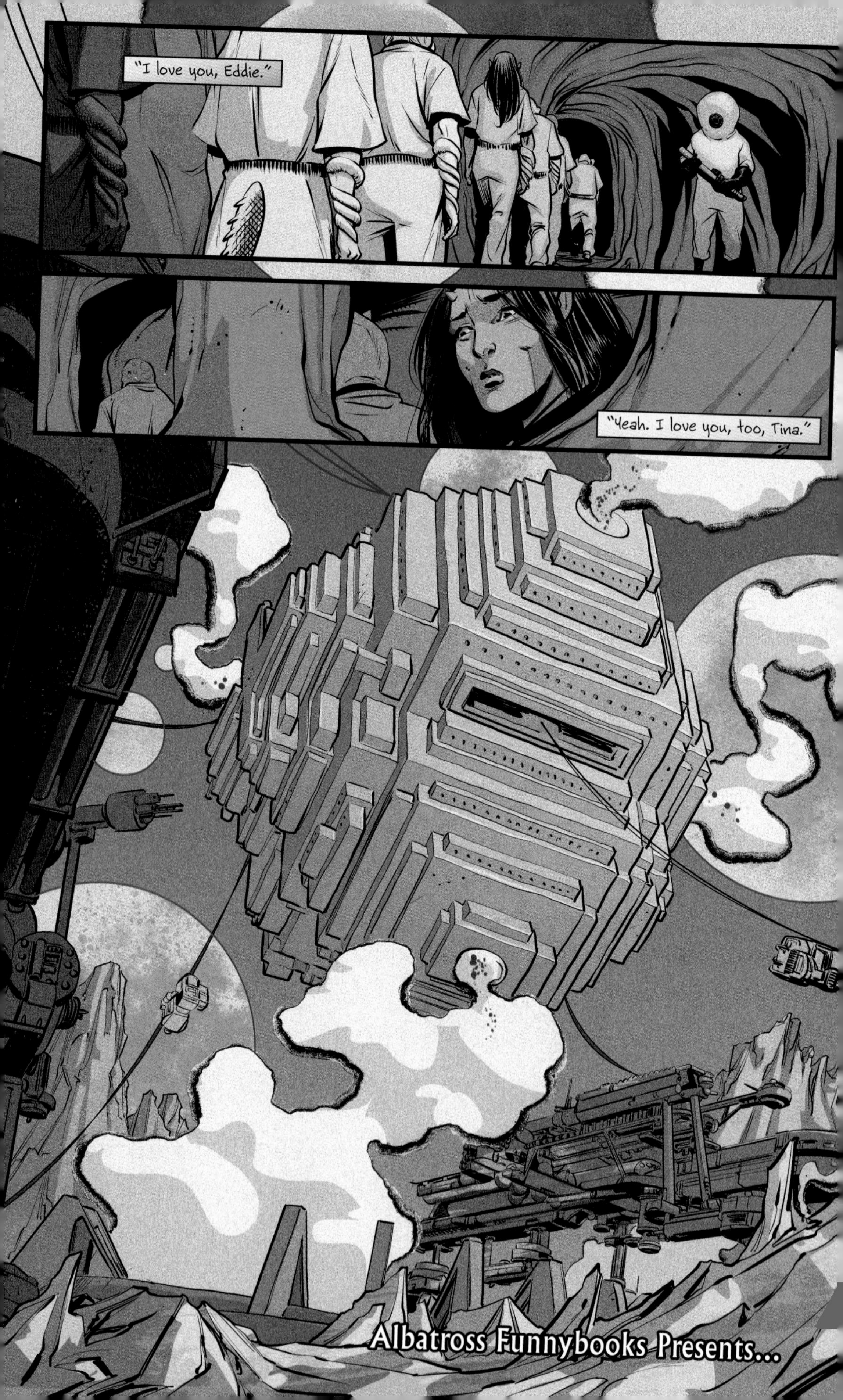

"I love you, Eddie."
"Yeah. I love you, too, Tina."
Albatross Funnybooks Presents...

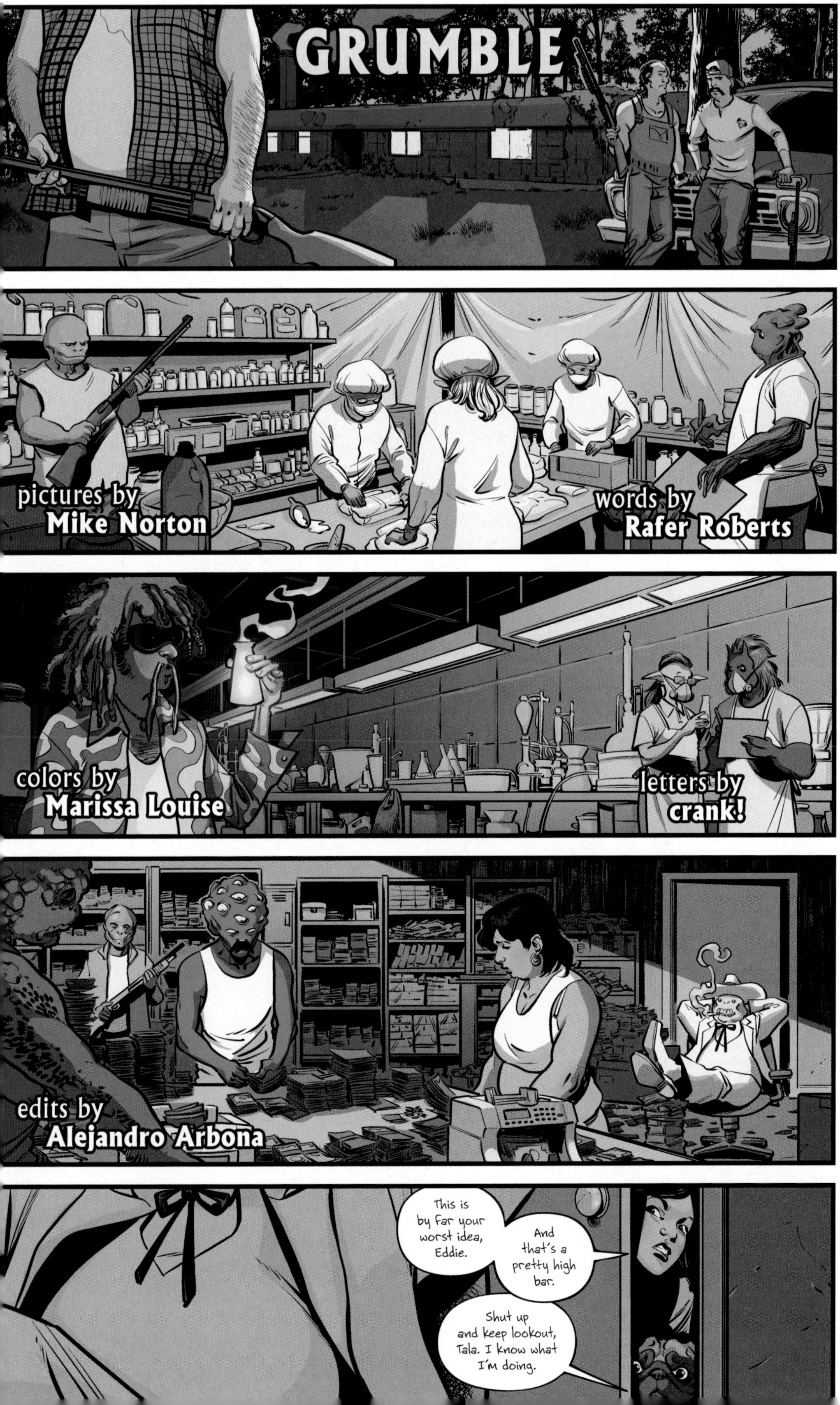
GRUMBLE
pictures by Mike Norton
words by Rafer Roberts
colors by Marissa Louise
letters by crank!
edits by Alejandro Arbona
This is by far your worst idea, Eddie.
And that's a pretty high bar.
Shut up and keep lookout, Tala. I know what I'm doing.

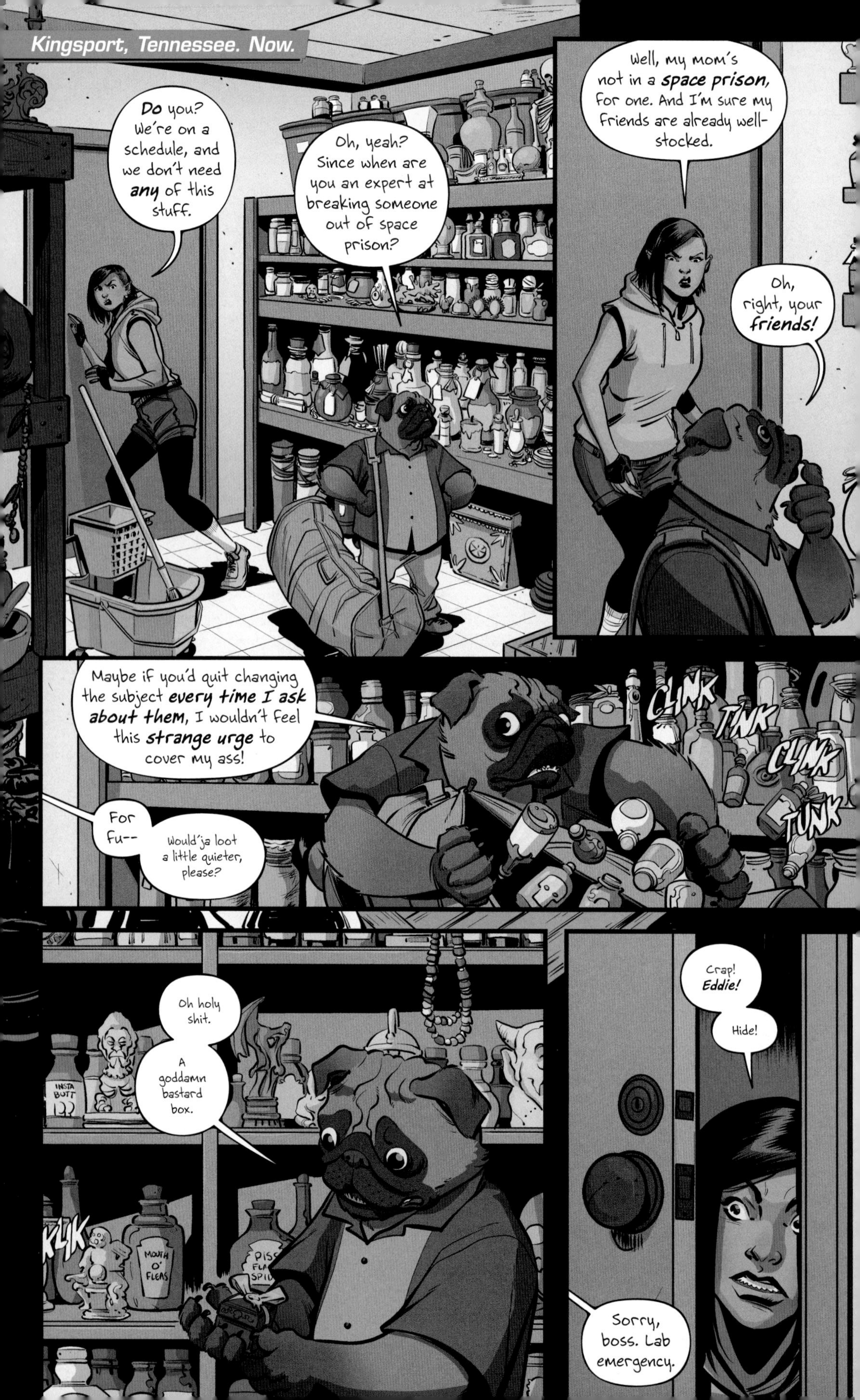

Kingsport, Tennessee. Now.
Do you? We're on a schedule, and we don't need any of this stuff.
Oh, yeah? Since when are you an expert at breaking someone out of space prison?
Well, my mom's not in a space prison, for one. And I'm sure my friends are already well-stocked.
Oh, right, your friends!
Maybe if you'd quit changing the subject every time I ask about them, I wouldn't feel this strange urge to cover my ass!
CLINK
TINK
CLINK
TUNK
For Fu--
Would'ja loot a little quieter, please?
Oh holy shit.
A goddamn bastard box.
INSTA BUTT
KLYK
MOUTH O' FLEAS
Crap! Eddie!
Hide!
Sorry, boss. Lab emergency.

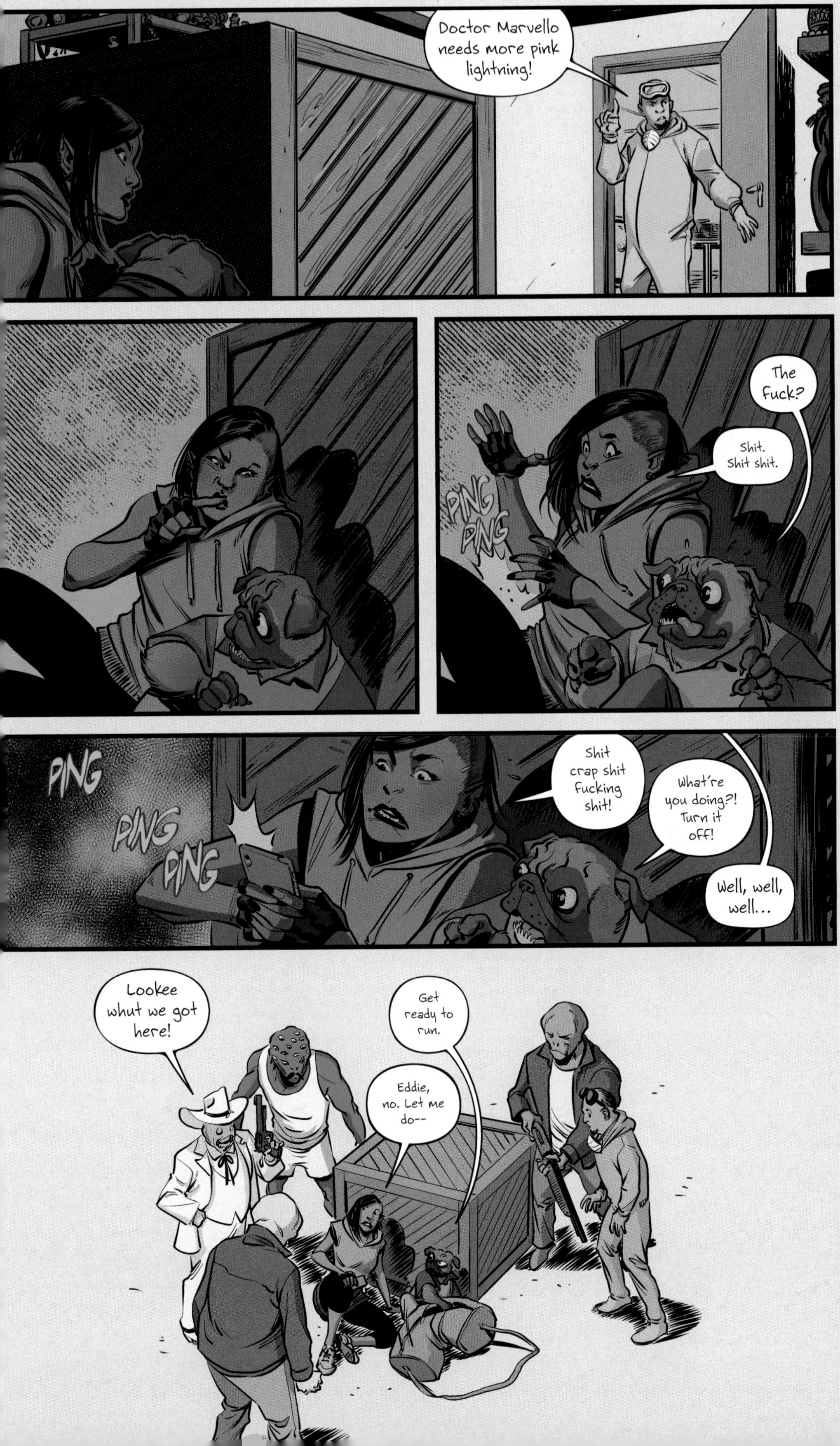

Doctor Marvello needs more pink lightning!
The Fuck?
Shit. Shit shit.
PING PING
PING PING PING
Shit crap shit Fucking shit!
What're you doing?! Turn it off!
Well, well, well...
Lookee whut we got here!
Get ready to run.
Eddie, no. Let me do--

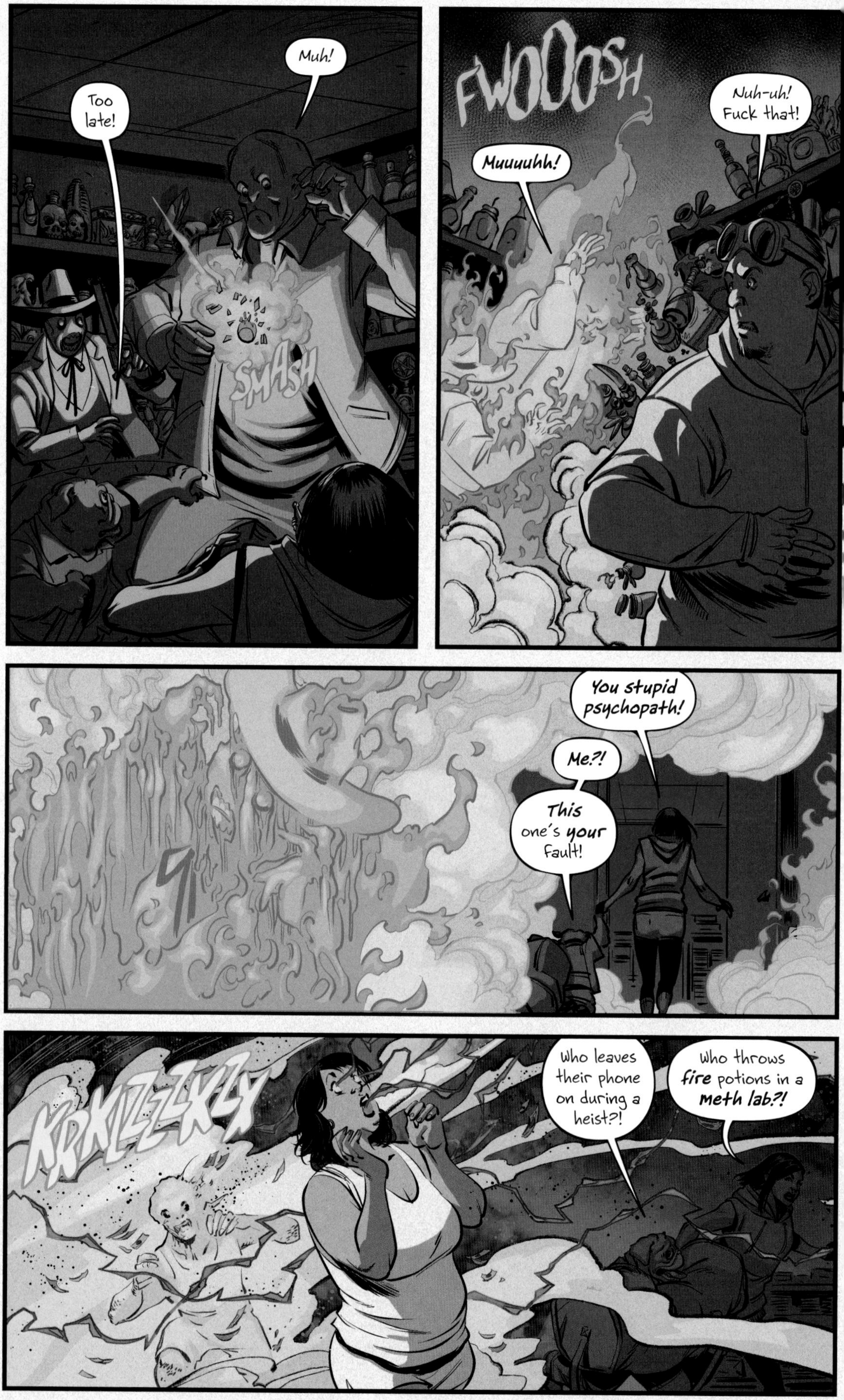

Muh!
Too late!
SMASH
FWOOOSH
Nuh-uh! Fuck that!
Muuuuhh!
You stupid psychopath!
Me?!
This one's your fault!
KRKLZZKLZ
Who leaves their phone on during a heist?!
Who throws fire potions in a meth lab?!

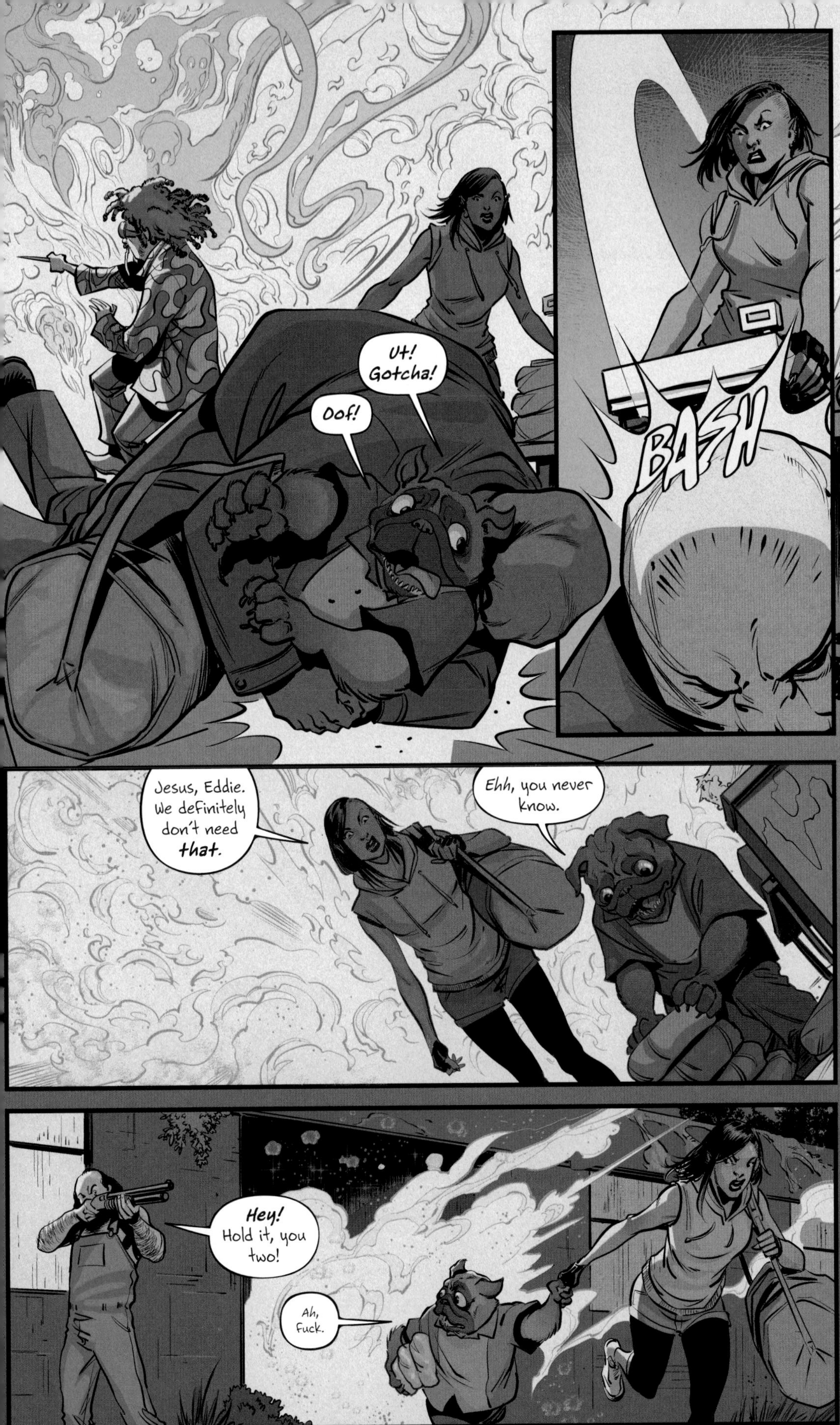

Ut! Gotcha!
Oof!
BASH
Jesus, Eddie. We definitely don't need **that**.
Ehh, you never know.
Hey! Hold it, you two!
Ah, Fuck.

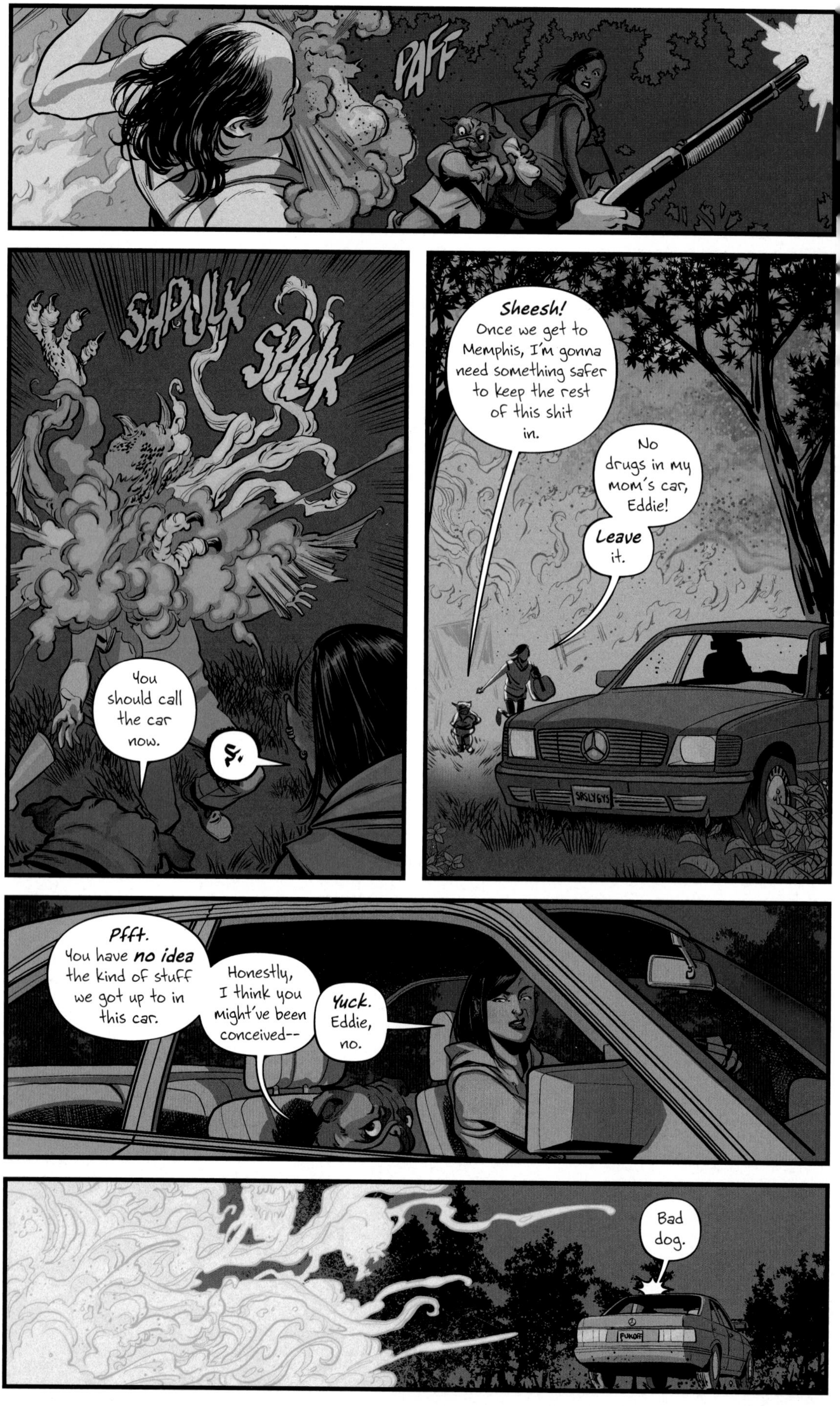
PAFF
SHPLUK
SPLUK
You should call the car now.
Sheesh! Once we get to Memphis, I'm gonna need something safer to keep the rest of this shit in.
No drugs in my mom's car, Eddie!
Leave it.
SRSLY6YS
Pfft. You have no idea the kind of stuff we got up to in this car.
Honestly, I think you might've been conceived--
Yuck. Eddie, no.
Bad dog.
FUKOFF

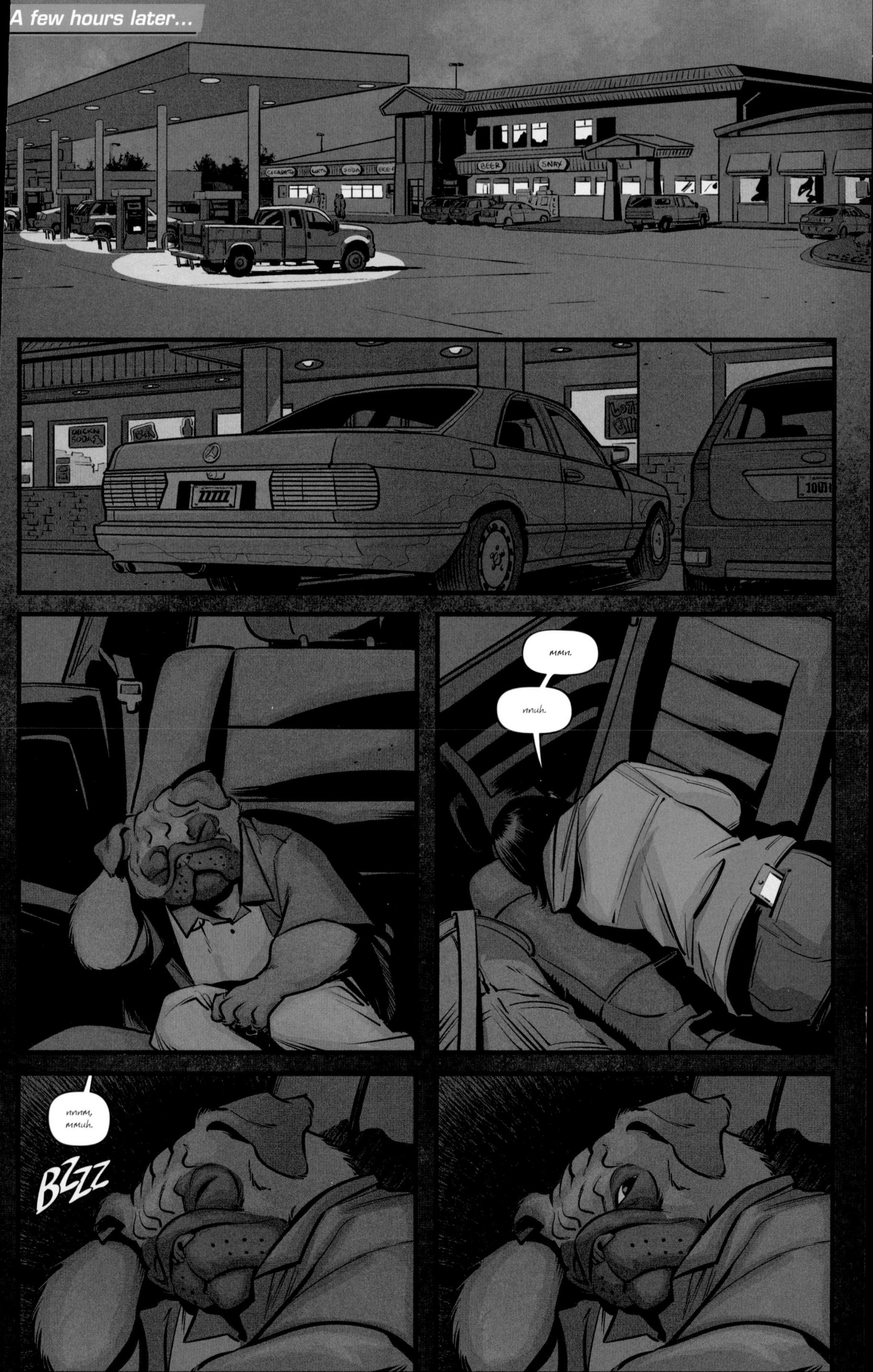
A few hours later...
BEER
SNAX
mmn.
nnuh.
nnnm, mmuh.
BZZZ

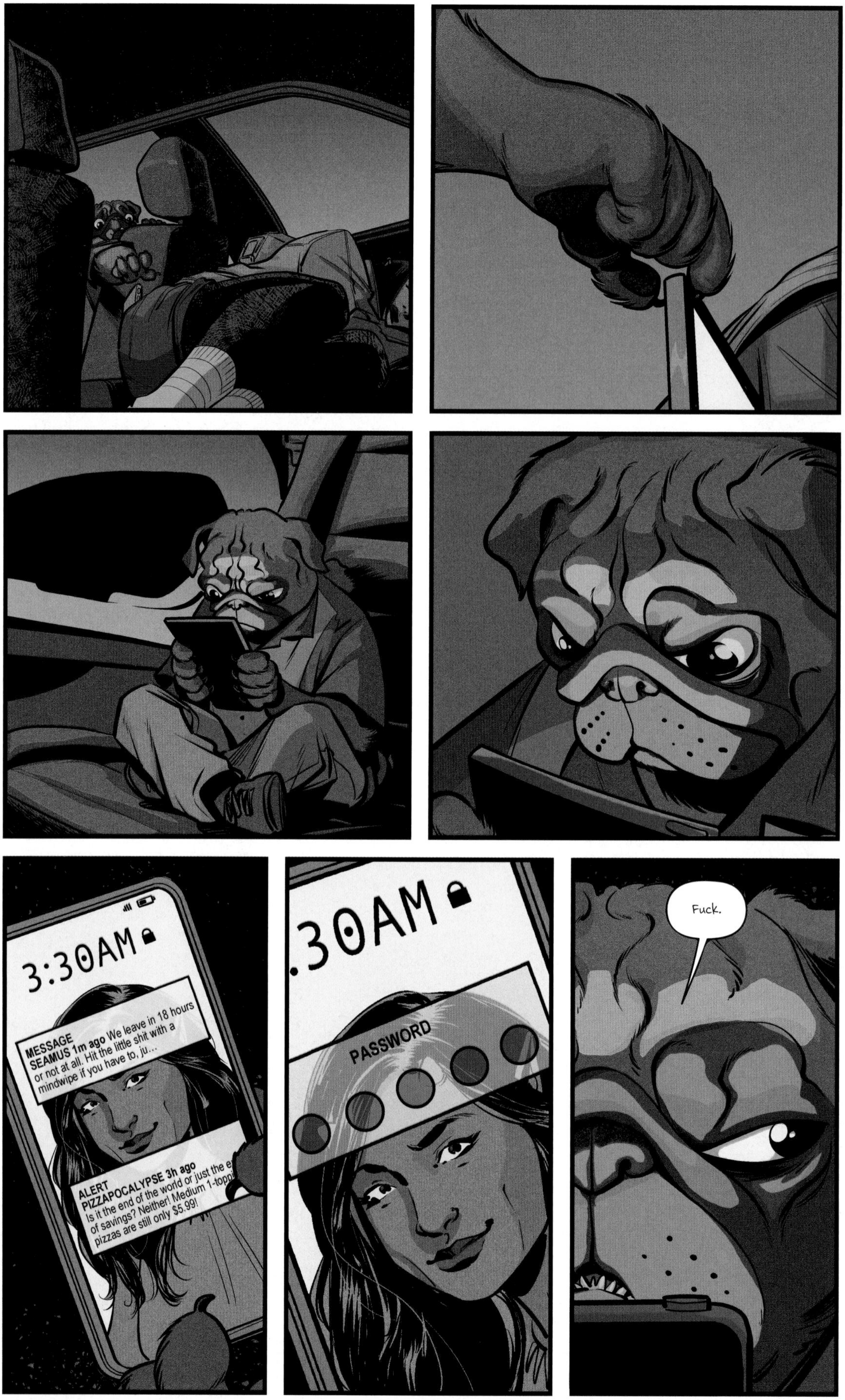
3:30AM
MESSAGE
SEAMUS 1m ago We leave in 18 hours or not at all. Hit the little shit with a mindwipe if you have to, ju...
ALERT
PIZZAPOCALYPSE 3h ago
Is it the end of the world or just the e of savings? Neither! Medium 1-toppi pizzas are still only $5.99!
.30AM
PASSWORD
Fuck.

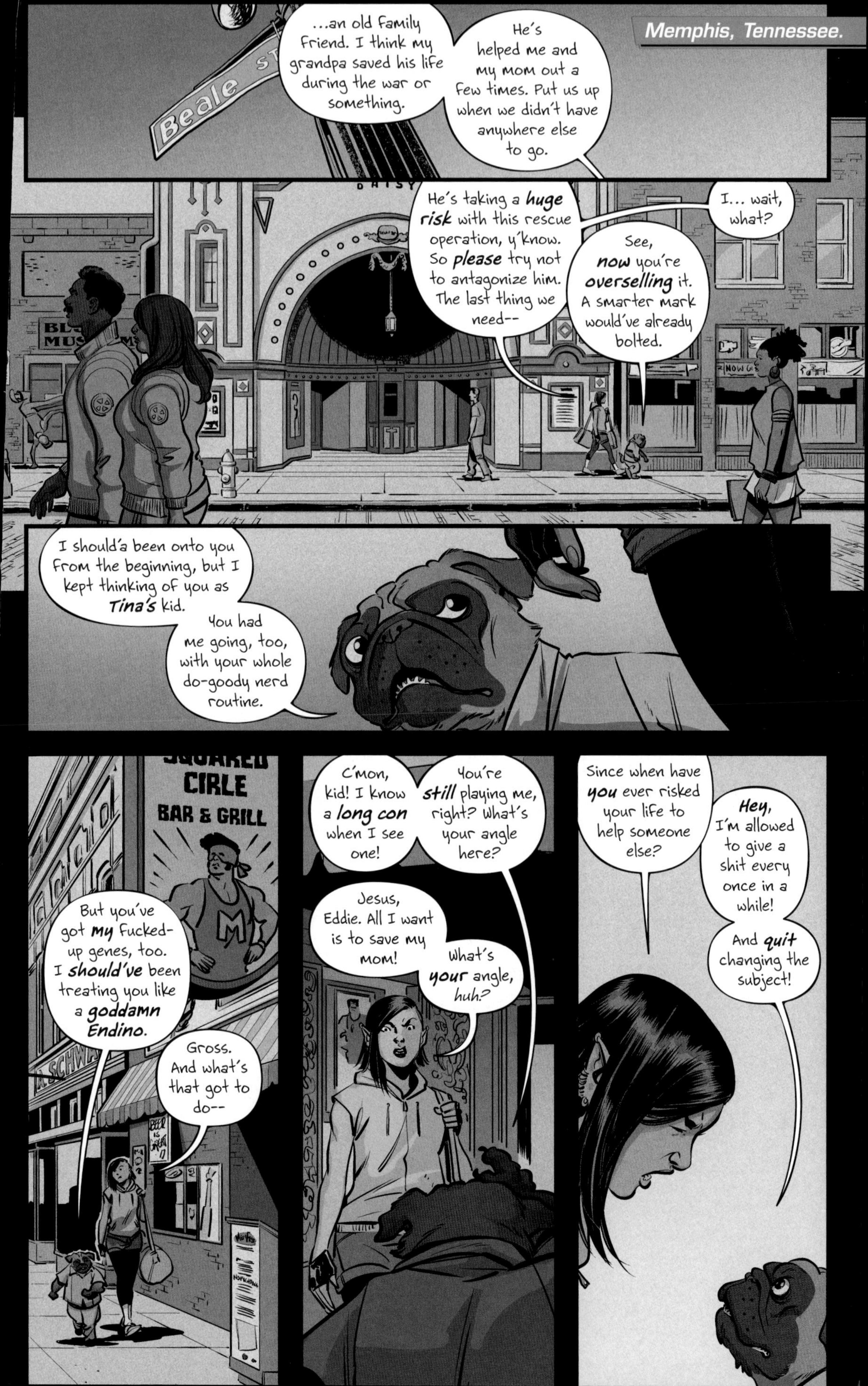
Memphis, Tennessee.
Beale St
...an old family friend. I think my grandpa saved his life during the war or something.
He's helped me and my mom out a few times. Put us up when we didn't have anywhere else to go.
He's taking a huge risk with this rescue operation, y'know. So please try not to antagonize him. The last thing we need--
I... wait, what?
See, now you're overselling it. A smarter mark would've already bolted.
I should'a been onto you from the beginning, but I kept thinking of you as Tina's kid.
You had me going, too, with your whole do-goody nerd routine.
CIRLE
BAR & GRILL
But you've got my fucked-up genes, too. I should've been treating you like a goddamn Endino.
Gross. And what's that got to do--
C'mon, kid! I know a long con when I see one!
You're still playing me, right? What's your angle here?
Jesus, Eddie. All I want is to save my mom!
What's your angle, huh?
Since when have you ever risked your life to help someone else?
Hey, I'm allowed to give a shit every once in a while!
And quit changing the subject!

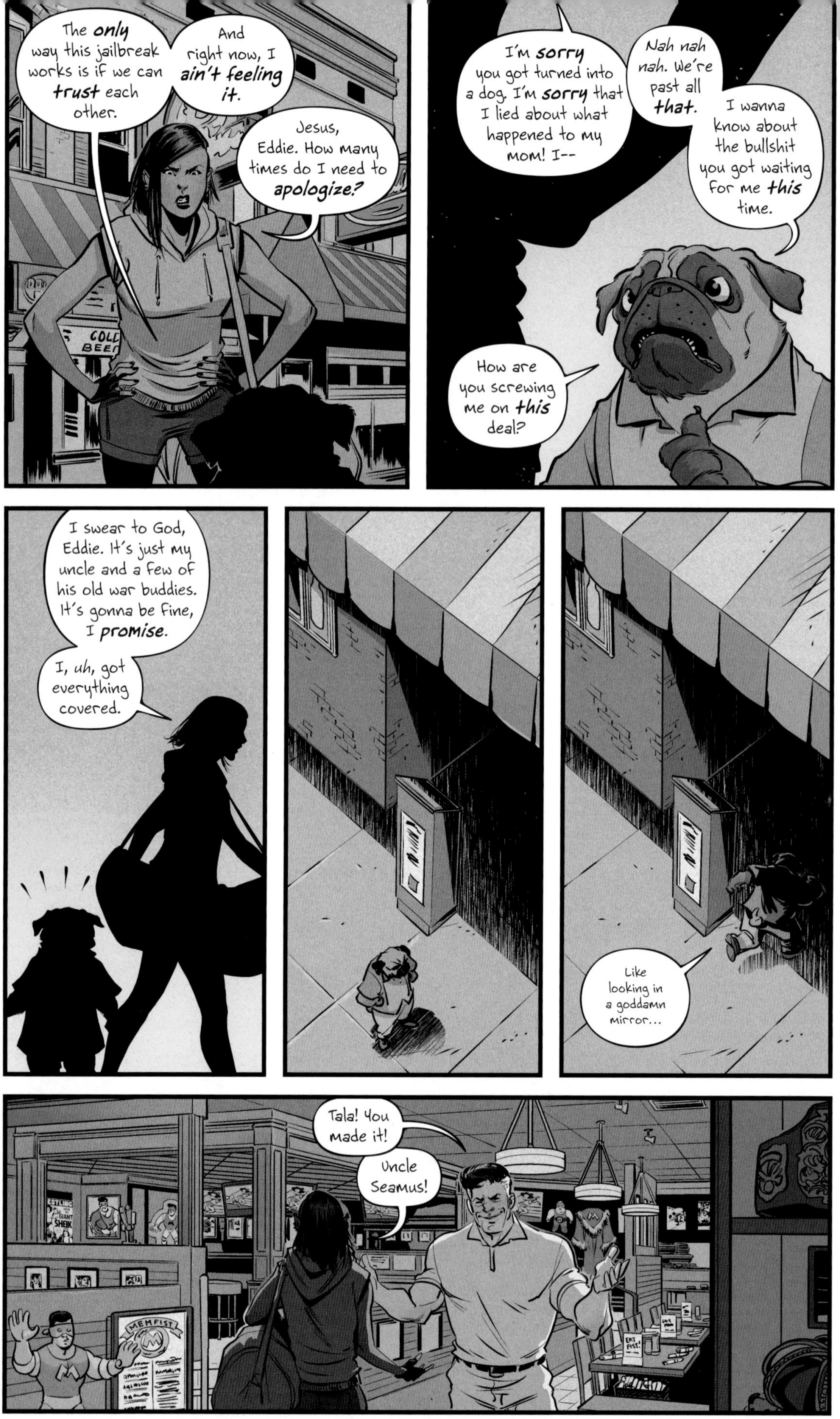
The **only** way this jailbreak works is if we can **trust** each other.
And right now, I **ain't feeling it.**
Jesus, Eddie. How many times do I need to **apologize?**
I'm **sorry** you got turned into a dog. I'm **sorry** that I lied about what happened to my mom! I--
Nah nah nah. We're past all **that.**
I wanna know about the bullshit you got waiting for me **this** time.
How are you screwing me on **this** deal?
I swear to God, Eddie. It's just my uncle and a few of his old war buddies. It's gonna be fine, I **promise.**
I, uh, got everything covered.
Like looking in a goddamn mirror...
Tala! You made it!
Uncle Seamus!

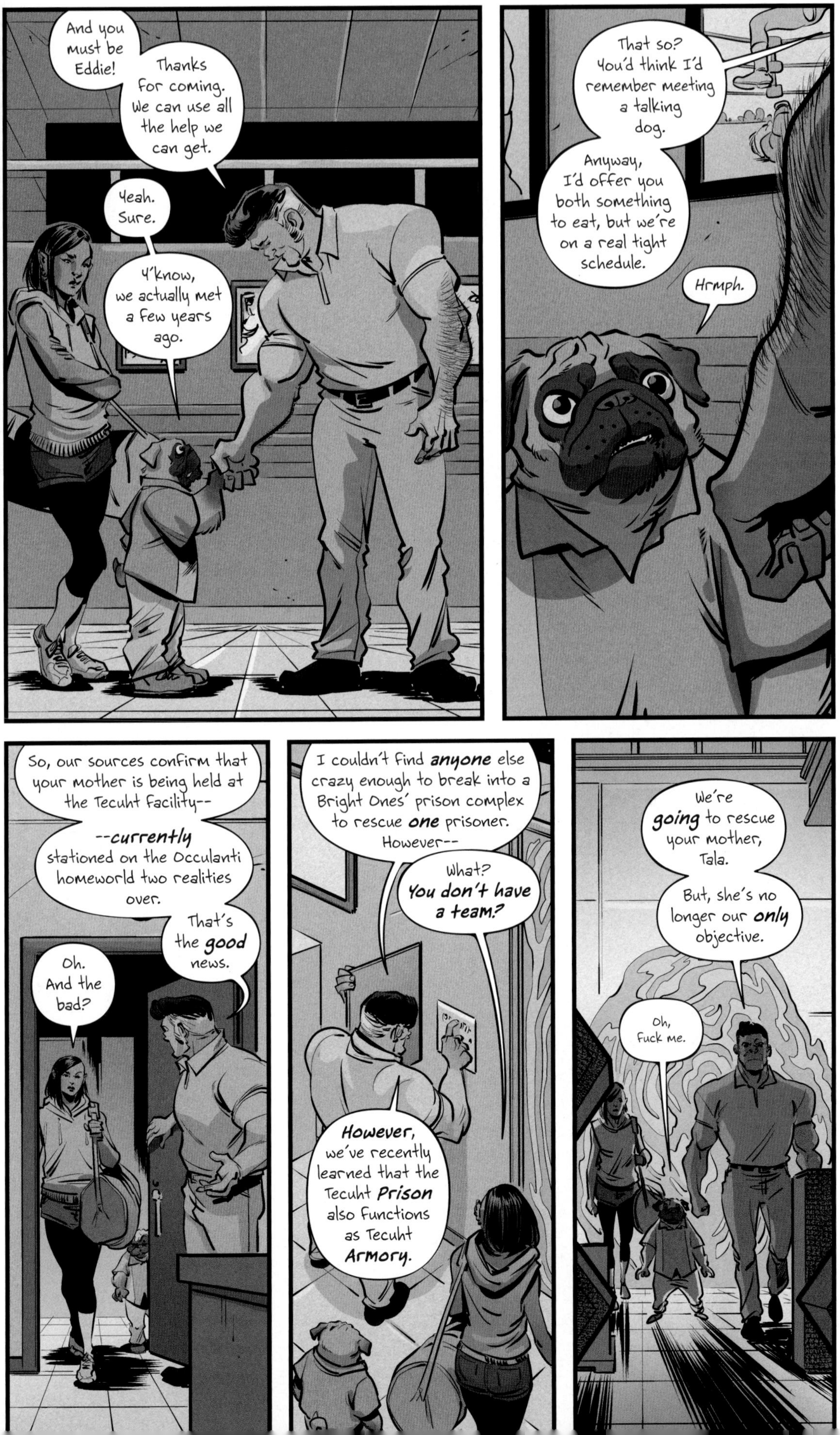
And you must be Eddie!
Thanks for coming. We can use all the help we can get.
Yeah. Sure.
Y'know, we actually met a few years ago.
That so? You'd think I'd remember meeting a talking dog.
Anyway, I'd offer you both something to eat, but we're on a real tight schedule.
Hrmph.
So, our sources confirm that your mother is being held at the Tecuht Facility--
--currently stationed on the Occulanti homeworld two realities over.
That's the good news.
Oh. And the bad?
I couldn't find anyone else crazy enough to break into a Bright Ones' prison complex to rescue one prisoner. However--
What? You don't have a team?
However, we've recently learned that the Tecuht Prison also functions as Tecuht Armory.
We're going to rescue your mother, Tala.
But, she's no longer our only objective.
Oh, fuck me.

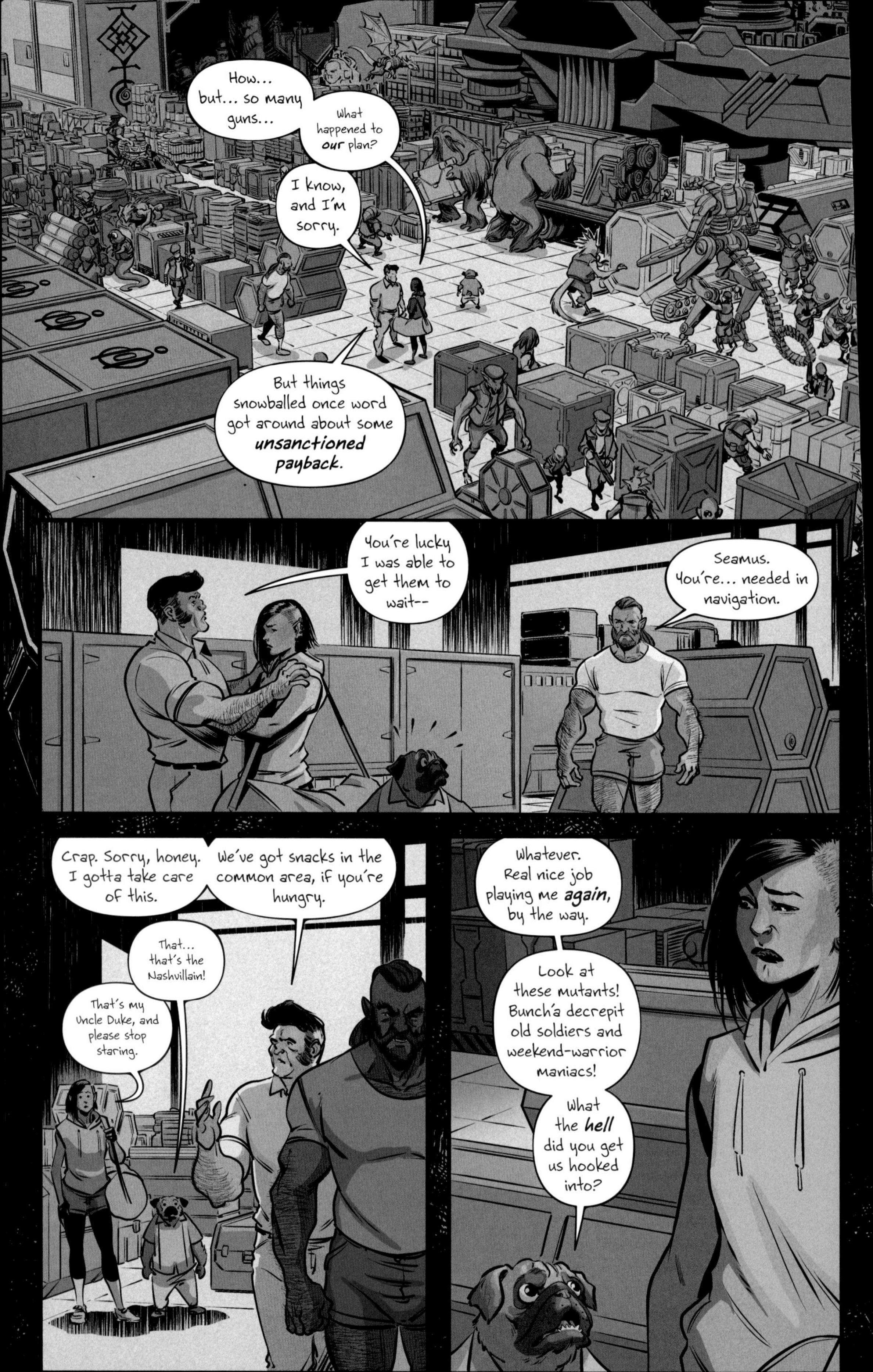
How... but... so many guns...
What happened to our plan?
I know, and I'm sorry.
But things snowballed once word got around about some ***unsanctioned payback***.
You're lucky I was able to get them to wait--
Seamus. You're... needed in navigation.
Crap. Sorry, honey. I gotta take care of this.
We've got snacks in the common area, if you're hungry.
That... that's the Nashvillain!
That's my Uncle Duke, and please stop staring.
Whatever. Real nice job playing me **again**, by the way.
Look at these mutants! Bunch'a decrepit old soldiers and weekend-warrior maniacs!
What the ***hell*** did you get us hooked into?

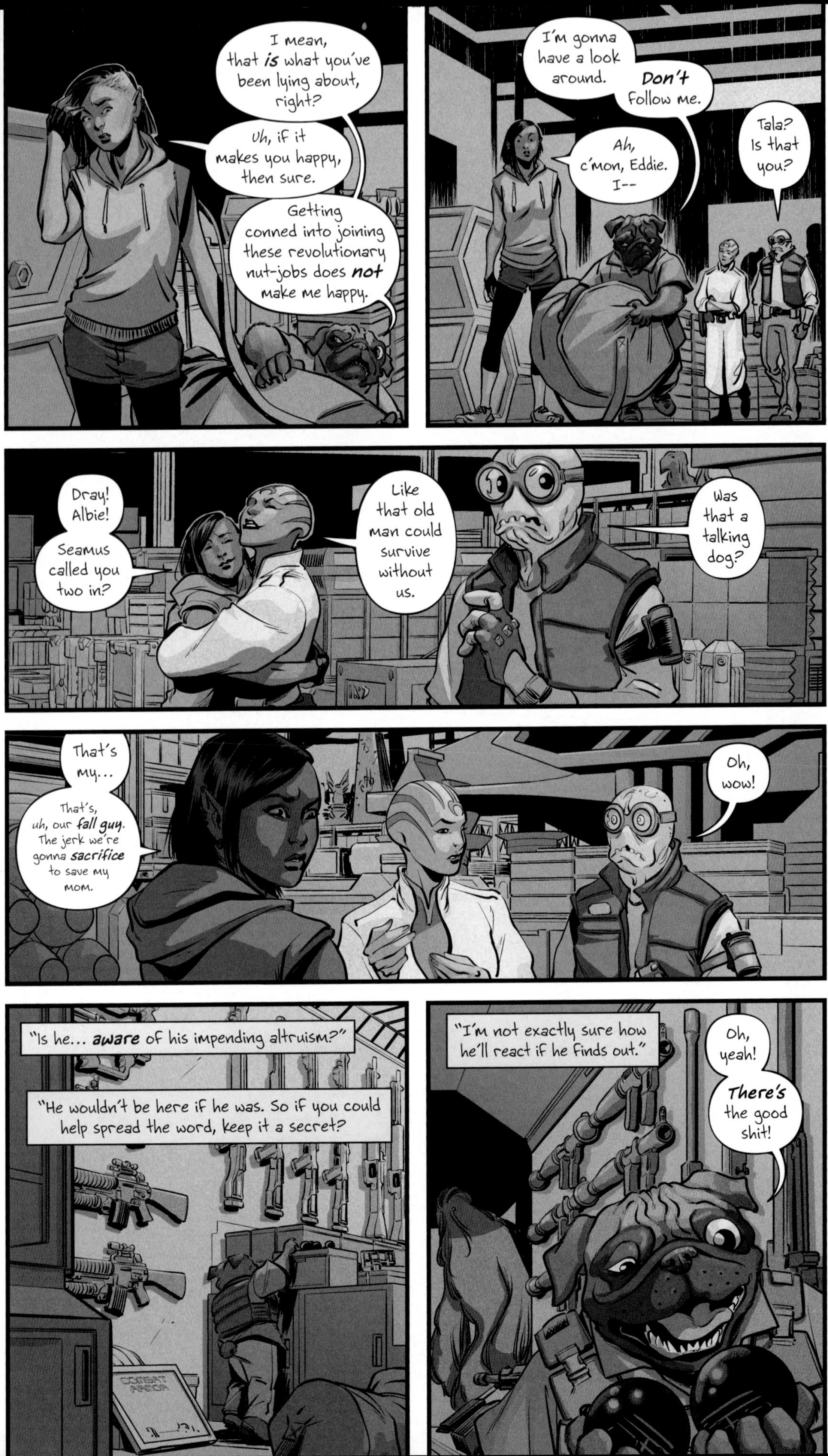
I mean, that *is* what you've been lying about, right?
Uh, if it makes you happy, then sure.
Getting conned into joining these revolutionary nut-jobs does **not** make me happy.
I'm gonna have a look around. **Don't** follow me.
Ah, c'mon, Eddie. I--
Tala? Is that you?
Dray! Albie!
Seamus called you two in?
Like that old man could survive without us.
Was that a talking dog?
That's my...
That's, uh, our **fall guy**. The jerk we're gonna **sacrifice** to save my mom.
Oh, wow!
"Is he... **aware** of his impending altruism?"
"He wouldn't be here if he was. So if you could help spread the word, keep it a secret?
"I'm not exactly sure how he'll react if he finds out."
Oh, yeah!
There's the good shit!

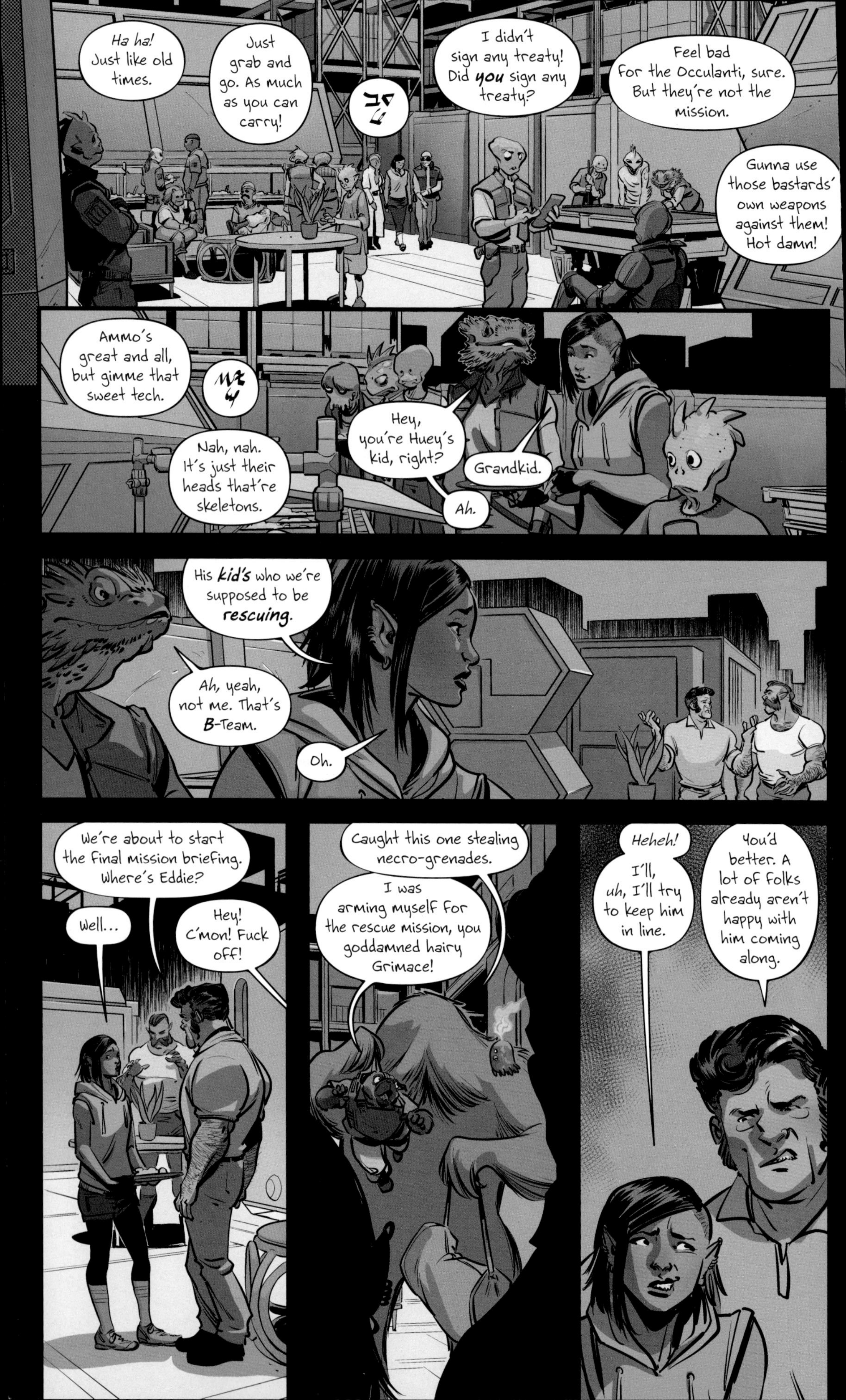
Ha ha! Just like old times.
Just grab and go. As much as you can carry!
I didn't sign any treaty! Did you sign any treaty?
Feel bad for the Occulanti, sure. But they're not the mission.
Gunna use those bastards' own weapons against them! Hot damn!
Ammo's great and all, but gimme that sweet tech.
Nah, nah. It's just their heads that're skeletons.
Hey, you're Huey's kid, right?
Grandkid.
Ah.
His kid's who we're supposed to be rescuing.
Ah, yeah, not me. That's B-Team.
Oh.
We're about to start the final mission briefing. Where's Eddie?
Well...
Hey! C'mon! Fuck off!
Caught this one stealing necro-grenades.
I was arming myself for the rescue mission, you goddamned hairy Grimace!
Heheh!
I'll, uh, I'll try to keep him in line.
You'd better. A lot of folks already aren't happy with him coming along.

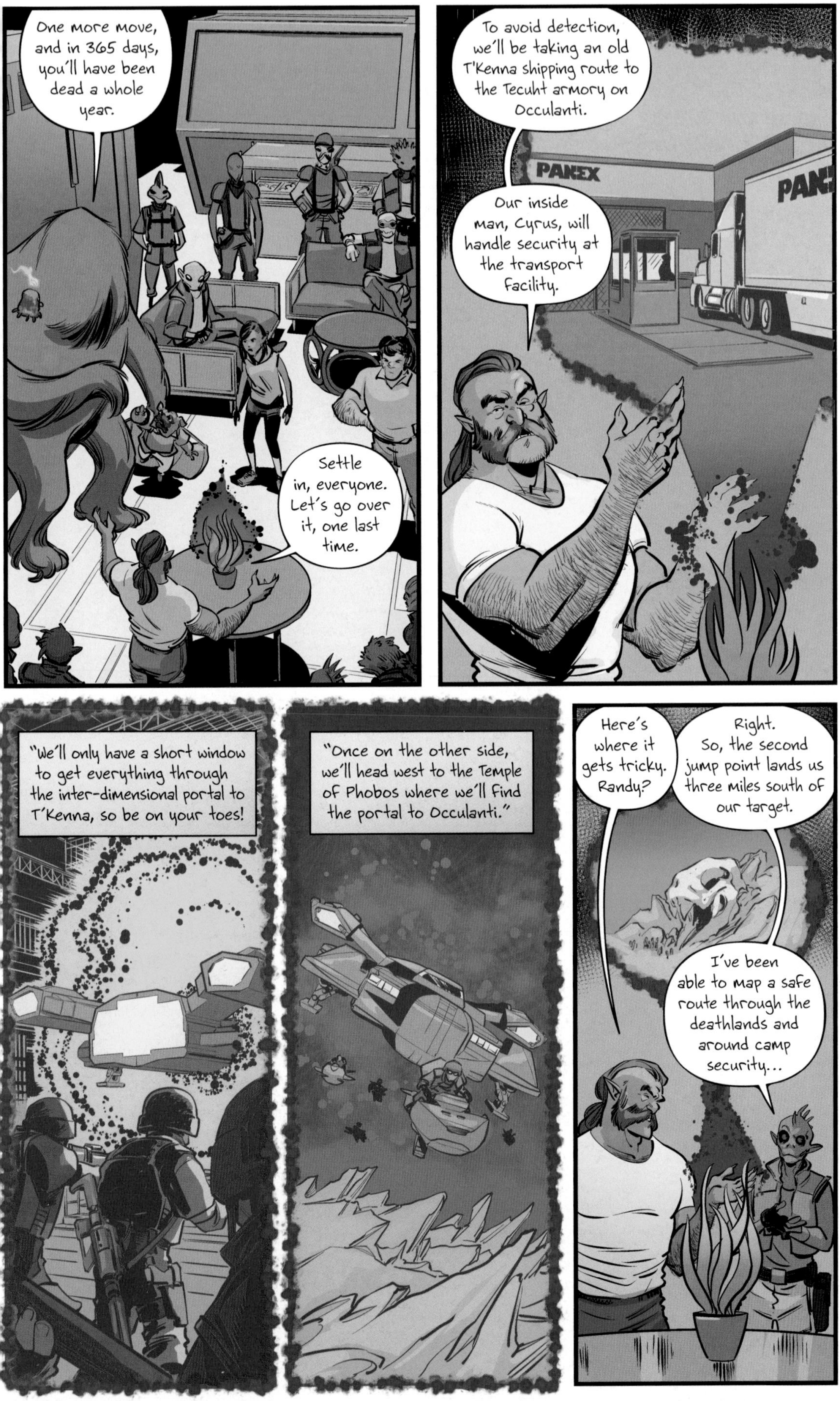
One more move, and in 365 days, you'll have been dead a whole year.
Settle in, everyone. Let's go over it, one last time.
To avoid detection, we'll be taking an old T'Kenna shipping route to the Tecuht armory on Occulanti.
PANEX
Our inside man, Cyrus, will handle security at the transport facility.
"We'll only have a short window to get everything through the inter-dimensional portal to T'Kenna, so be on your toes!
"Once on the other side, we'll head west to the Temple of Phobos where we'll find the portal to Occulanti."
Here's where it gets tricky. Randy?
Right. So, the second jump point lands us three miles south of our target.
I've been able to map a safe route through the deathlands and around camp security...

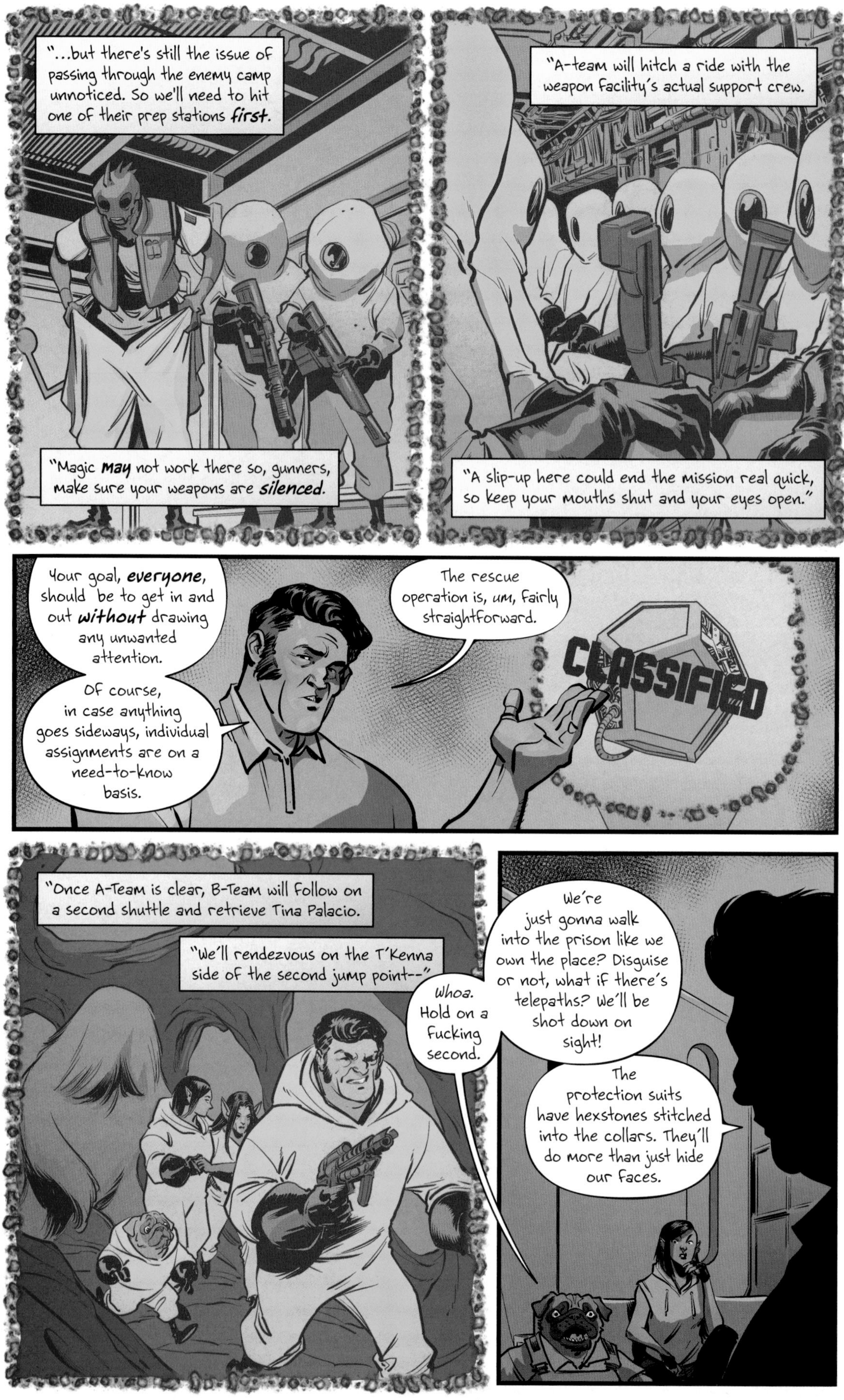
"...but there's still the issue of passing through the enemy camp unnoticed. So we'll need to hit one of their prep stations first.
"Magic may not work there so, gunners, make sure your weapons are silenced.
"A-team will hitch a ride with the weapon facility's actual support crew.
"A slip-up here could end the mission real quick, so keep your mouths shut and your eyes open."
Your goal, everyone, should be to get in and out without drawing any unwanted attention.
Of course, in case anything goes sideways, individual assignments are on a need-to-know basis.
The rescue operation is, um, fairly straightforward.
CLASSIFIED
"Once A-Team is clear, B-Team will follow on a second shuttle and retrieve Tina Palacio.
"We'll rendezvous on the T'Kenna side of the second jump point--"
Whoa. Hold on a fucking second.
We're just gonna walk into the prison like we own the place? Disguise or not, what if there's telepaths? We'll be shot down on sight!
The protection suits have hexstones stitched into the collars. They'll do more than just hide our faces.

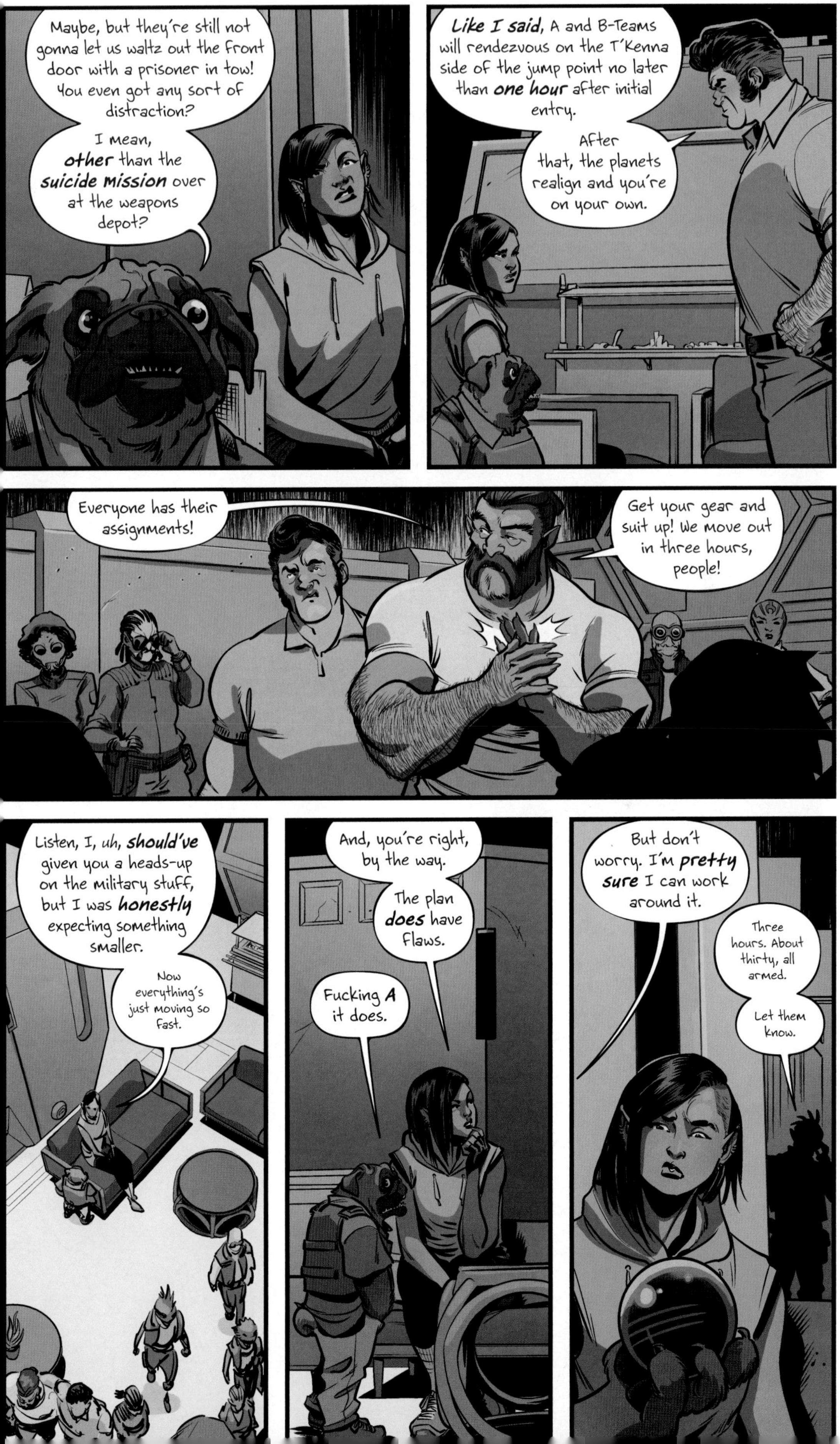
Maybe, but they're still not gonna let us waltz out the front door with a prisoner in tow! You even got any sort of distraction?
I mean, **other** than the **suicide mission** over at the weapons depot?
Like I said, A and B-Teams will rendezvous on the T'Kenna side of the jump point no later than **one hour** after initial entry.
After that, the planets realign and you're on your own.
Everyone has their assignments!
Get your gear and suit up! We move out in three hours, people!
Listen, I, uh, **should've** given you a heads-up on the military stuff, but I was **honestly** expecting something smaller.
Now everything's just moving so fast.
And, you're right, by the way.
The plan **does** have flaws.
Fucking **A** it does.
But don't worry. I'm **pretty sure** I can work around it.
Three hours. About thirty, all armed.
Let them know.

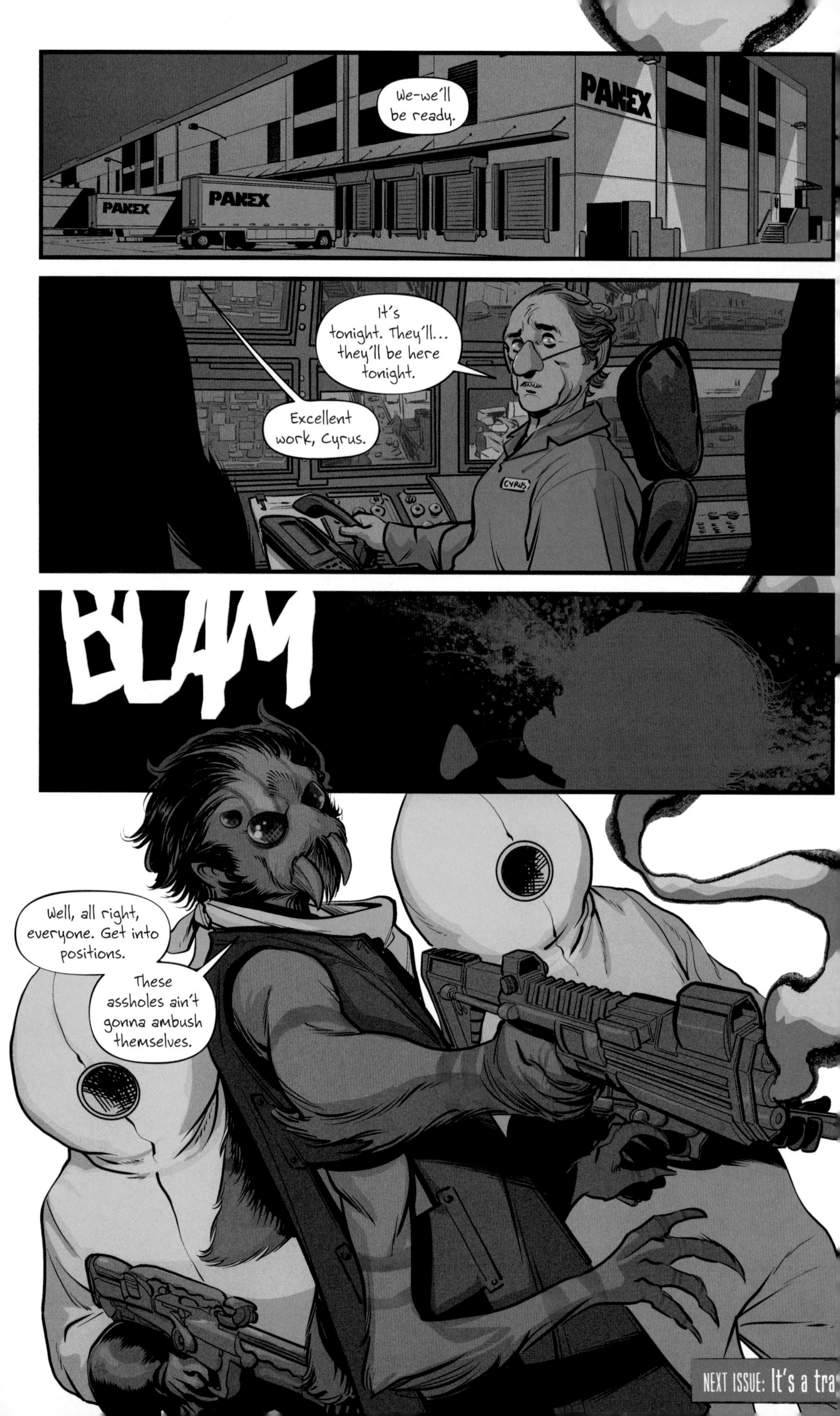
We-we'll be ready.
PANEX
PANEX
PANEX
It's tonight. They'll... they'll be here tonight.
Excellent work, Cyrus.
CYRUS
BLAM
Well, all right, everyone. Get into positions.
These assholes ain't gonna ambush themselves.
NEXT ISSUE: It's a tra

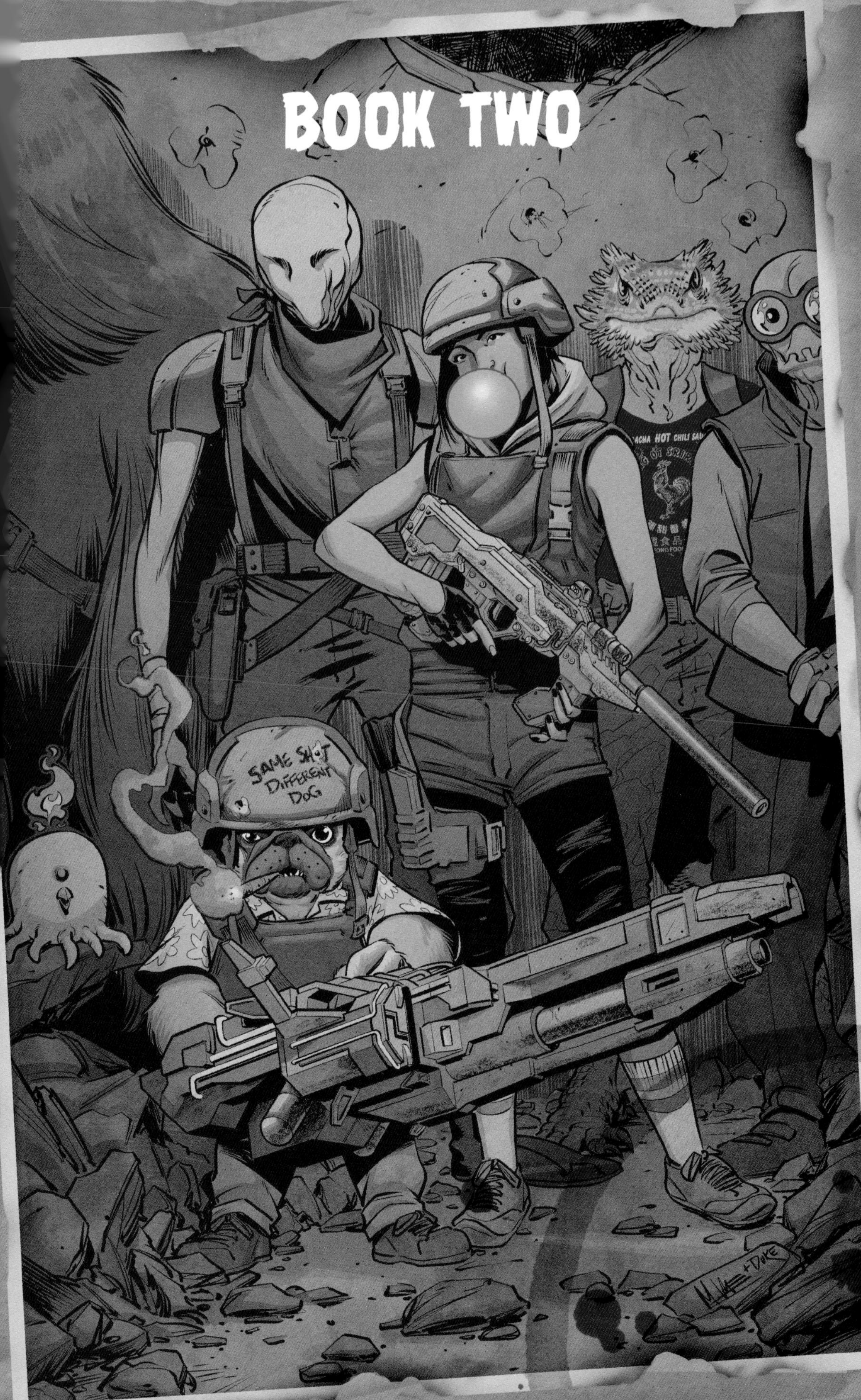
BOOK TWO
SAME SH T
DIFFERENT
DOG

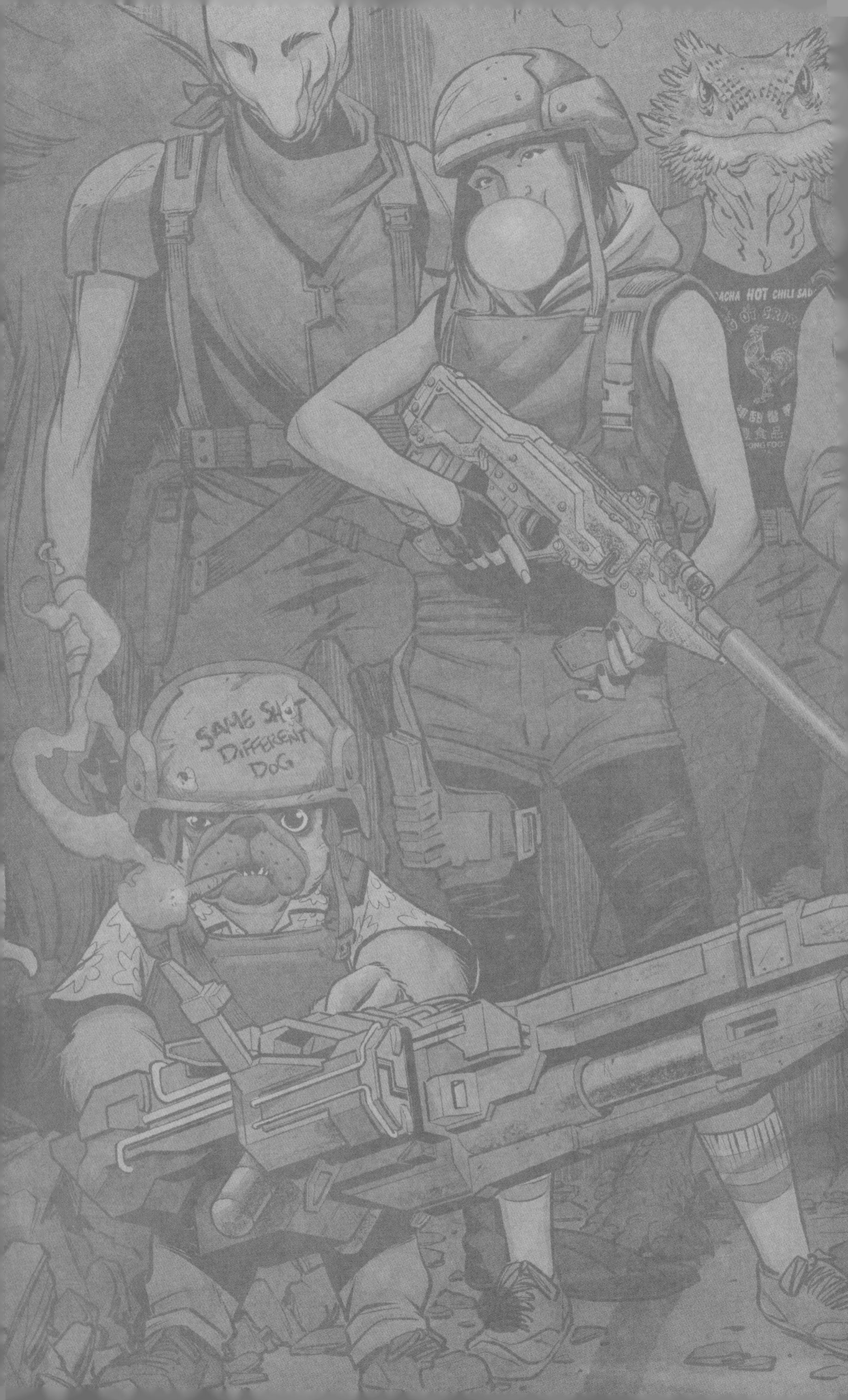
CACHA HOT CHILI SAU
SAME SH T
DIFFERENT
DOG

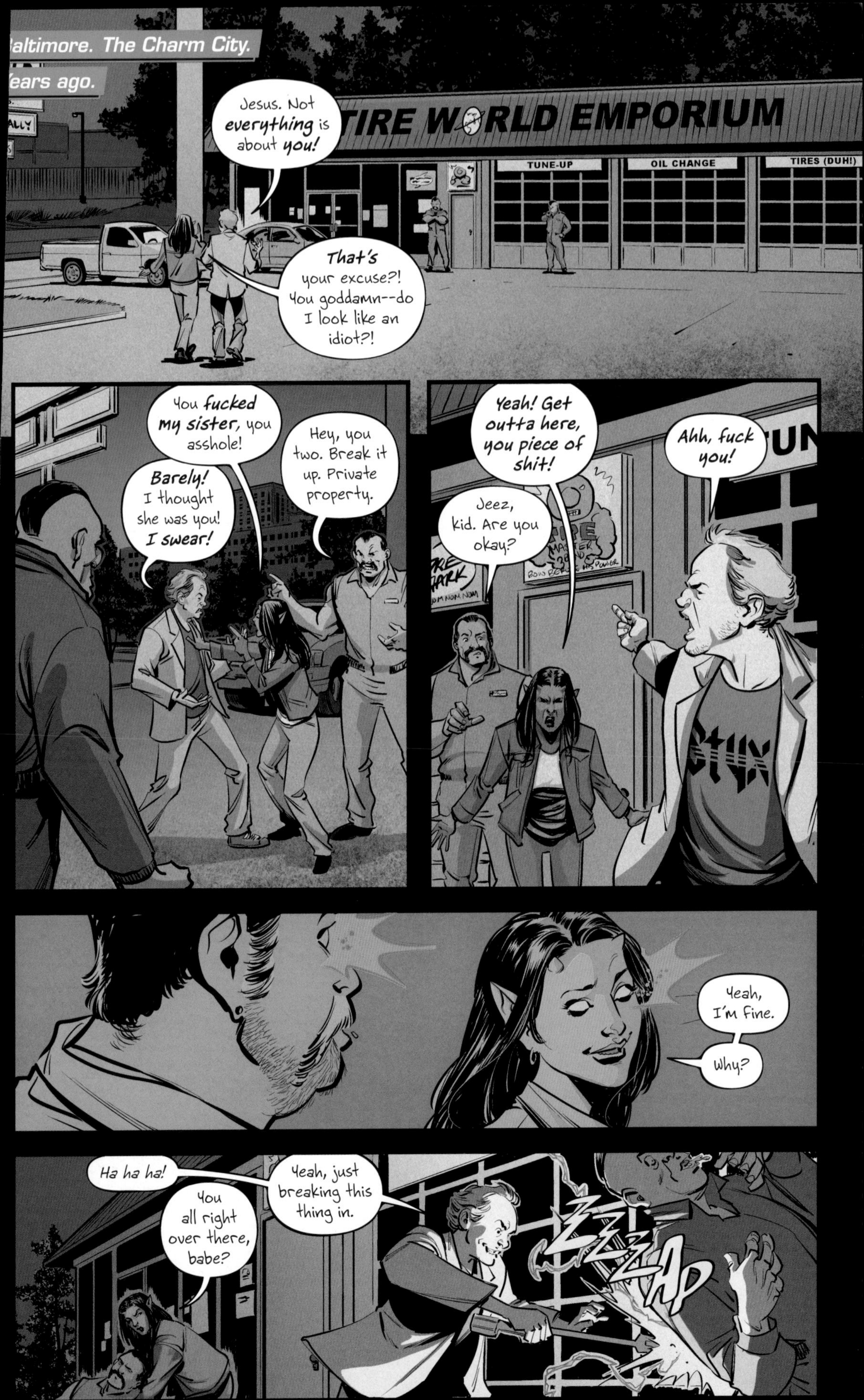

Baltimore. The Charm City.
Years ago.
TIRE WORLD EMPORIUM
TUNE-UP
OIL CHANGE
TIRES (DUH!)
Jesus. Not everything is about you!
That's your excuse?! You goddamn--do I look like an idiot?!
You fucked my sister, you asshole!
Barely! I thought she was you! I swear!
Hey, you two. Break it up. Private property.
Yeah! Get outta here, you piece of shit!
Ahh, fuck you!
Jeez, kid. Are you okay?
Styx
Yeah, I'm fine.
Why?
Ha ha ha!
You all right over there, babe?
Yeah, just breaking this thing in.
ZZZZAP

I dunno. Thought it would have more kick, y'know?

Well, a cattle prod's less murdery than stabbing people all the time, Eddie, so maybe give it a chance?

Mehh.

ZAP

Quit griping. You won't even need it once we hit L.A. Nothing but sunny skies, palm trees, *retirement*--

Yeah, yeah. That all sounds great, Tina. Sucks that we can't just skip town and go!

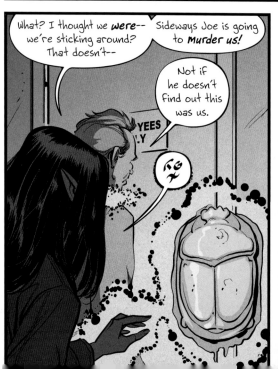

What? I thought we **were**-- we're sticking around? That doesn't--

Sideways Joe is going to **Murder us!**

Not if he doesn't find out this was us.

And going on the run right after one of his drophouses gets hit would be a pretty good tip-off.

He'd send Simon.

I'm not afraid of that big pussycat.

You should be.

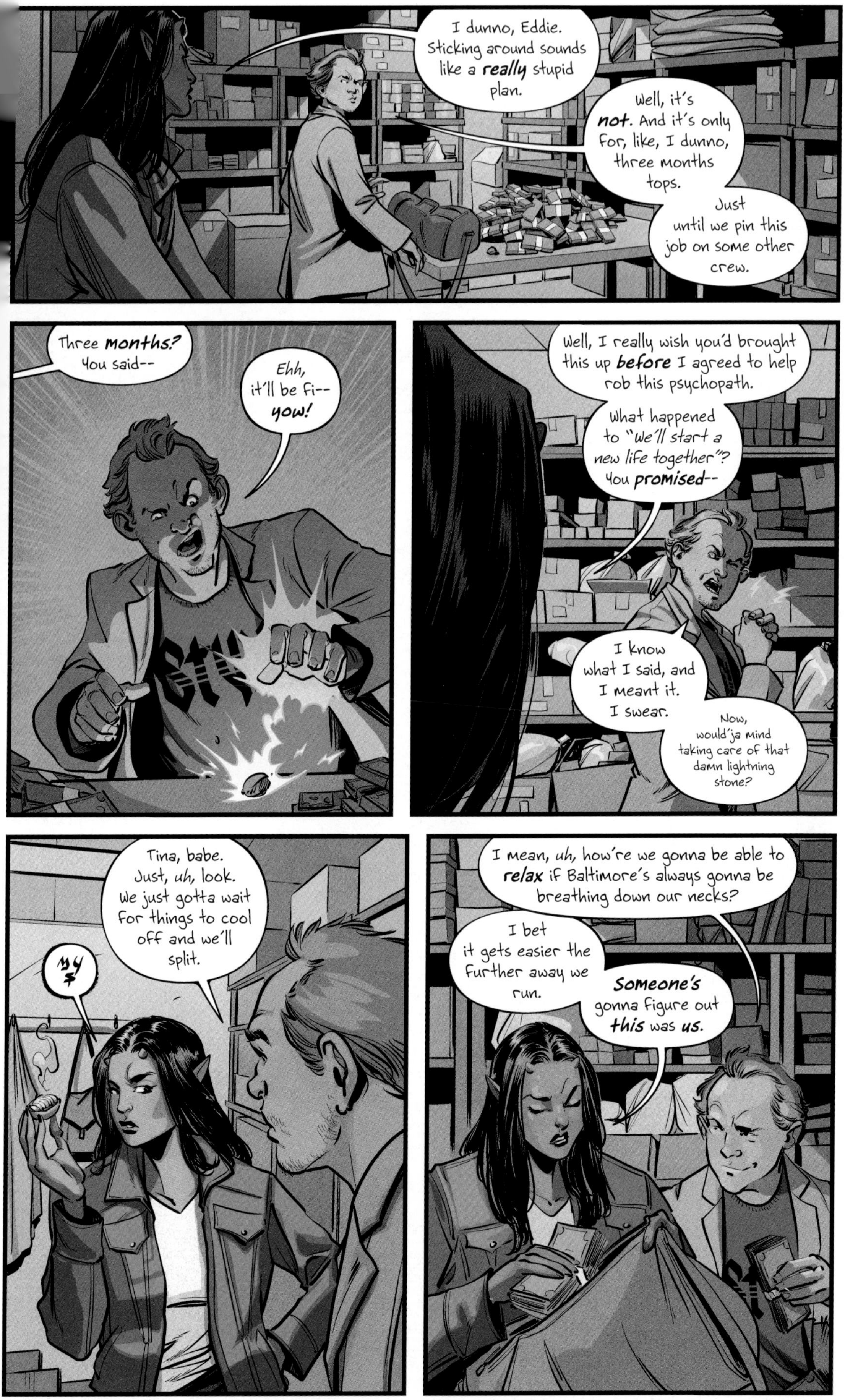
I dunno, Eddie. Sticking around sounds like a **really** stupid plan.
Well, it's **not**. And it's only for, like, I dunno, three months tops.
Just until we pin this job on some other crew.
Three **months?** You said--
Ehh, it'll be fi-- **yow!**
Well, I really wish you'd brought this up **before** I agreed to help rob this psychopath.
What happened to *"We'll start a new life together"*? You **promised**--
I know what I said, and I meant it. I swear.
Now, would'ja mind taking care of that damn lightning stone?
Tina, babe. Just, *uh*, look. We just gotta wait for things to cool off and we'll split.
I mean, *uh*, how're we gonna be able to **relax** if Baltimore's always gonna be breathing down our necks?
I bet it gets easier the further away we run.
Someone's gonna figure out **this** was **us**.

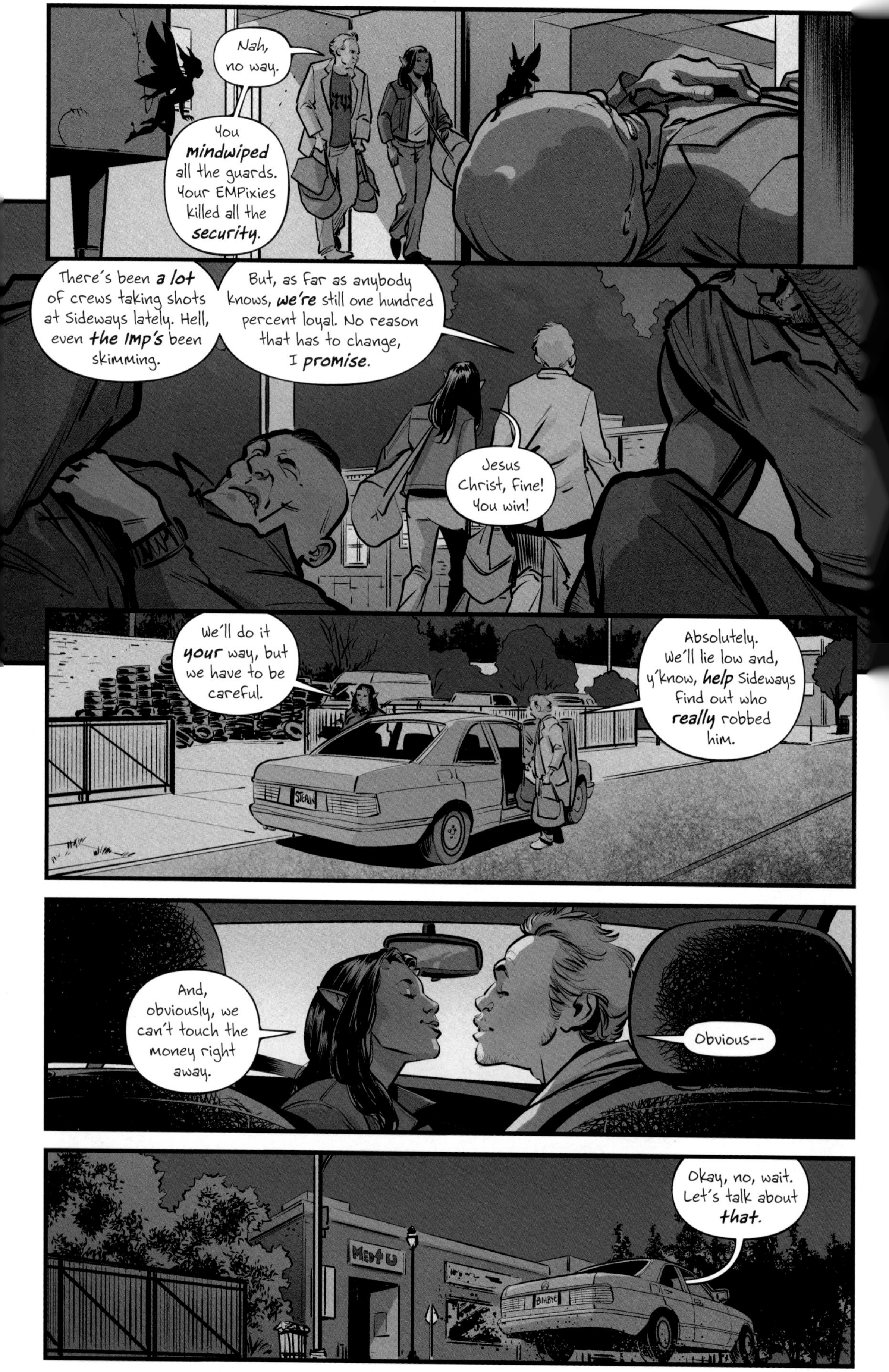
Nah, no way.
You mindwiped all the guards. Your EMPixies killed all the security.
There's been a lot of crews taking shots at Sideways lately. Hell, even the Imp's been skimming.
But, as far as anybody knows, we're still one hundred percent loyal. No reason that has to change, I promise.
Jesus Christ, Fine! You win!
We'll do it your way, but we have to be careful.
Absolutely. We'll lie low and, y'know, help Sideways find out who really robbed him.
And, obviously, we can't touch the money right away.
Obvious--
Okay, no, wait. Let's talk about that.

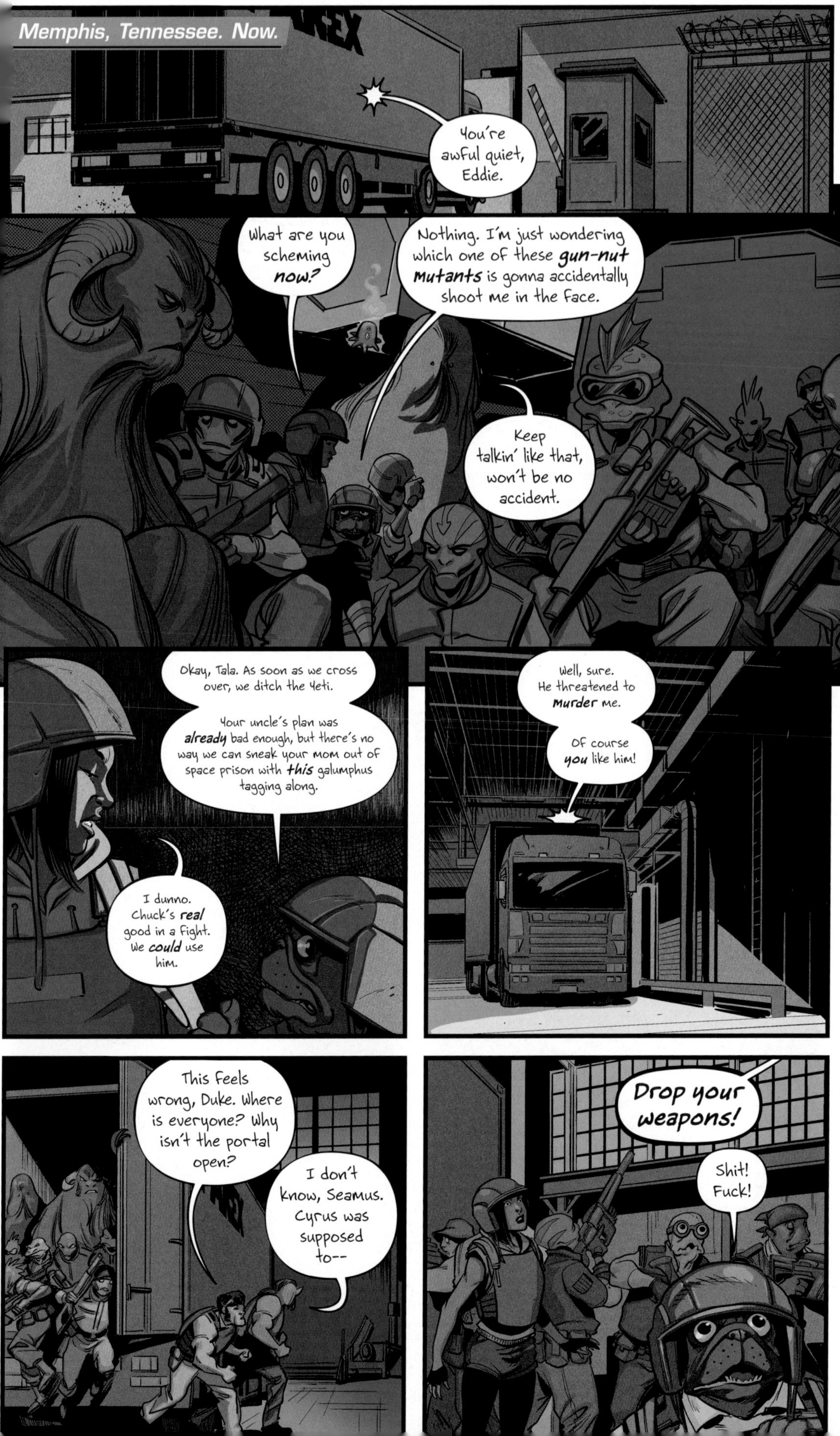
Memphis, Tennessee. Now.
You're awful quiet, Eddie.
What are you scheming now?
Nothing. I'm just wondering which one of these gun-nut mutants is gonna accidentally shoot me in the face.
Keep talkin' like that, won't be no accident.
Okay, Tala. As soon as we cross over, we ditch the Yeti.
Your uncle's plan was already bad enough, but there's no way we can sneak your mom out of space prison with this galumphus tagging along.
I dunno. Chuck's real good in a fight. We could use him.
Well, sure. He threatened to murder me.
Of course you like him!
This feels wrong, Duke. Where is everyone? Why isn't the portal open?
I don't know, Seamus. Cyrus was supposed to--
Drop your weapons!
Shit! Fuck!

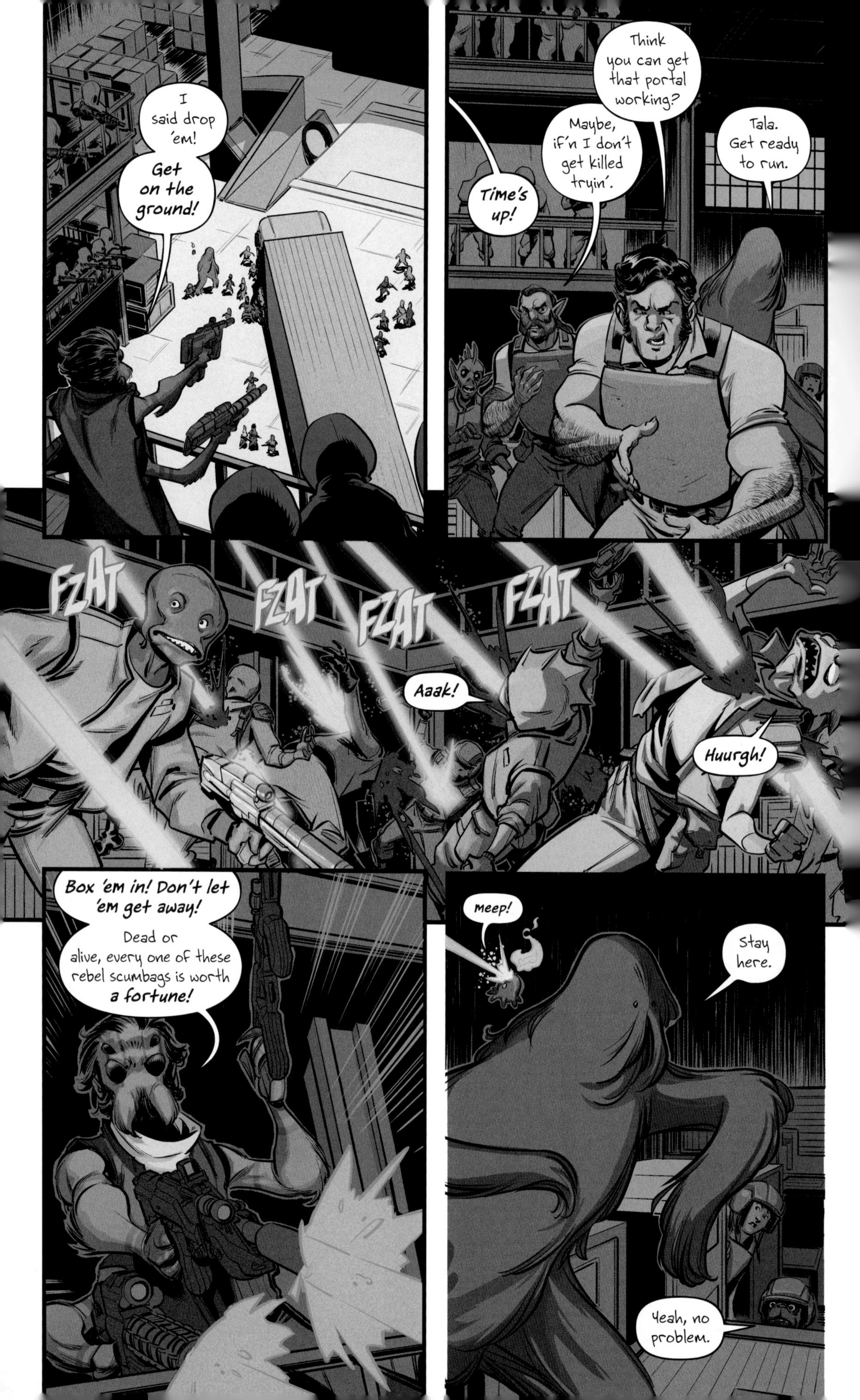

I said drop 'em!
Get on the ground!
Think you can get that portal working?
Maybe, if'n I don't get killed tryin'.
Time's up!
Tala. Get ready to run.
FZAT
FZAT
FZAT
FZAT
Aaak!
Huurgh!
Box 'em in! Don't let 'em get away!
Dead or alive, every one of these rebel scumbags is worth a fortune!
Meep!
Stay here.
Yeah, no problem.

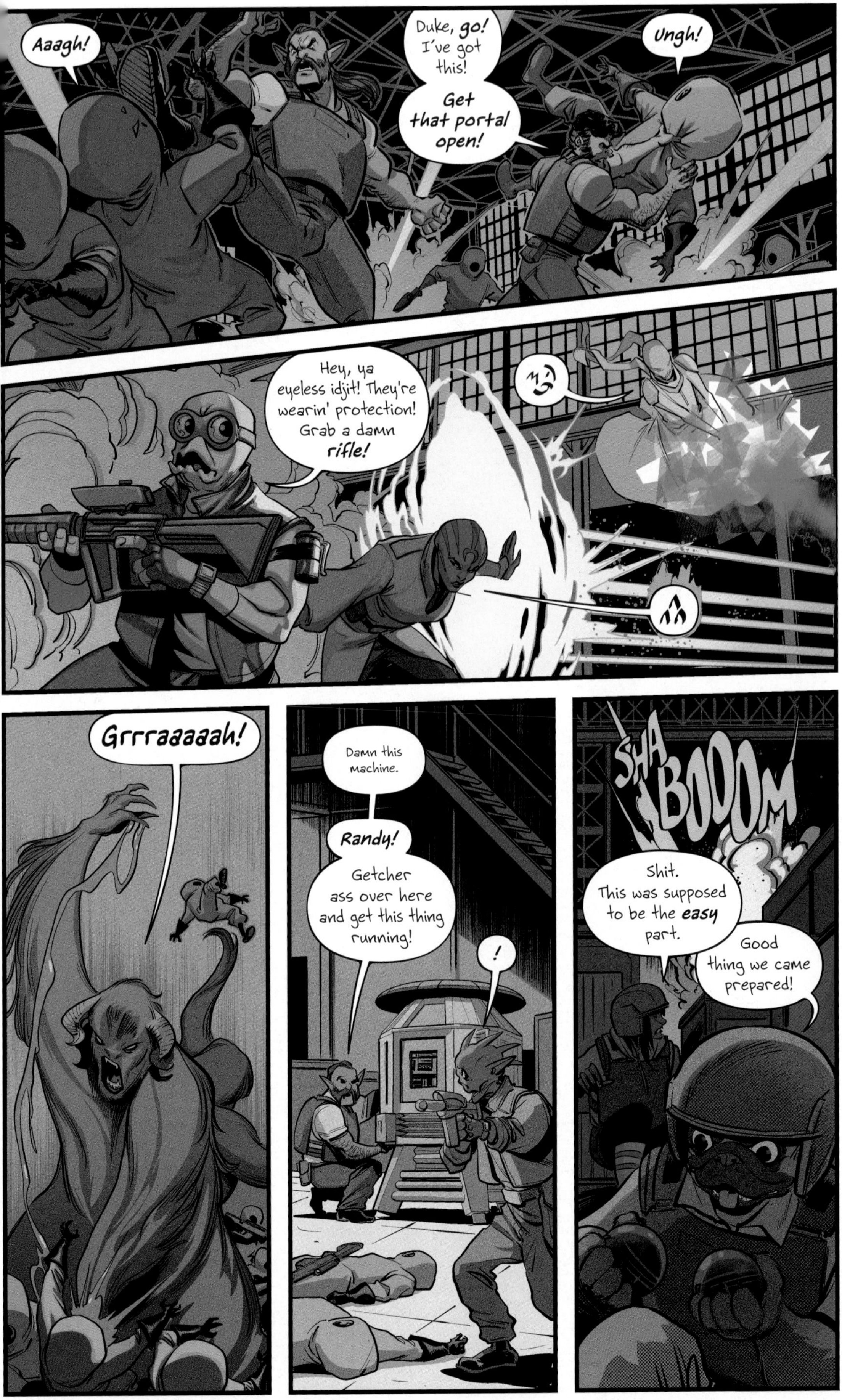
Aaagh!
Duke, go! I've got this!
Get that portal open!
Ungh!
Hey, ya eyeless idjit! They're wearin' protection! Grab a damn rifle!
Grrraaaaaah!
Damn this machine.
Randy!
Getcher ass over here and get this thing running!
!
SHA BOOOM
Shit. This was supposed to be the easy part.
Good thing we came prepared!

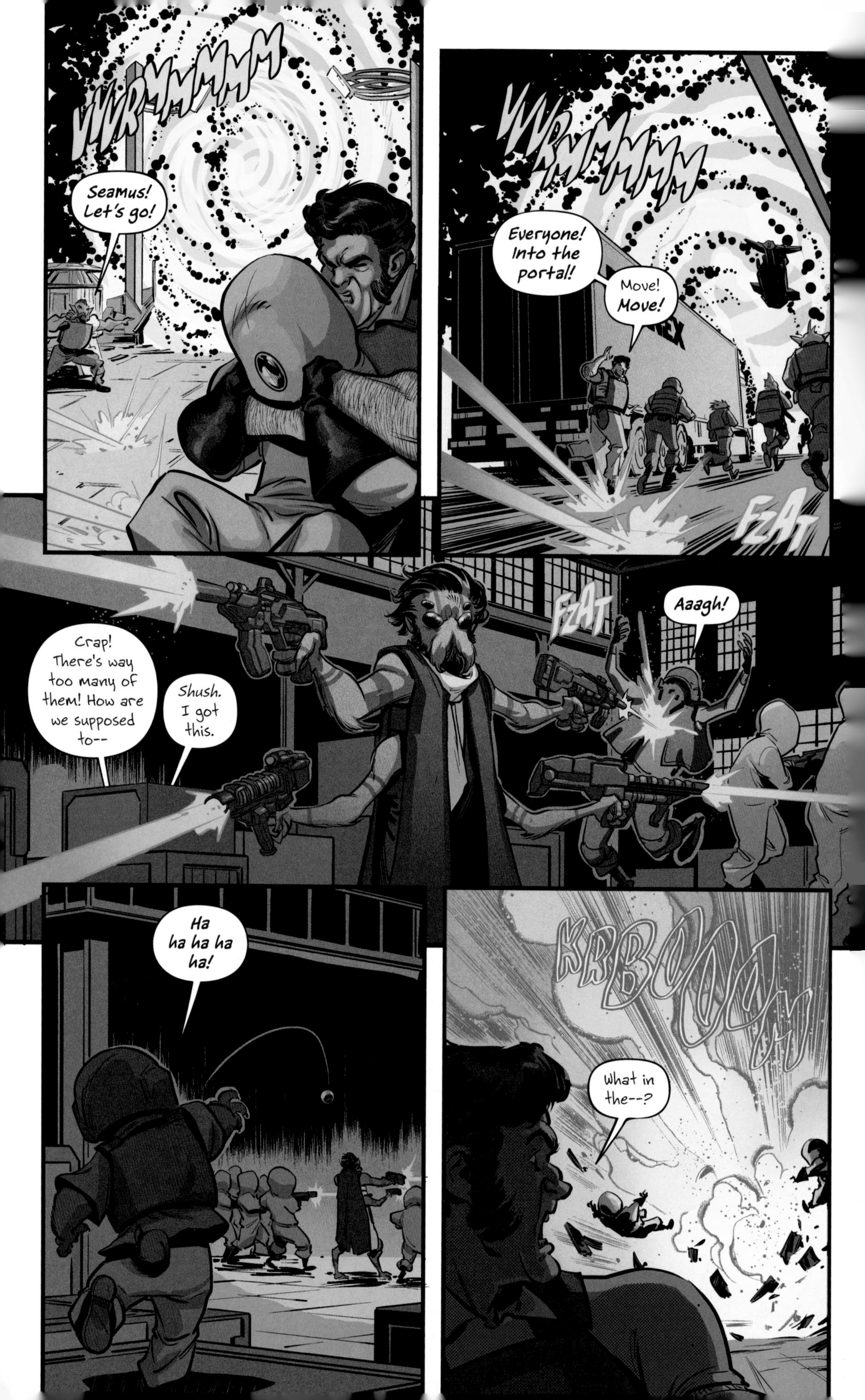
VVVRMMMMMM
Seamus! Let's go!
VVVRMMMMMM
Everyone! Into the portal!
Move! Move!
FZAT
FZAT
Aaagh!
Crap! There's way too many of them! How are we supposed to--
Shush. I got this.
Ha ha ha ha ha!
KRBOOOOM
What in the--?

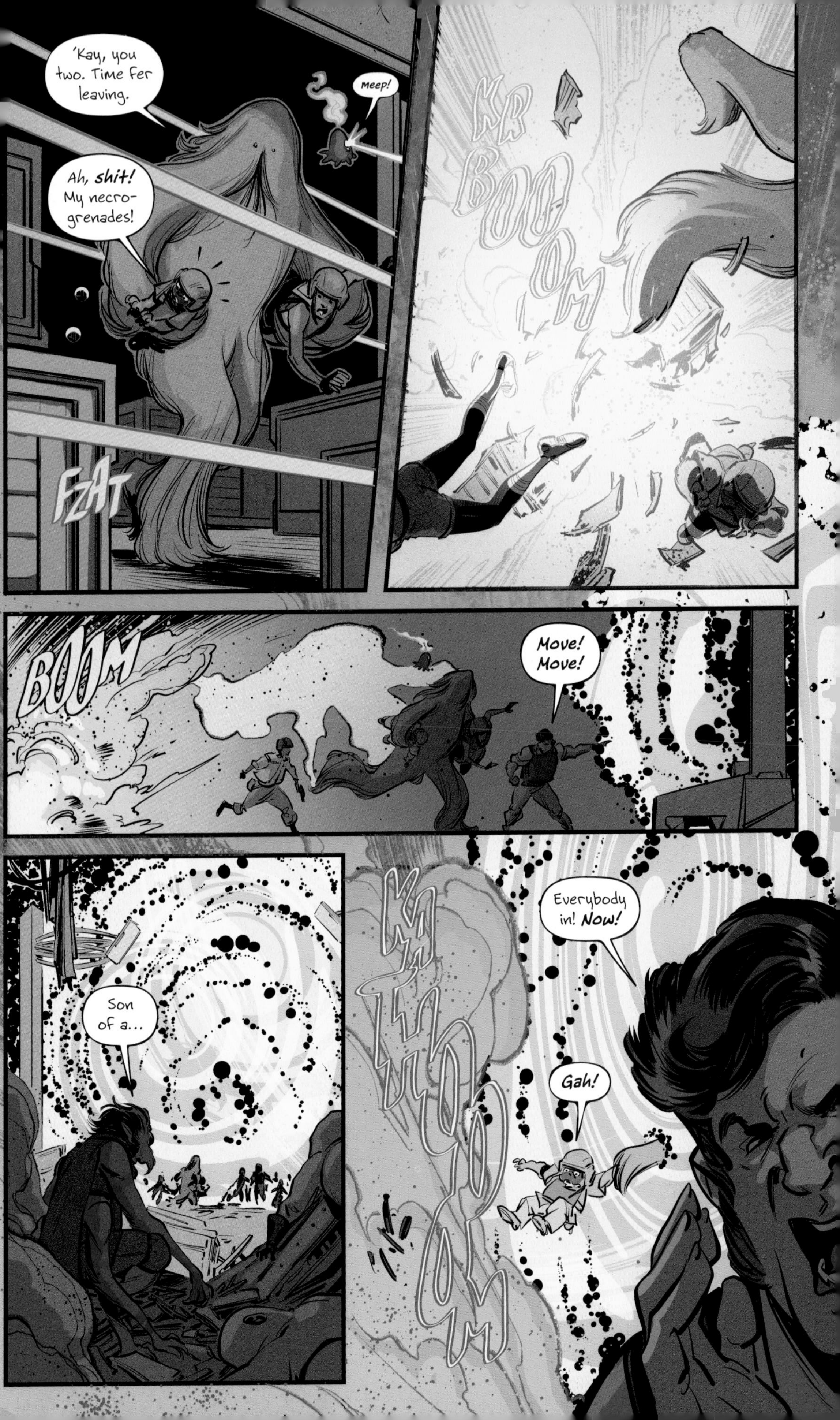
'Kay, you two. Time fer leaving.
Meep!
Ah, shit! My necro-grenades!
FZAT
KRBOOOOM
BOOM
Move! Move!
Son of a...
Everybody in! Now!
Gah!

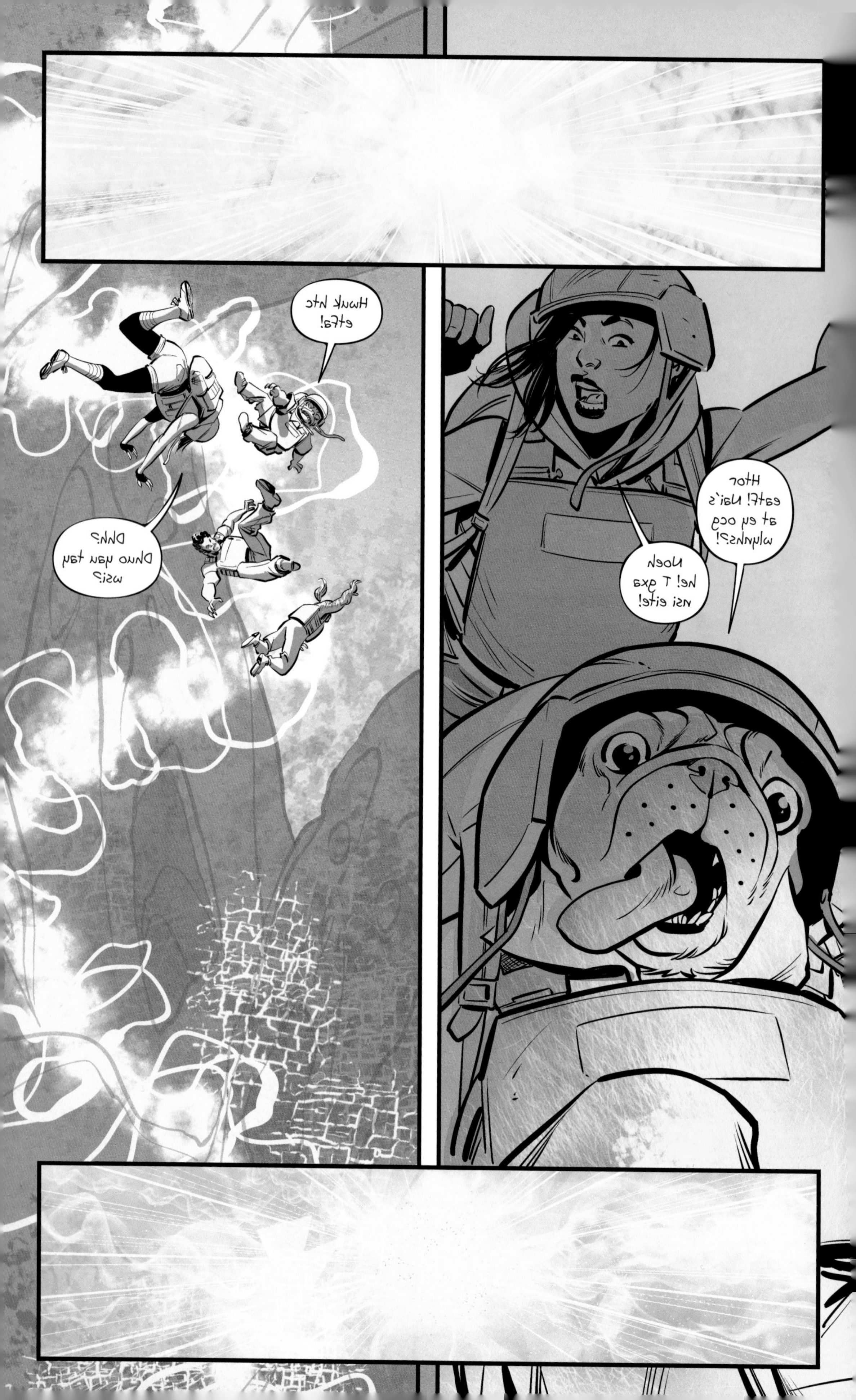

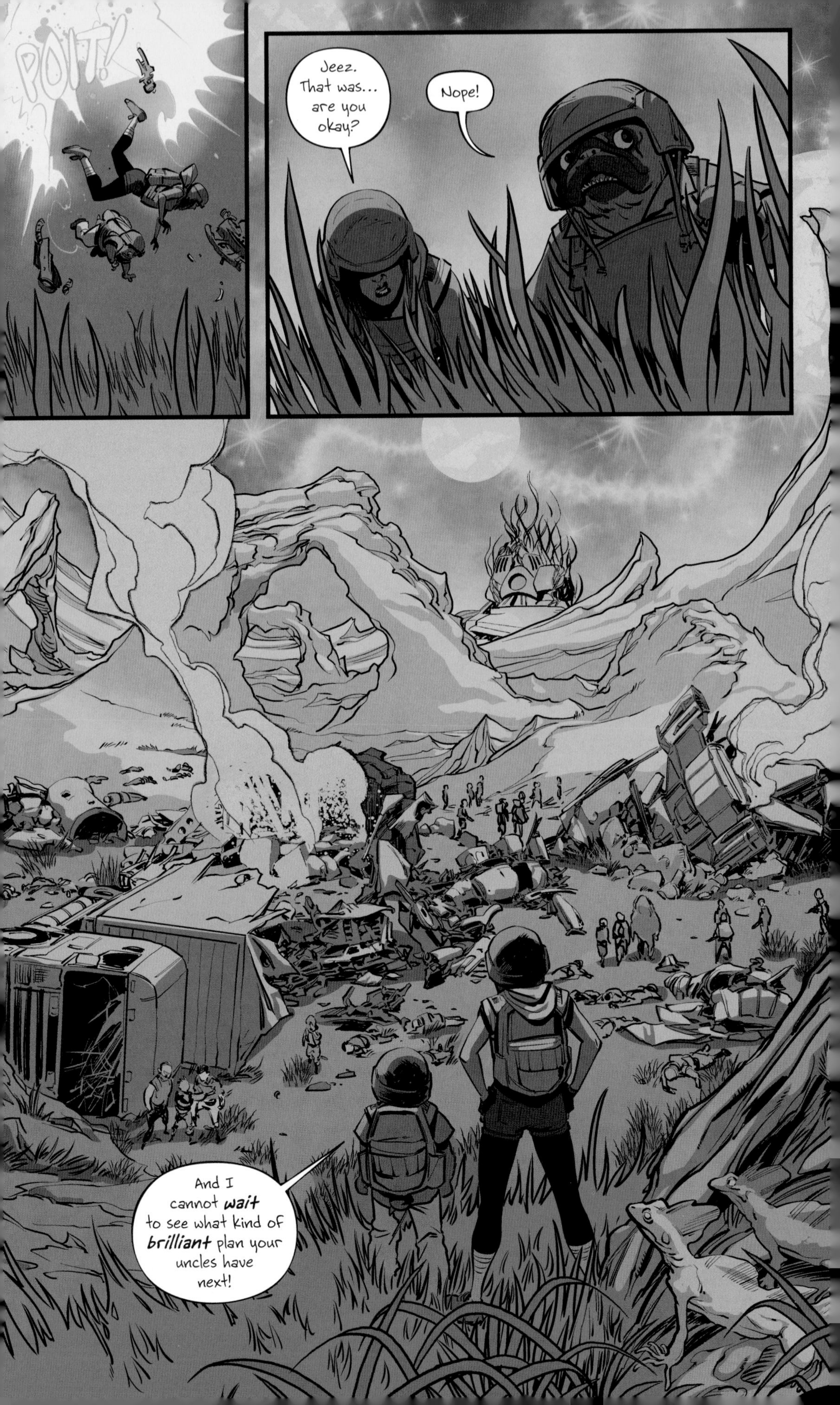
POIT!
Jeez. That was... are you okay?
Nope!
And I cannot **wait** to see what kind of **brilliant** plan your uncles have next!

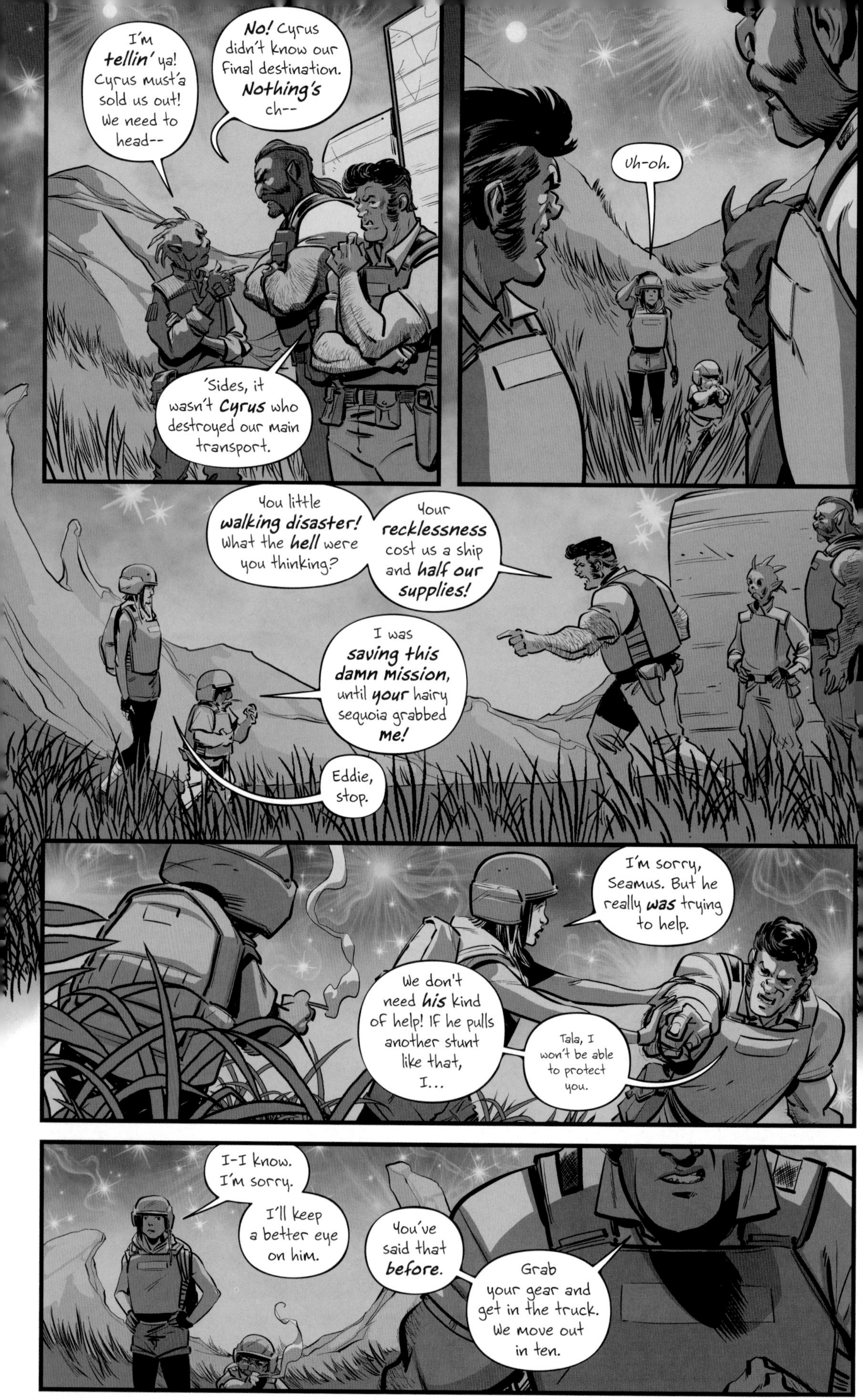
I'm tellin' ya! Cyrus must'a sold us out! We need to head--
No! Cyrus didn't know our final destination. Nothing's ch--
'Sides, it wasn't Cyrus who destroyed our main transport.
Uh-oh.
You little walking disaster! What the hell were you thinking?
Your recklessness cost us a ship and half our supplies!
I was saving this damn mission, until your hairy sequoia grabbed me!
Eddie, stop.
I'm sorry, Seamus. But he really was trying to help.
We don't need his kind of help! If he pulls another stunt like that, I...
Tala, I won't be able to protect you.
I-I know. I'm sorry.
I'll keep a better eye on him.
You've said that before.
Grab your gear and get in the truck. We move out in ten.

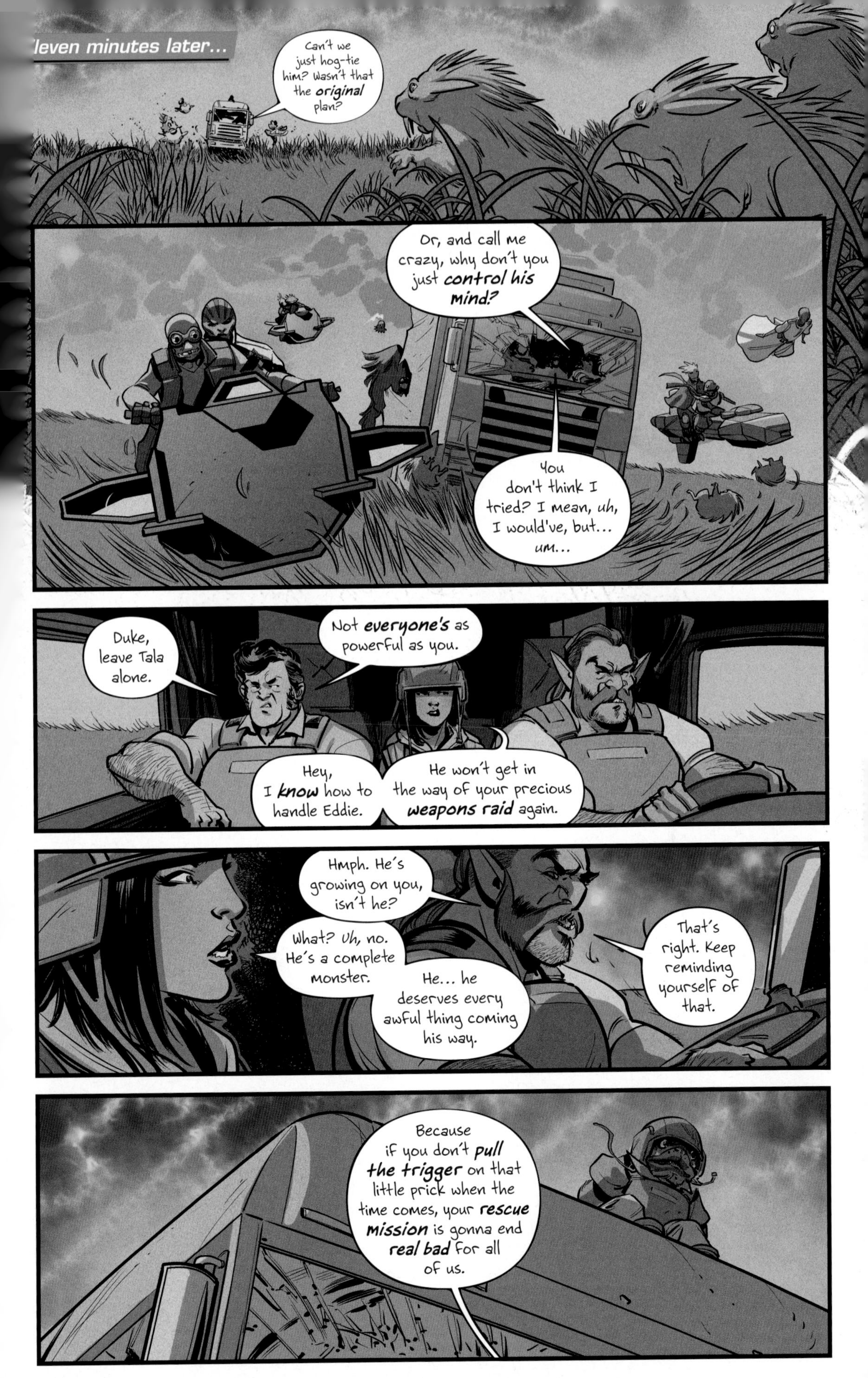
leven minutes later...
Can't we just hog-tie him? Wasn't that the original plan?
Or, and call me crazy, why don't you just control his mind?
You don't think I tried? I mean, uh, I would've, but... um...
Duke, leave Tala alone.
Not everyone's as powerful as you.
Hey, I know how to handle Eddie.
He won't get in the way of your precious weapons raid again.
Hmph. He's growing on you, isn't he?
What? Uh, no. He's a complete monster.
He... he deserves every awful thing coming his way.
That's right. Keep reminding yourself of that.
Because if you don't pull the trigger on that little prick when the time comes, your rescue mission is gonna end real bad for all of us.

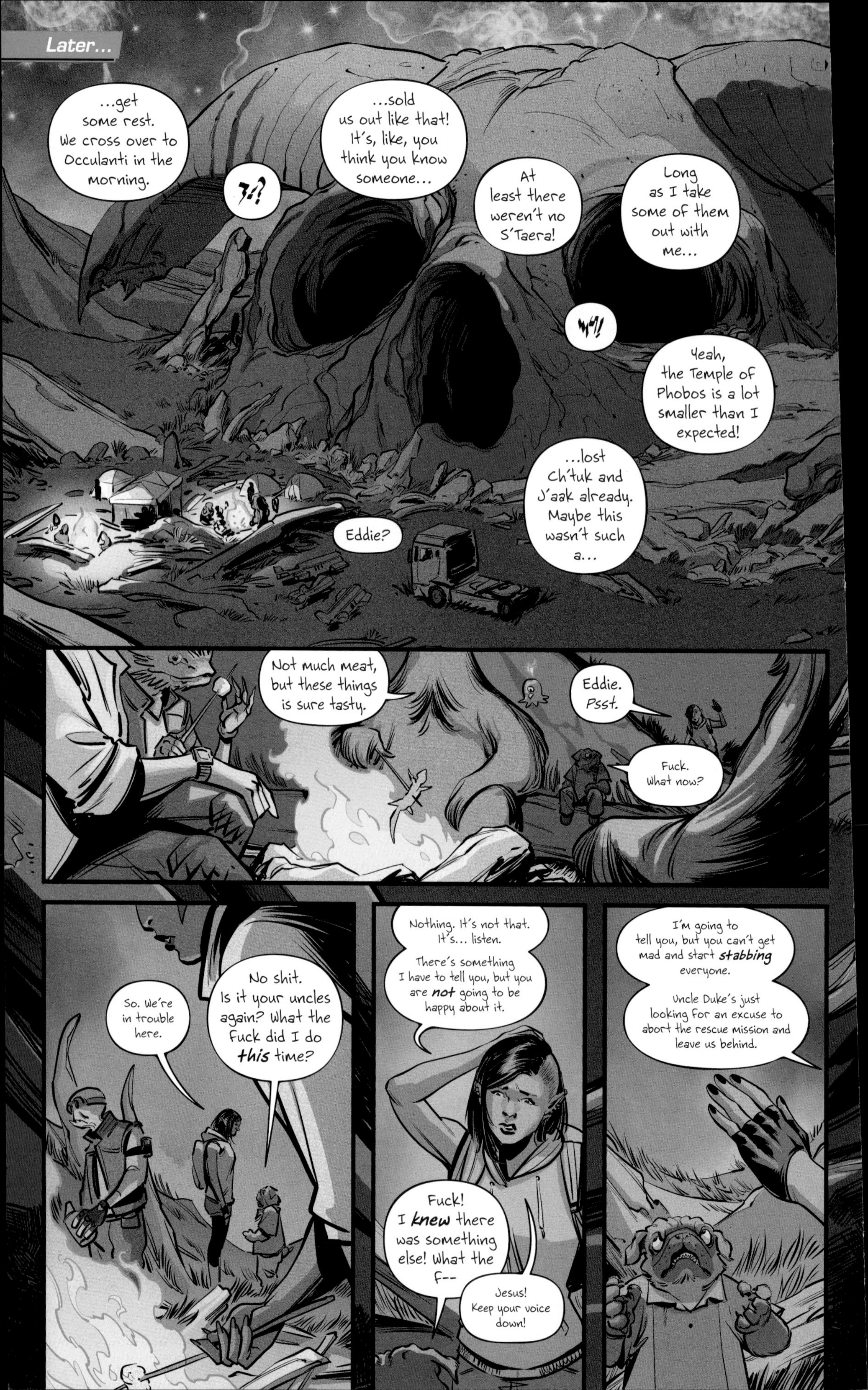
Later...
...get some rest. We cross over to Occulanti in the morning.
?!?
...sold us out like that! It's, like, you think you know someone...
At least there weren't no S'Taera!
Long as I take some of them out with me...
!!
Yeah, the Temple of Phobos is a lot smaller than I expected!
...lost Ch'tuk and J'aak already. Maybe this wasn't such a...
Eddie?
Not much meat, but these things is sure tasty.
Eddie. Psst.
Fuck. What now?
So. We're in trouble here.
No shit. Is it your uncles again? What the Fuck did I do this time?
Nothing. It's not that. It's... listen.
There's something I have to tell you, but you are not going to be happy about it.
Fuck! I knew there was something else! What the f--
Jesus! Keep your voice down!
I'm going to tell you, but you can't get mad and start stabbing everyone.
Uncle Duke's just looking for an excuse to abort the rescue mission and leave us behind.

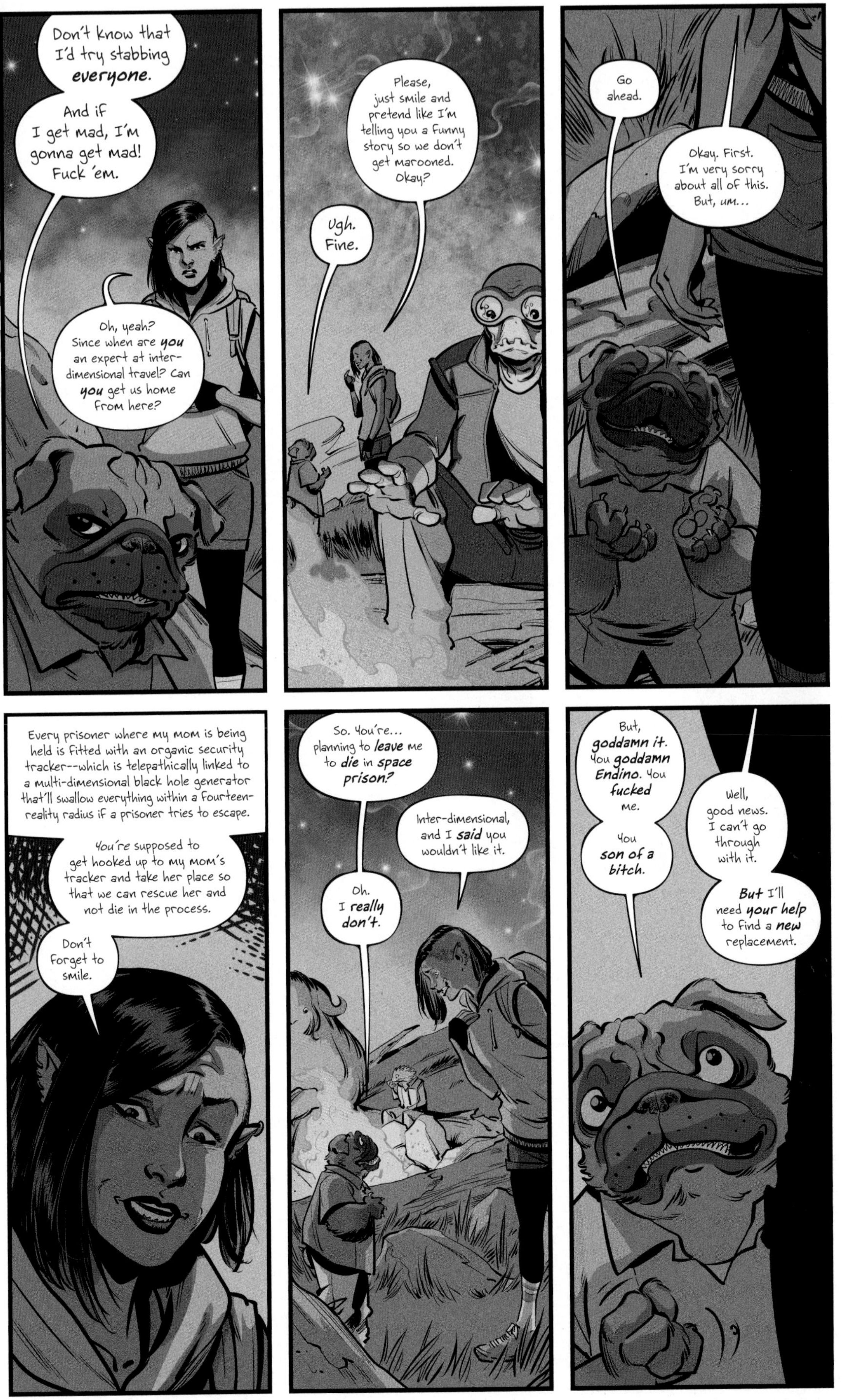
Don't know that I'd try stabbing **everyone**.
And if I get mad, I'm gonna get mad! Fuck 'em.
Oh, yeah? Since when are **you** an expert at inter-dimensional travel? Can **you** get us home from here?
Please, just smile and pretend like I'm telling you a funny story so we don't get marooned. Okay?
Ugh. Fine.
Go ahead.
Okay. First. I'm very sorry about all of this. But, um...
Every prisoner where my mom is being held is fitted with an organic security tracker--which is telepathically linked to a multi-dimensional black hole generator that'll swallow everything within a fourteen-reality radius if a prisoner tries to escape.
You're supposed to get hooked up to my mom's tracker and take her place so that we can rescue her and not die in the process.
Don't forget to smile.
So. You're... planning to **leave** me to **die** in **space prison?**
Inter-dimensional, and I **said** you wouldn't like it.
Oh. I **really don't**.
But, **goddamn it**. You **goddamn Endino**. You **fucked** me.
You **son of a bitch**.
Well, good news. I can't go through with it.
But I'll need **your help** to find a **new** replacement.

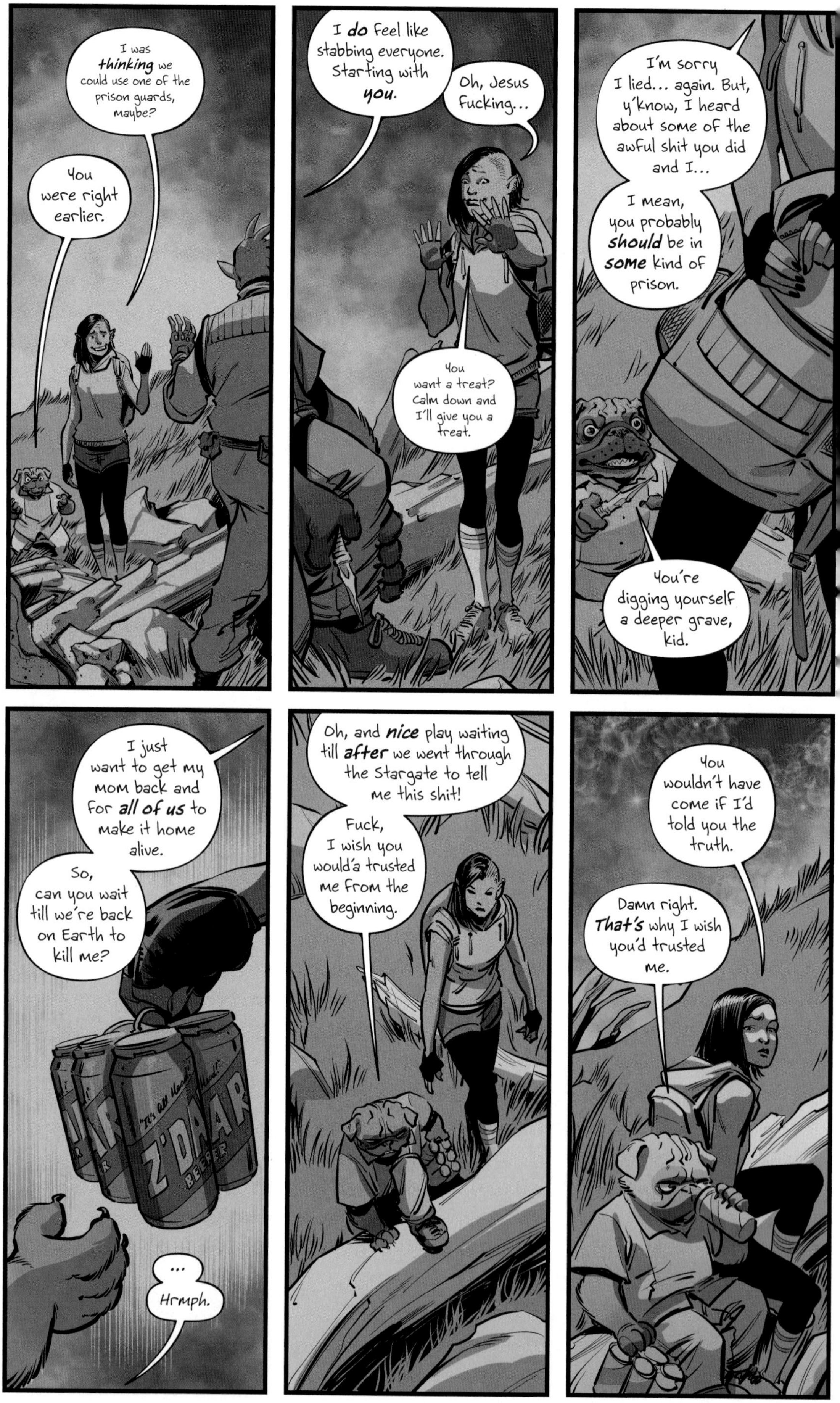
I was thinking we could use one of the prison guards, maybe?
You were right earlier.
I do feel like stabbing everyone. Starting with you.
Oh, Jesus Fucking...
You want a treat? Calm down and I'll give you a treat.
I'm sorry I lied... again. But, y'know, I heard about some of the awful shit you did and I...
I mean, you probably should be in some kind of prison.
You're digging yourself a deeper grave, kid.
I just want to get my mom back and for all of us to make it home alive.
So, can you wait till we're back on Earth to kill me?
"It's All Hands!"
Z'DAAR BEER
...
Hrmph.
Oh, and nice play waiting till after we went through the Stargate to tell me this shit!
Fuck, I wish you would'a trusted me from the beginning.
You wouldn't have come if I'd told you the truth.
Damn right. That's why I wish you'd trusted me.

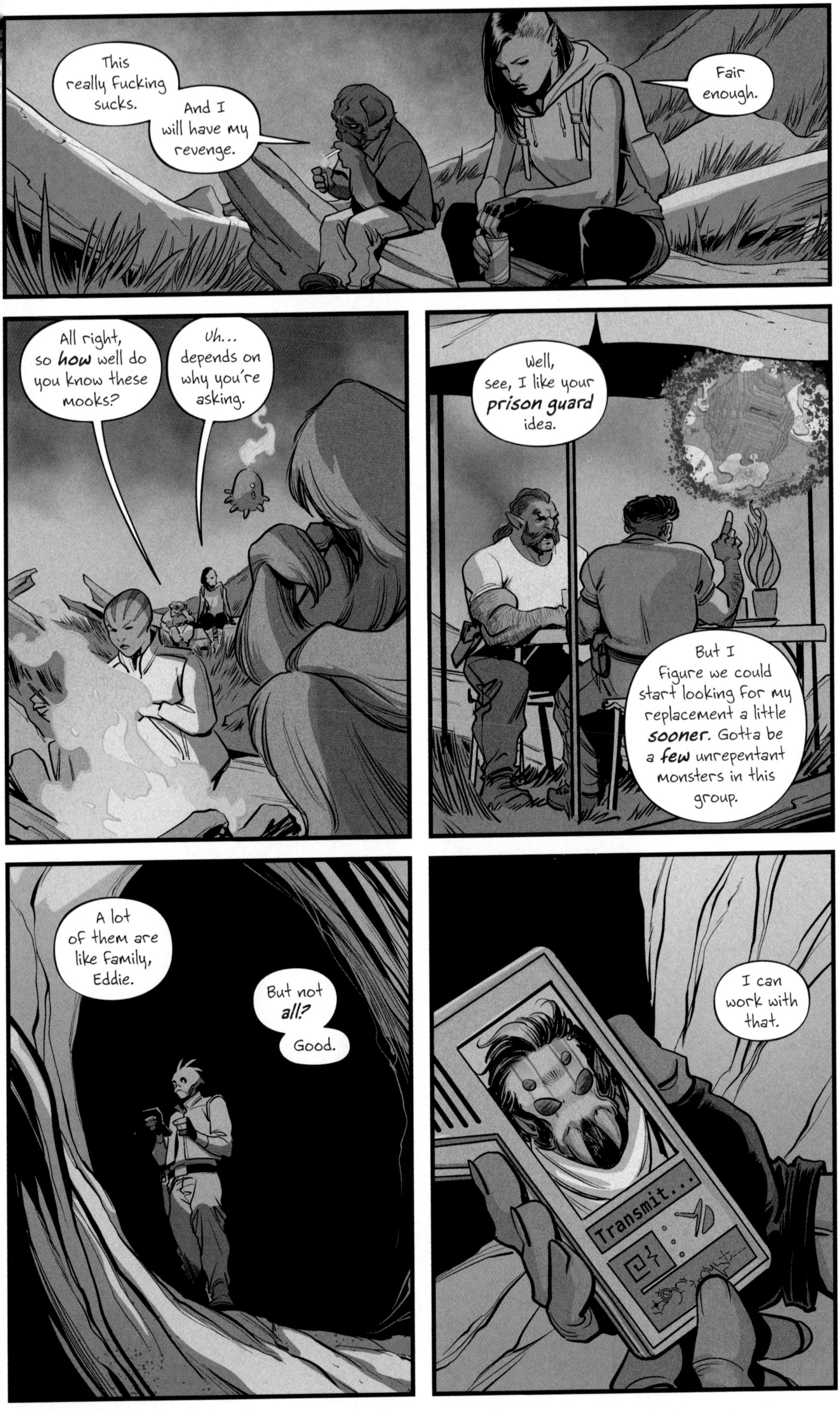

This really Fucking sucks.
And I will have my revenge.
Fair enough.
All right, so how well do you know these mooks?
Uh... depends on why you're asking.
Well, see, I like your prison guard idea.
But I figure we could start looking for my replacement a little sooner. Gotta be a few unrepentant monsters in this group.
A lot of them are like family, Eddie.
But not all?
Good.
Transmit...
I can work with that.

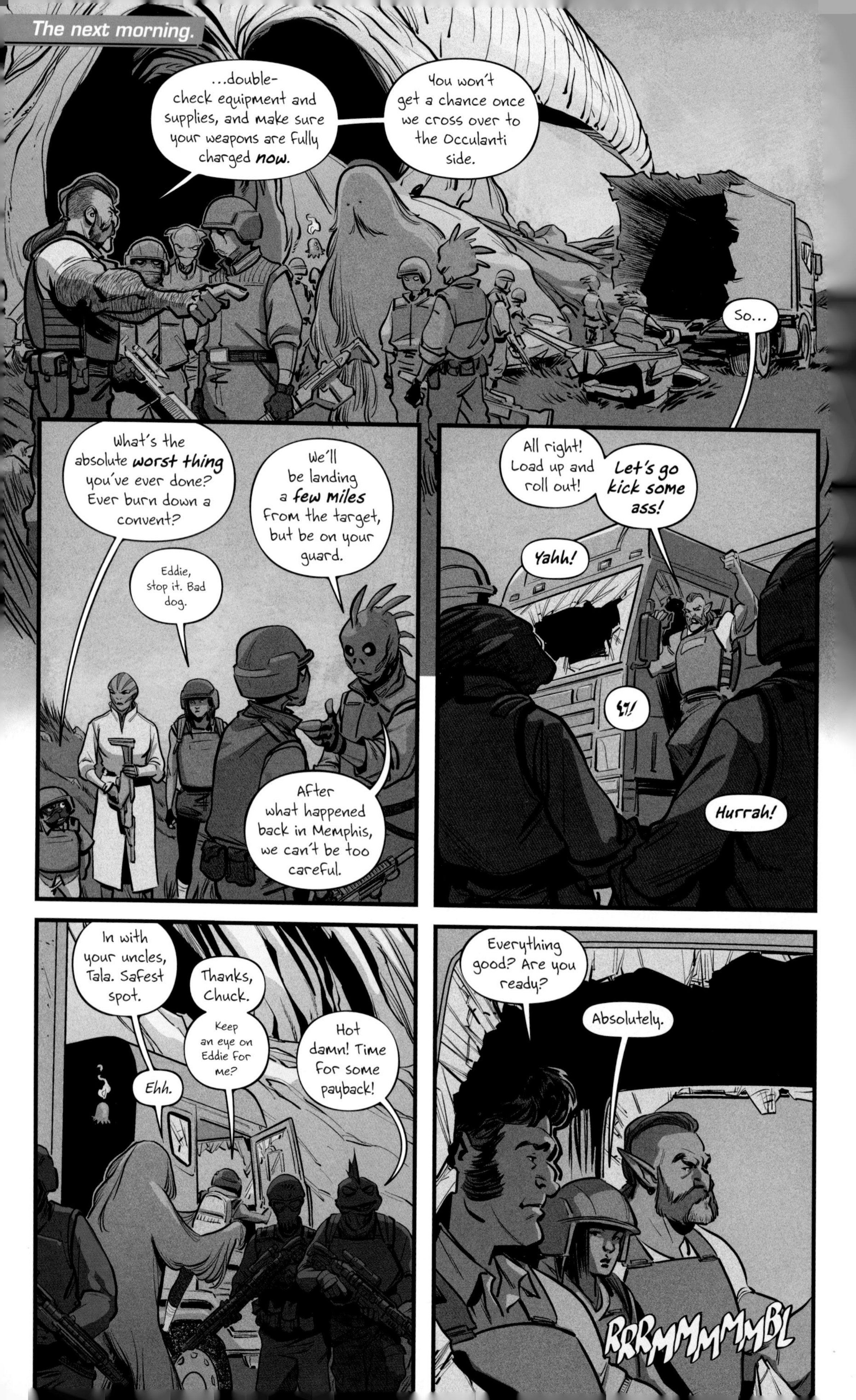
The next morning.
...double-check equipment and supplies, and make sure your weapons are fully charged now.
You won't get a chance once we cross over to the Occulanti side.
So...
What's the absolute worst thing you've ever done? Ever burn down a convent?
Eddie, stop it. Bad dog.
We'll be landing a few miles from the target, but be on your guard.
After what happened back in Memphis, we can't be too careful.
All right! Load up and roll out!
Let's go kick some ass!
Yahh!
Hurrah!
In with your uncles, Tala. Safest spot.
Thanks, Chuck.
Keep an eye on Eddie for me?
Ehh.
Hot damn! Time for some payback!
Everything good? Are you ready?
Absolutely.
RRRMMMMMBL

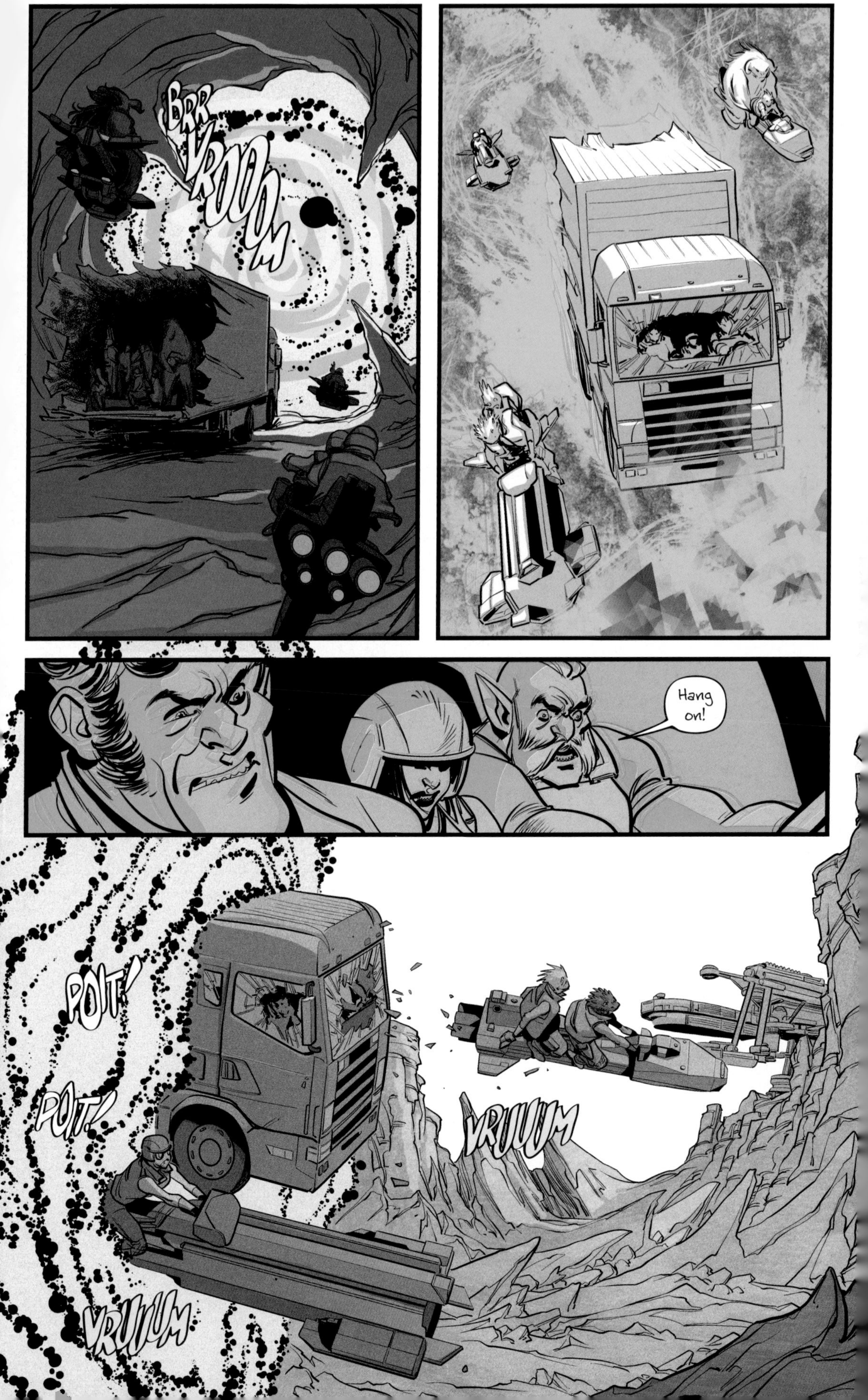
BRR VROOOOM
Hang on!
POIT!
POIT!
VRUUUM
VRUUUM

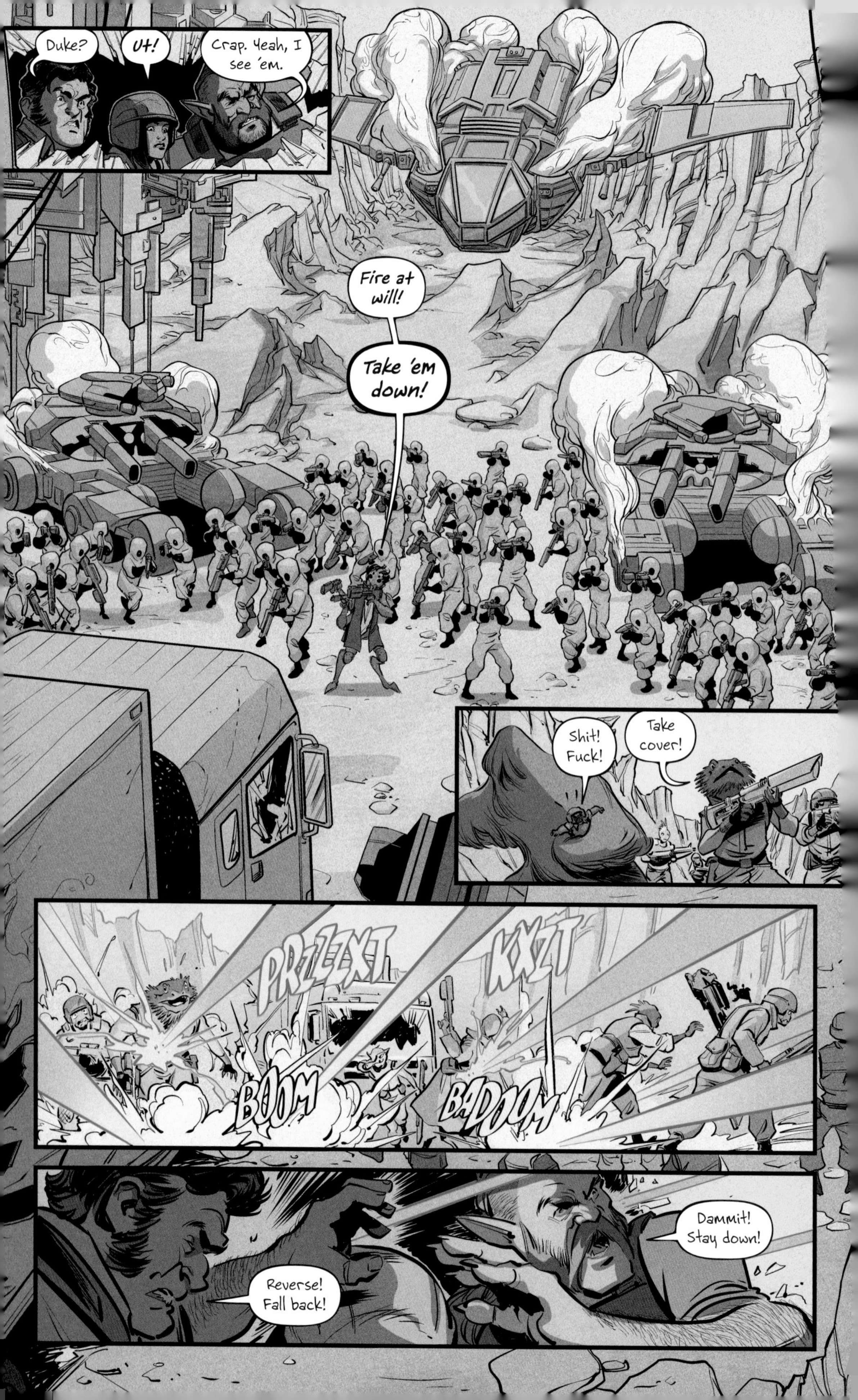
Duke?
Ut!
Crap. Yeah, I see 'em.
Fire at will!
Take 'em down!
Shit! Fuck!
Take cover!
PRZZZXT
KXZT
BOOM
BADOOM
Dammit! Stay down!
Reverse! Fall back!

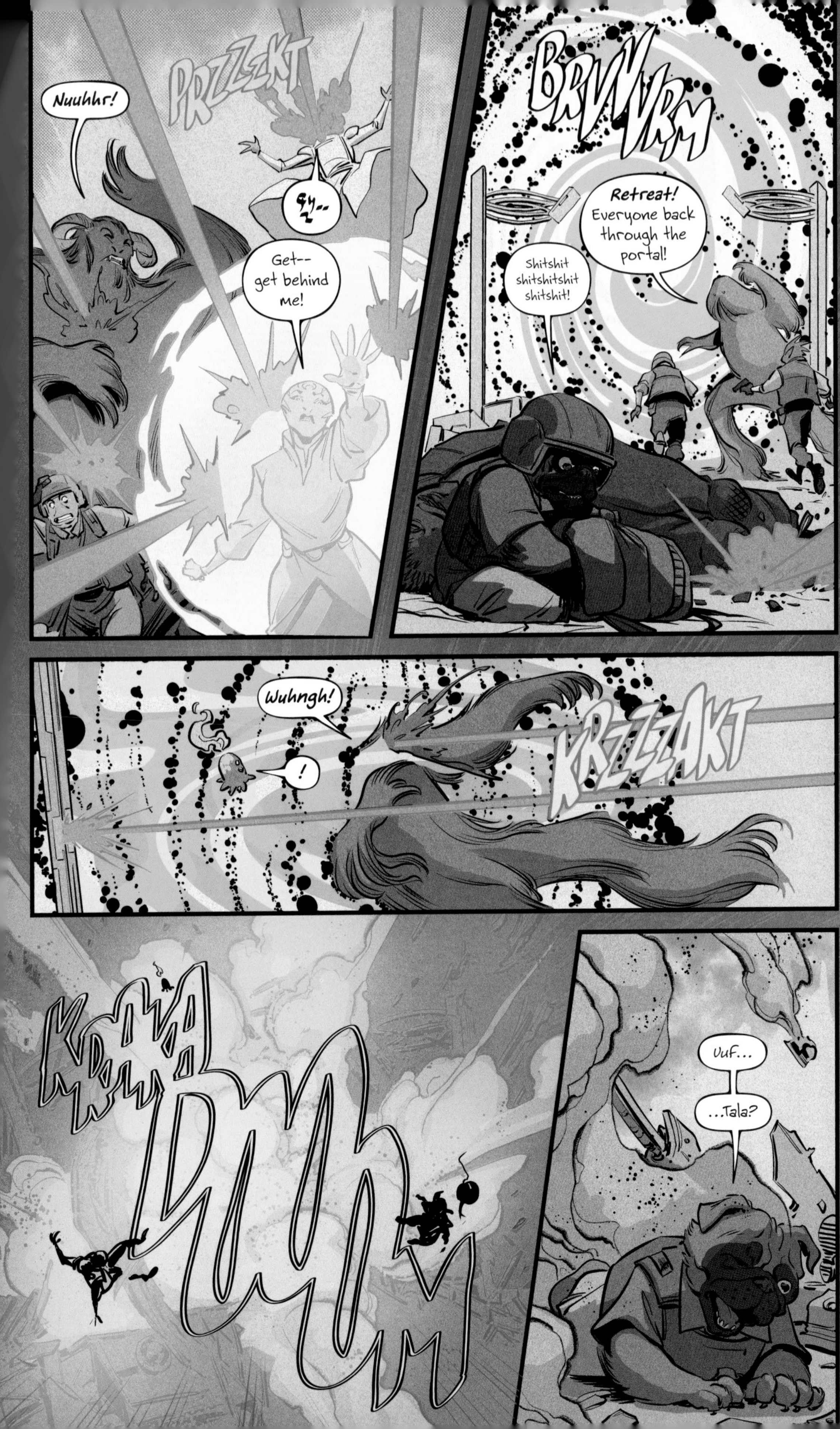
PRZZZKT
Nuuhhr!
Gy--
Get--
get behind
me!
BRVVVRM
Retreat!
Everyone back
through the
portal!
Shitshit
shitshitshitshit
shitshit!
Wuhngh!
!
KRZZZAKT
KRMM
Uuf...
...Tala?

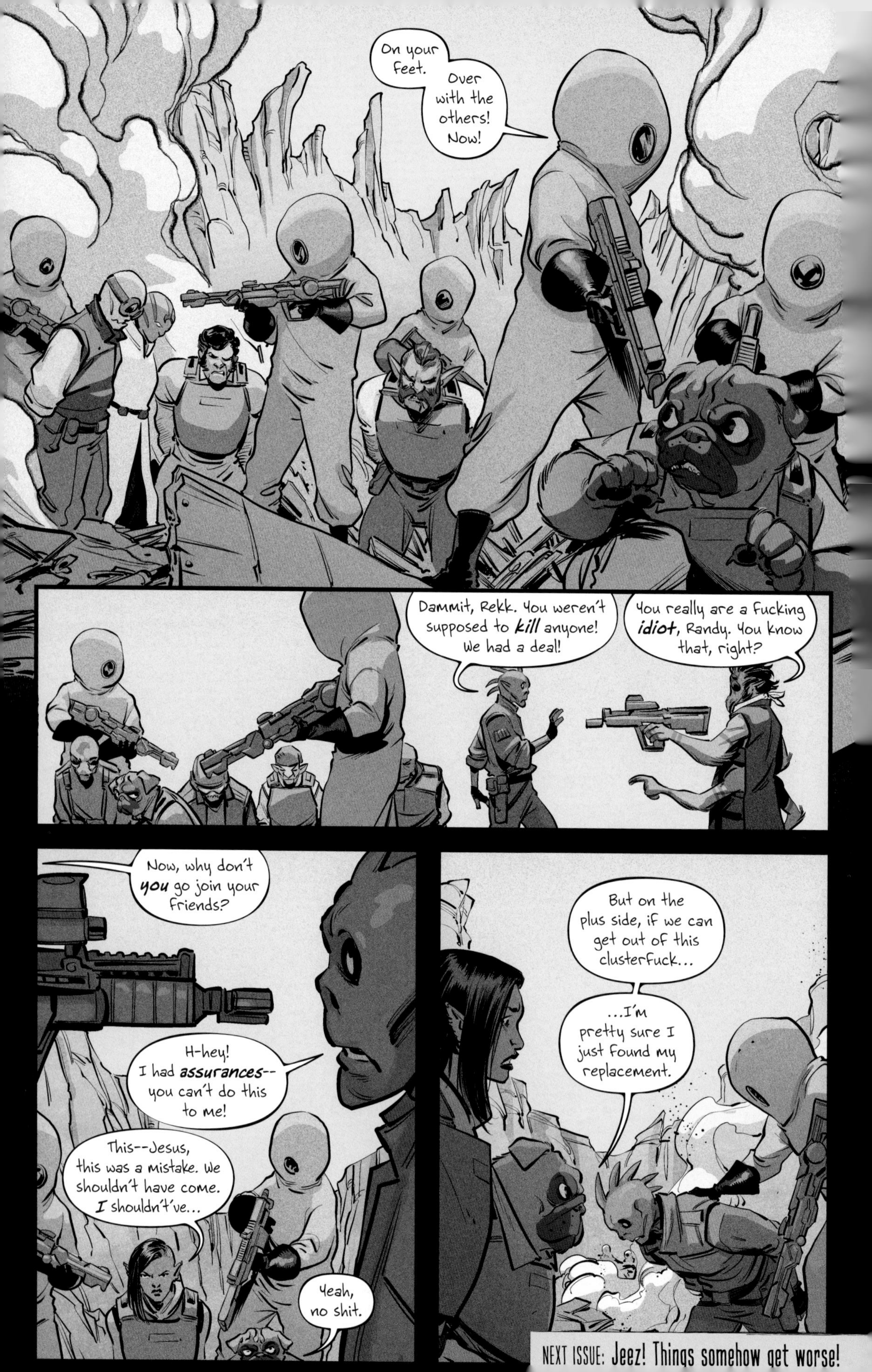
On your feet.
Over with the others! Now!
Dammit, Rekk. You weren't supposed to kill anyone! We had a deal!
You really are a fucking idiot, Randy. You know that, right?
Now, why don't you go join your friends?
H-hey! I had assurances--you can't do this to me!
This--Jesus, this was a mistake. We shouldn't have come. I shouldn't've...
Yeah, no shit.
But on the plus side, if we can get out of this clusterfuck...
...I'm pretty sure I just found my replacement.
NEXT ISSUE: Jeez! Things somehow get worse!

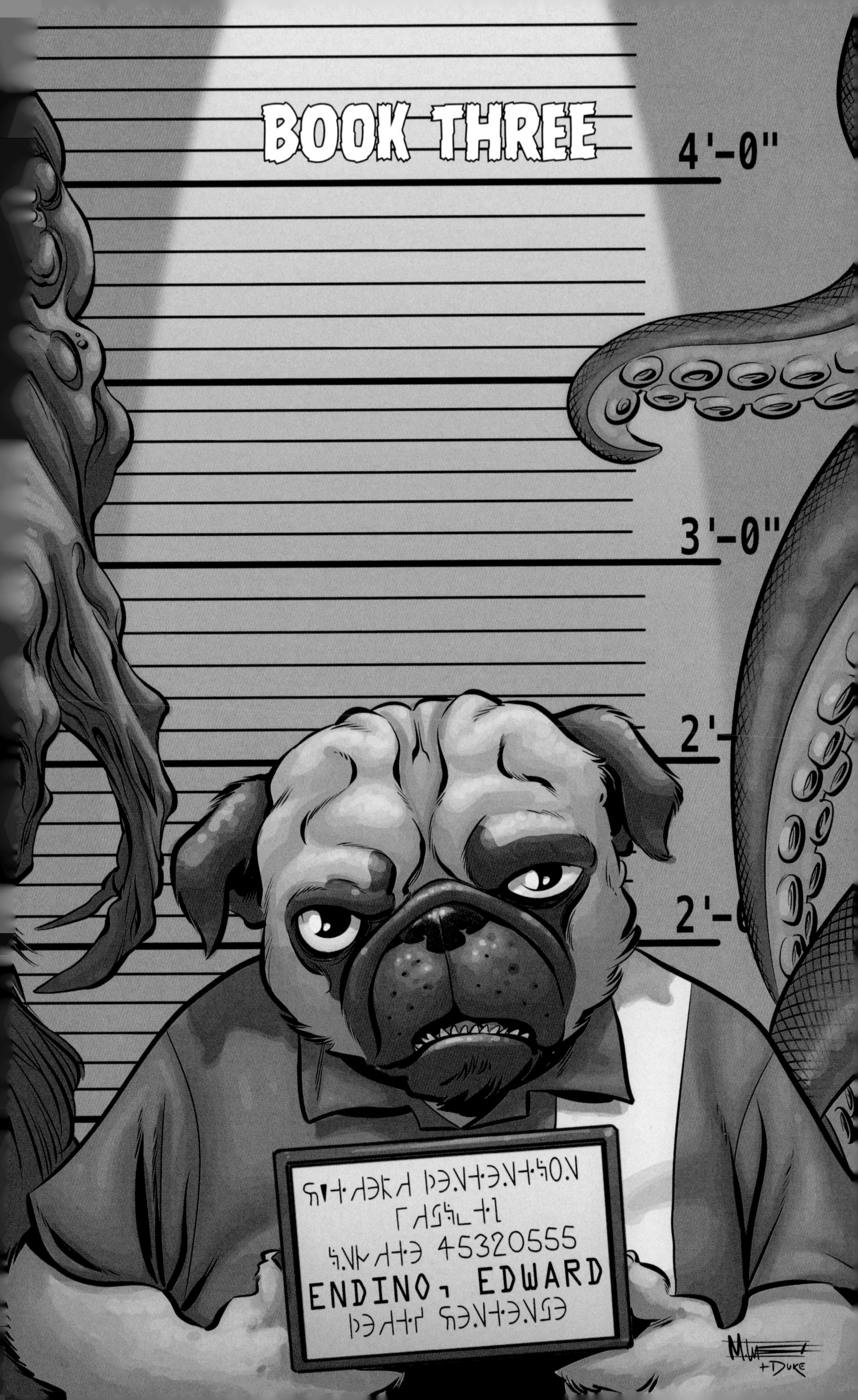
BOOK THREE
4'-0"
3'-0"
45320555
ENDINO, EDWARD

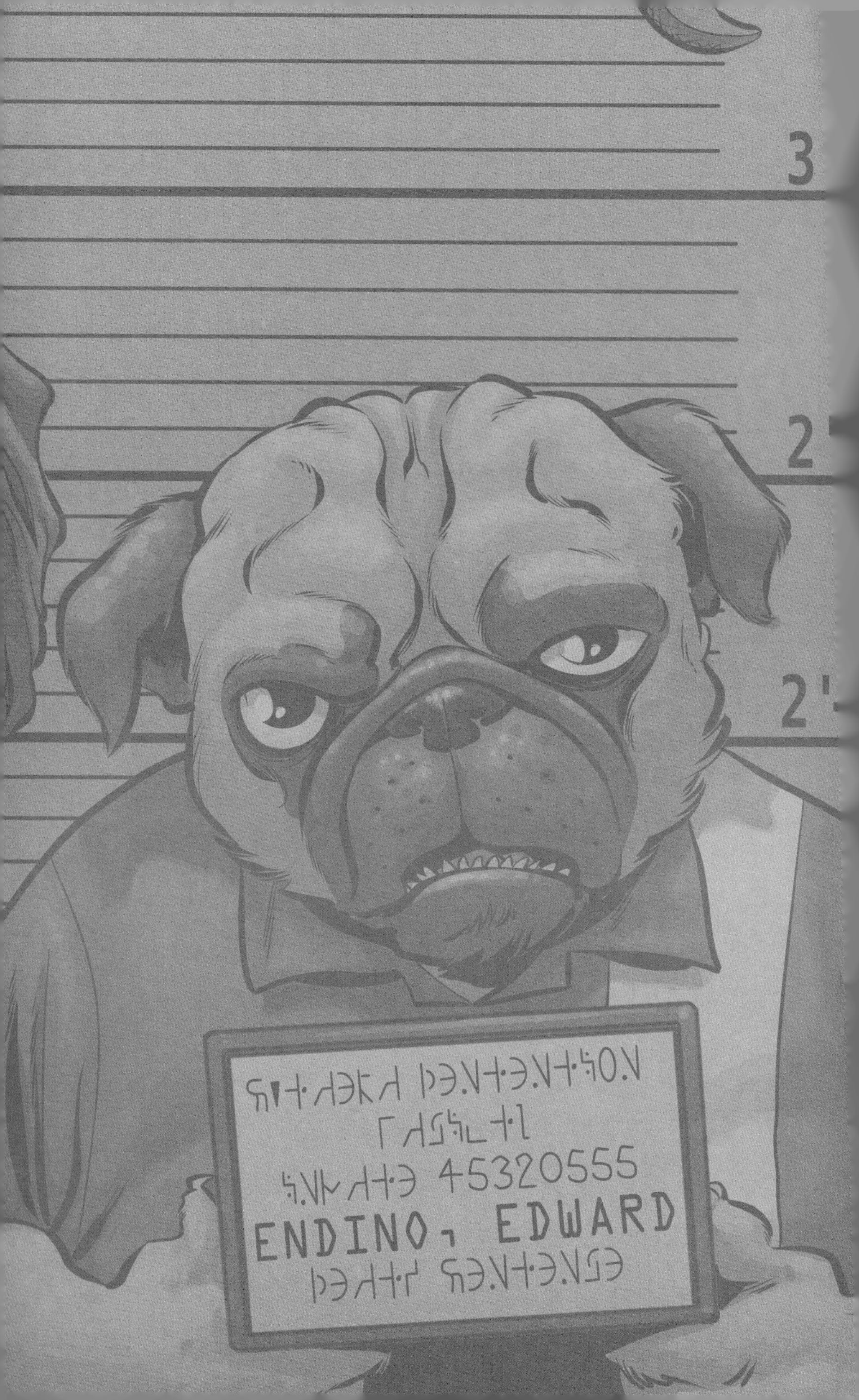
45320555
ENDINO, EDWARD

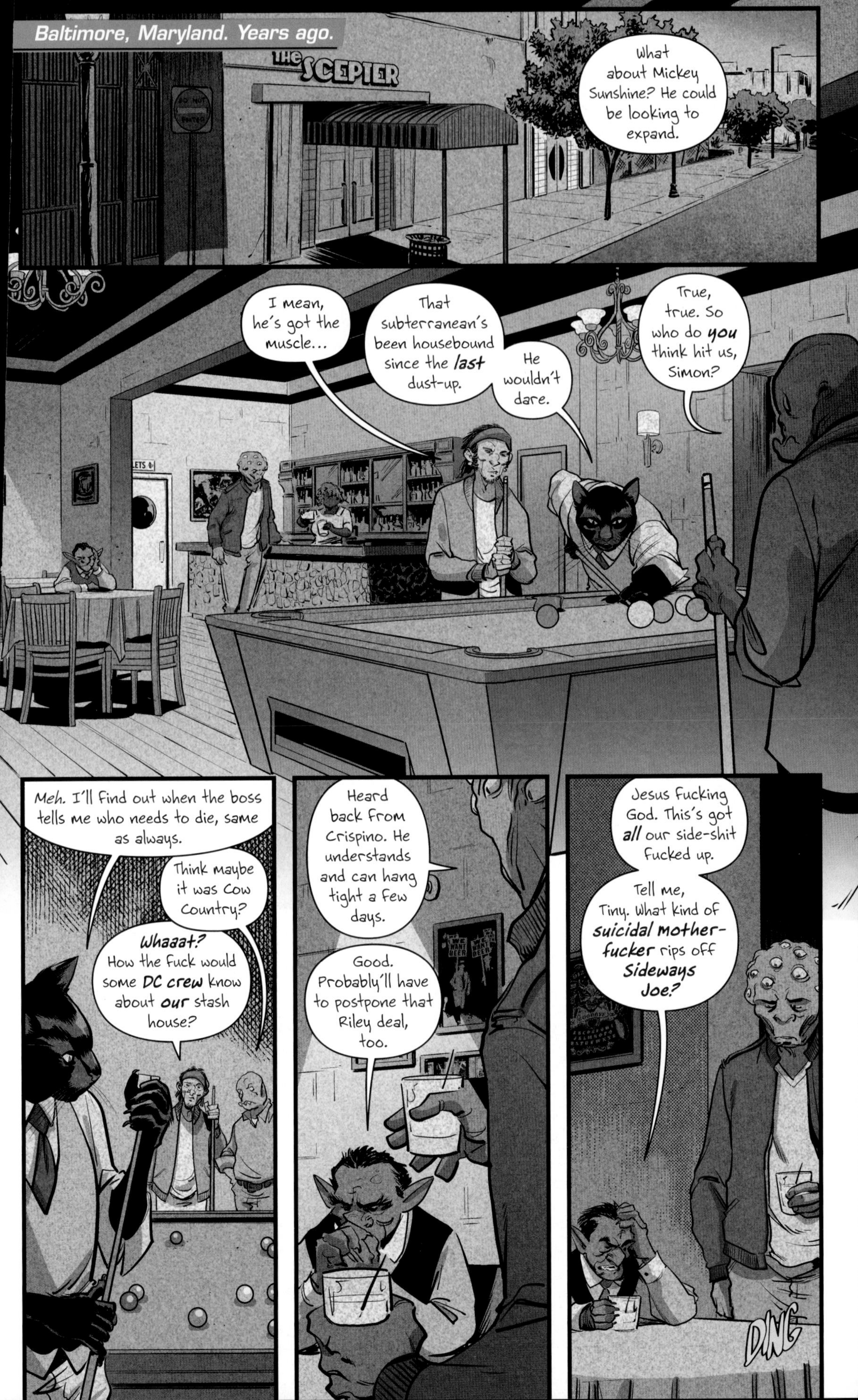
Baltimore, Maryland. Years ago.
THE SCEPTER
What about Mickey Sunshine? He could be looking to expand.
I mean, he's got the muscle...
That subterranean's been housebound since the last dust-up.
He wouldn't dare.
True, true. So who do you think hit us, Simon?
Meh. I'll find out when the boss tells me who needs to die, same as always.
Think maybe it was Cow Country?
Whaaat? How the fuck would some DC crew know about our stash house?
Heard back from Crispino. He understands and can hang tight a few days.
Good. Probably'll have to postpone that Riley deal, too.
Jesus Fucking God. This's got all our side-shit fucked up.
Tell me, Tiny. What kind of suicidal mother-fucker rips off Sideways Joe?
DING

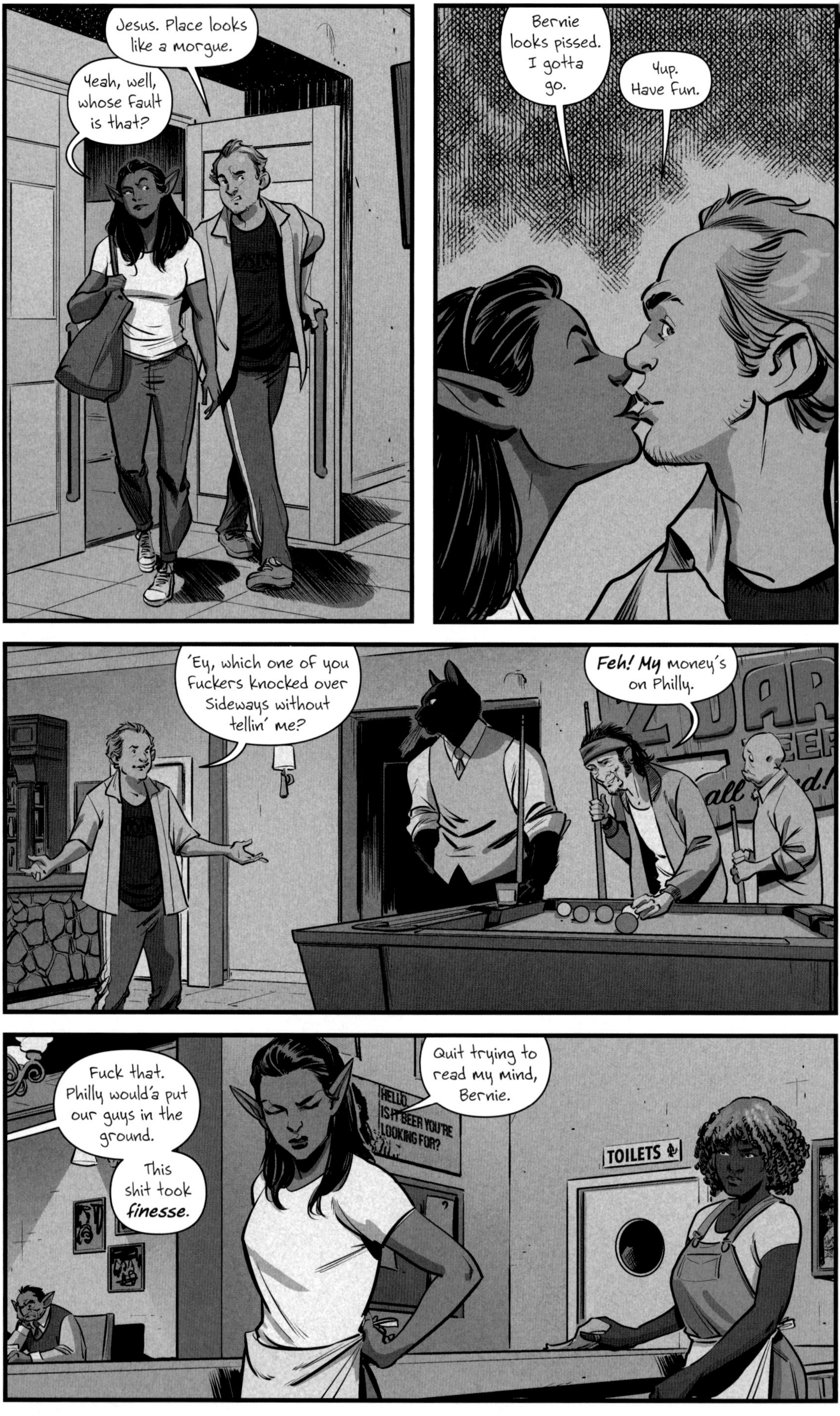
Jesus. Place looks like a morgue.
Yeah, well, whose fault is that?
Bernie looks pissed. I gotta go.
Yup. Have fun.
'Ey, which one of you fuckers knocked over Sideways without tellin' me?
Feh! My money's on Philly.
Fuck that. Philly would'a put our guys in the ground.
This shit took ***finesse***.
Quit trying to read my mind, Bernie.
HELLO IS IT BEER YOU'RE LOOKING FOR?
TOILETS

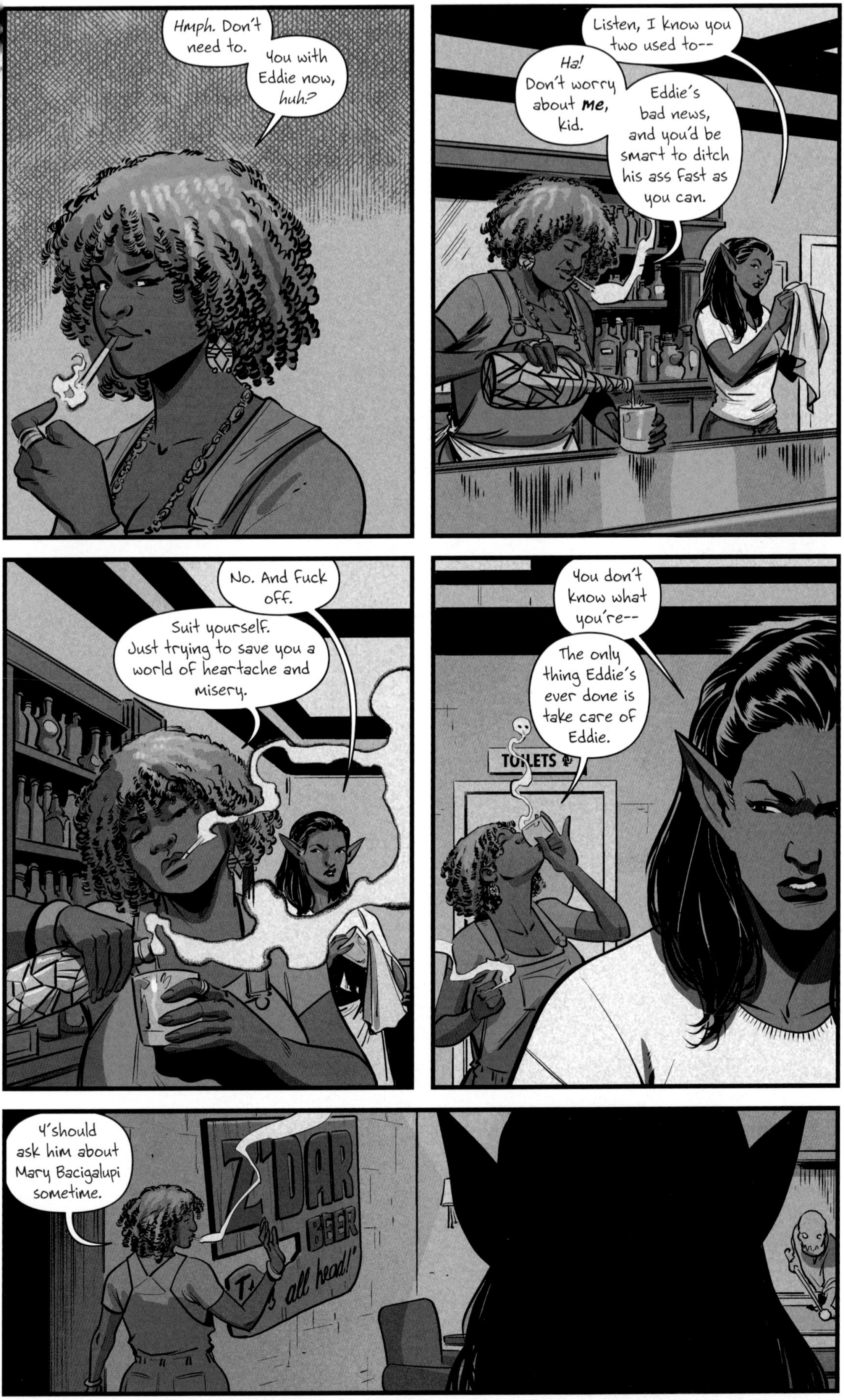
Hmph. Don't need to.
You with Eddie now, huh?
Listen, I know you two used to--
Ha! Don't worry about **me**, kid.
Eddie's bad news, and you'd be smart to ditch his ass fast as you can.
No. And fuck off.
Suit yourself. Just trying to save you a world of heartache and misery.
You don't know what you're--
The only thing Eddie's ever done is take care of Eddie.
TOILETS
Y'should ask him about Mary Bacigalupi sometime.
DAR
BEER
all head!

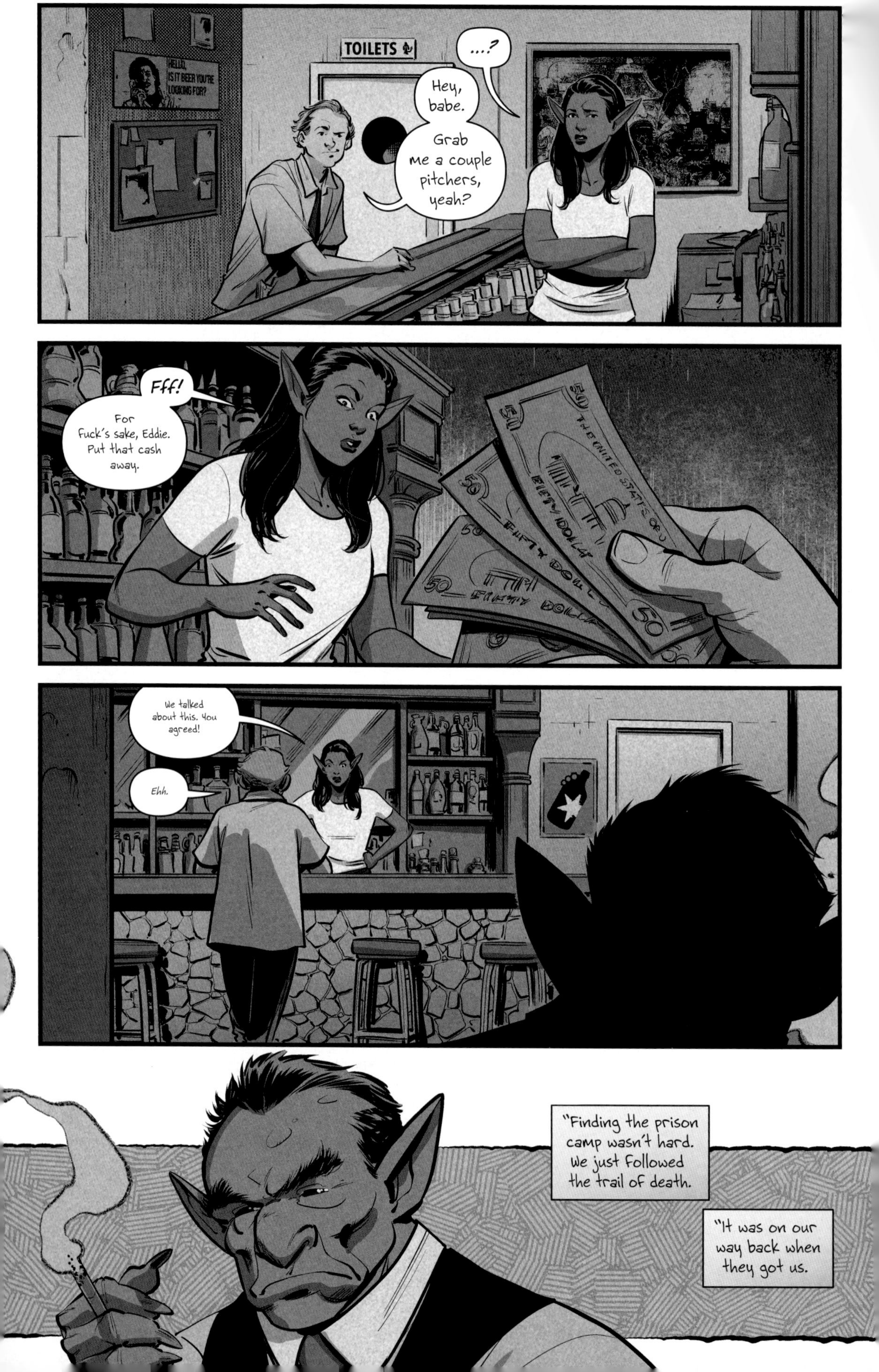
TOILETS
HELLO, IS IT BEER YOU'RE LOOKING FOR?
...?
Hey, babe.
Grab me a couple pitchers, yeah?
Fff!
For Fuck's sake, Eddie. Put that cash away.
We talked about this. You agreed!
Ehh.
"Finding the prison camp wasn't hard. We just followed the trail of death.
"It was on our way back when they got us.

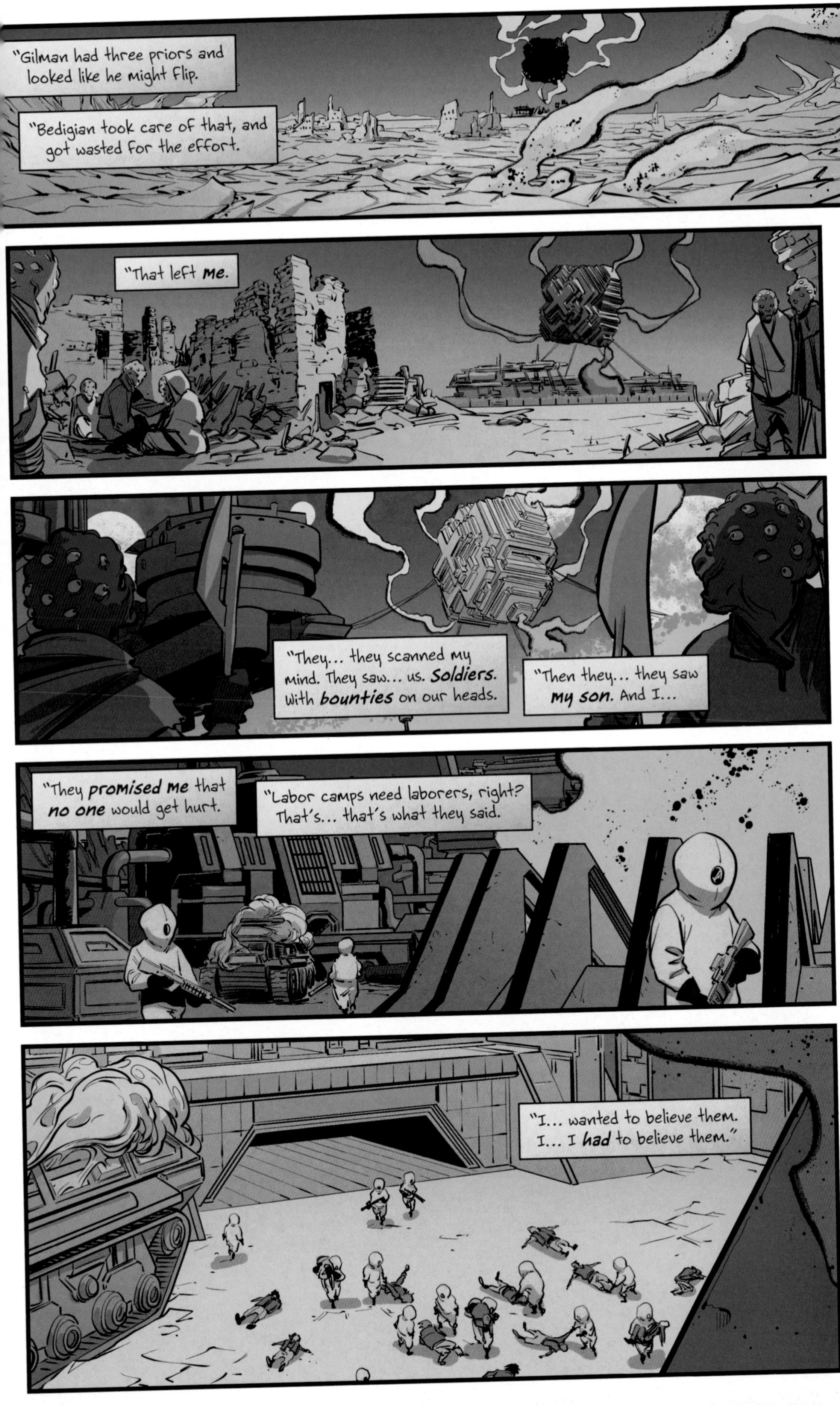
"Gilman had three priors and looked like he might flip.
"Bedigian took care of that, and got wasted for the effort.
"That left **me**.
"They... they scanned my mind. They saw... us. **Soldiers**. With **bounties** on our heads.
"Then they... they saw **my son**. And I...
"They **promised me** that **no one** would get hurt.
"Labor camps need laborers, right? That's... that's what they said.
"I... wanted to believe them. I... I **had** to believe them."

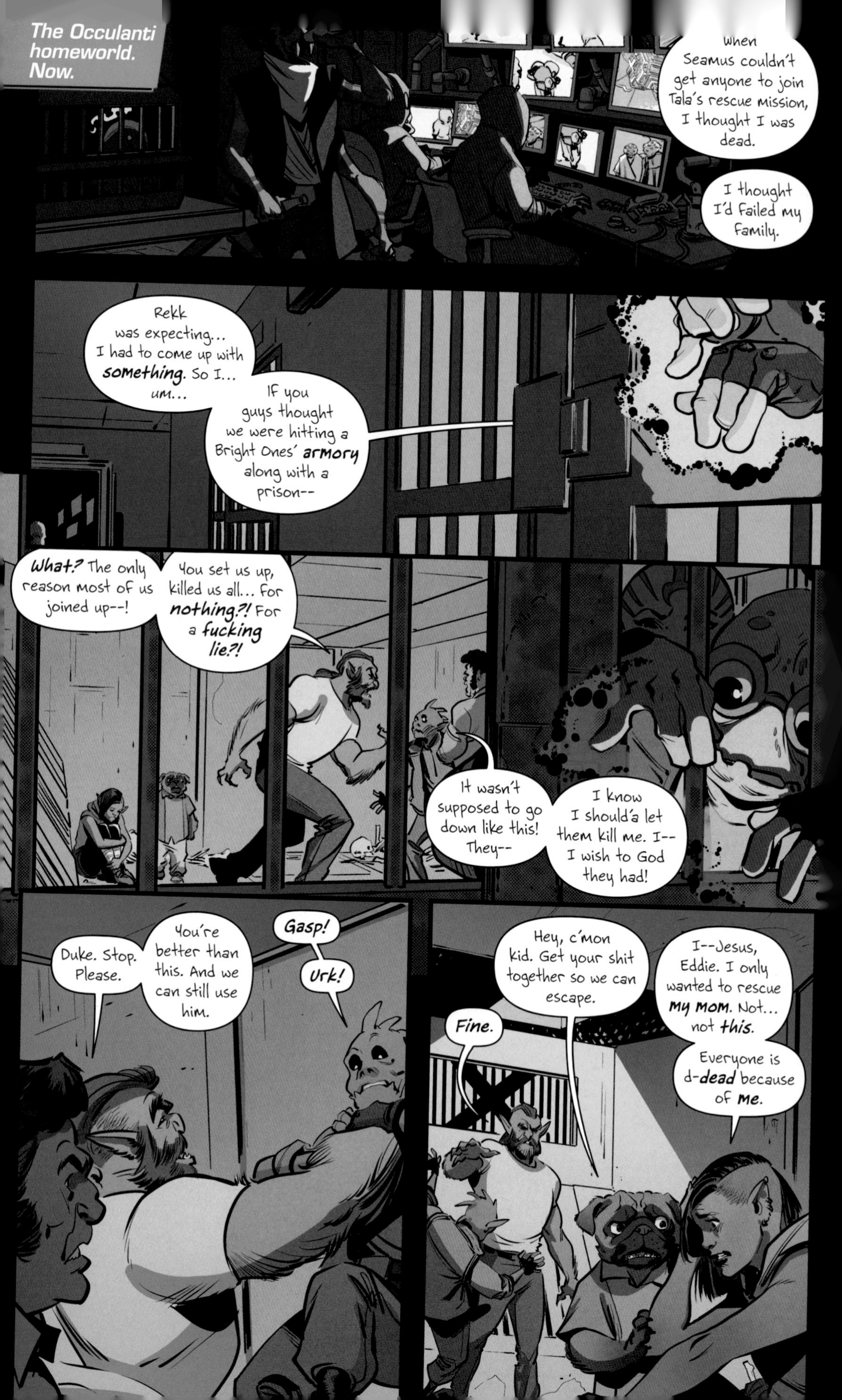

The Occulanti homeworld. Now.
when Seamus couldn't get anyone to join Tala's rescue mission, I thought I was dead.
I thought I'd failed my family.
Rekk was expecting... I had to come up with **something**. So I... um...
If you guys thought we were hitting a Bright Ones' **armory** along with a prison--
What? The only reason most of us joined up--!
You set us up, killed us all... for **nothing?!** For a **fucking lie?!**
It wasn't supposed to go down like this! They--
I know I should'a let them kill me. I-- I wish to God they had!
Duke. Stop. Please.
You're better than this. And we can still use him.
Gasp!
Urk!
Hey, c'mon kid. Get your shit together so we can escape.
Fine.
I--Jesus, Eddie. I only wanted to rescue **my mom**. Not... not **this**.
Everyone is d-**dead** because of **me**.

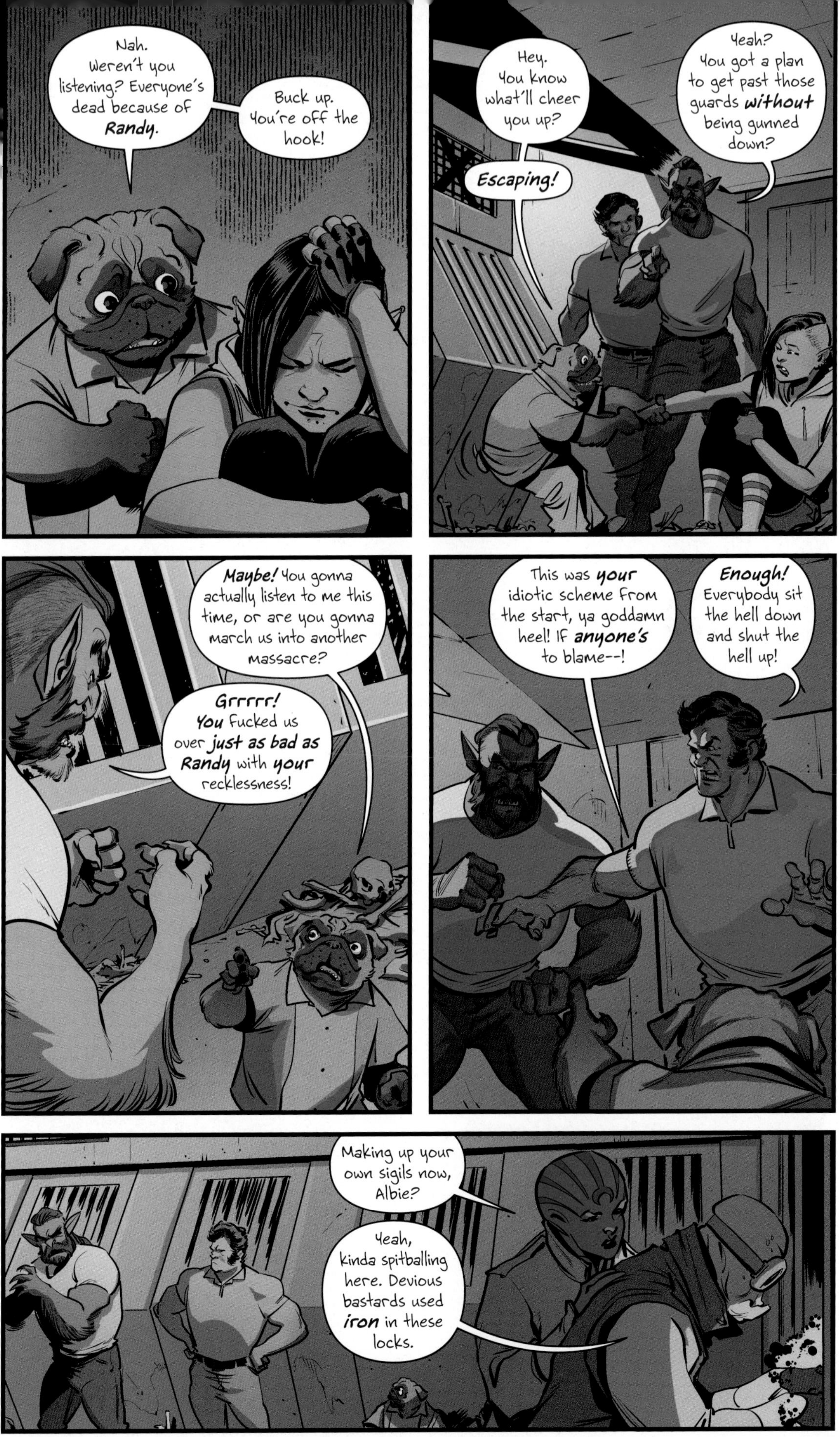
Nah. Weren't you listening? Everyone's dead because of Randy.
Buck up. You're off the hook!
Hey. You know what'll cheer you up?
Escaping!
Yeah? You got a plan to get past those guards without being gunned down?
Maybe! You gonna actually listen to me this time, or are you gonna march us into another massacre?
Grrrrr! You fucked us over just as bad as Randy with your recklessness!
This was your idiotic scheme from the start, ya goddamn heel! If anyone's to blame--!
Enough! Everybody sit the hell down and shut the hell up!
Making up your own sigils now, Albie?
Yeah, kinda spitballing here. Devious bastards used iron in these locks.

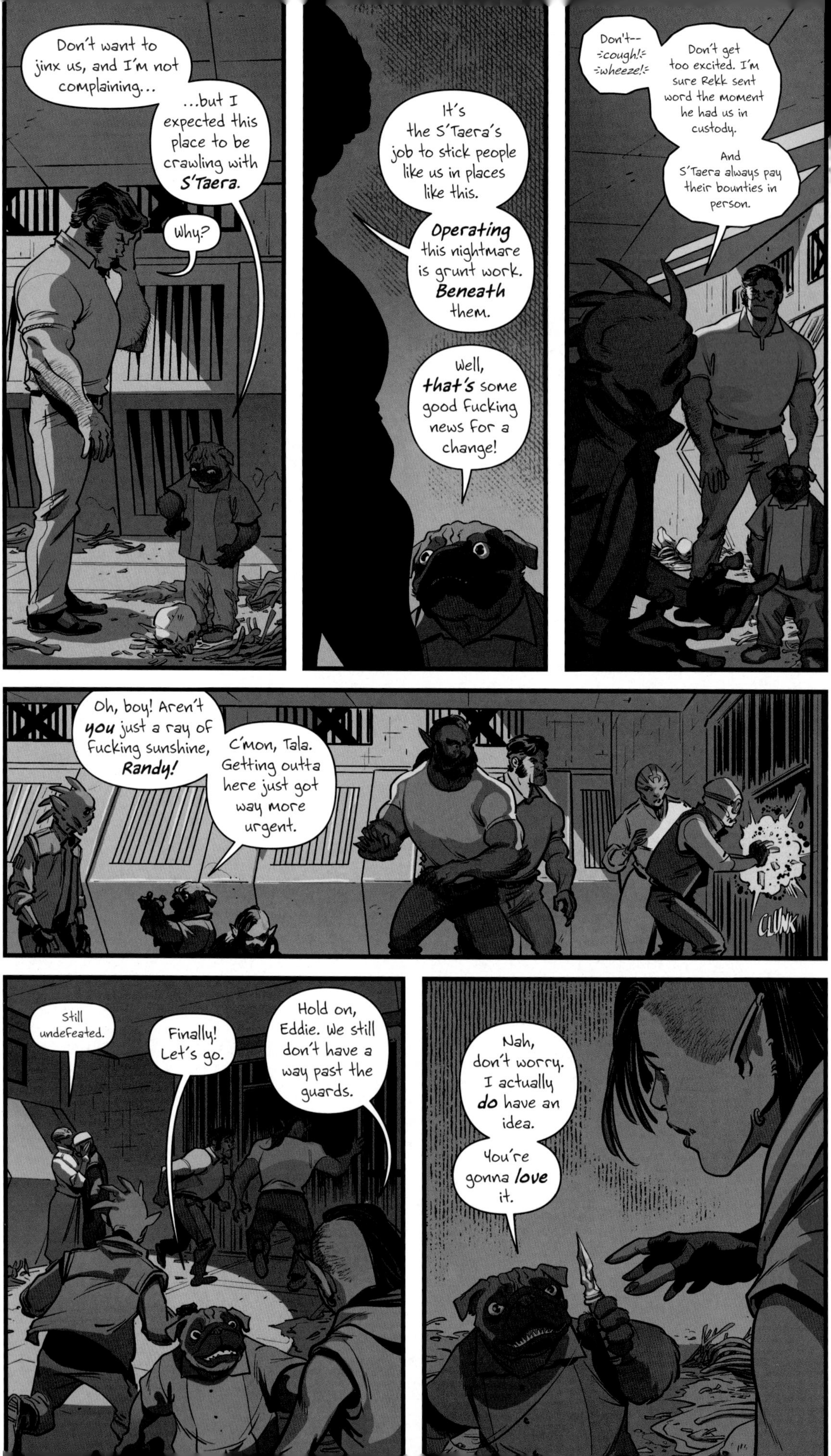
Don't want to jinx us, and I'm not complaining...
...but I expected this place to be crawling with **S'Taera.**
Why?
It's the S'Taera's job to stick people like us in places like this.
Operating this nightmare is grunt work. **Beneath** them.
Well, ***that's*** some good fucking news for a change!
Don't-- =cough!= =wheeze!=
Don't get too excited. I'm sure Rekk sent word the moment he had us in custody.
And S'Taera always pay their bounties in person.
Oh, boy! Aren't ***you*** just a ray of fucking sunshine, ***Randy!***
C'mon, Tala. Getting outta here just got way more urgent.
CLUNK
Still undefeated.
Finally! Let's go.
Hold on, Eddie. We still don't have a way past the guards.
Nah, don't worry. I actually **do** have an idea.
You're gonna ***love*** it.

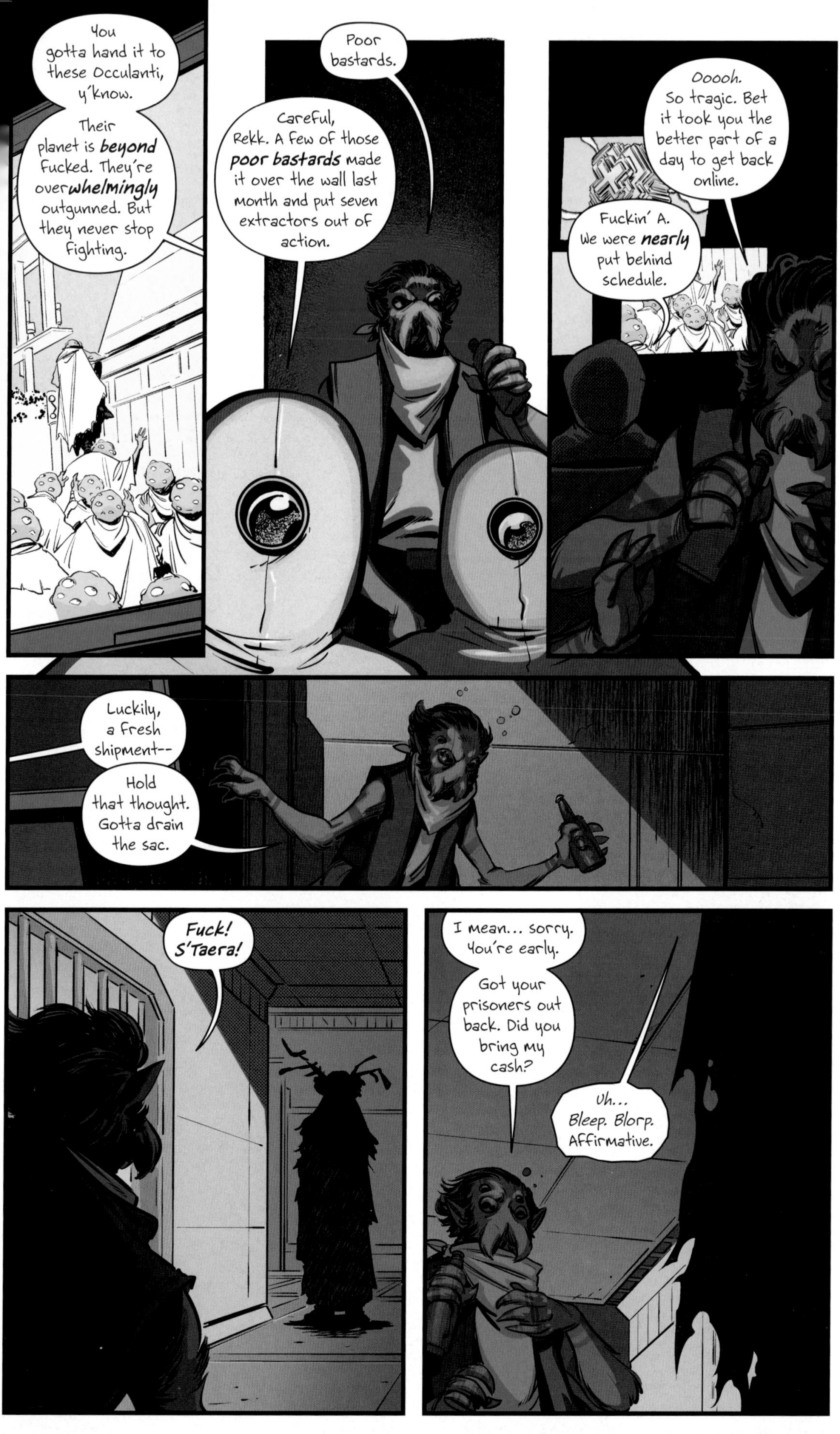
You gotta hand it to these Occulanti, y'know.
Their planet is **beyond** fucked. They're over**whelmingly** outgunned. But they never stop fighting.
Poor bastards.
Careful, Rekk. A few of those **poor bastards** made it over the wall last month and put seven extractors out of action.
Ooooh. So tragic. Bet it took you the better part of a day to get back online.
Fuckin' A. We were **nearly** put behind schedule.
Luckily, a fresh shipment--
Hold that thought. Gotta drain the sac.
Fuck! S'Taera!
I mean... sorry. You're early.
Got your prisoners out back. Did you bring my cash?
Uh... Bleep. Blorp. Affirmative.

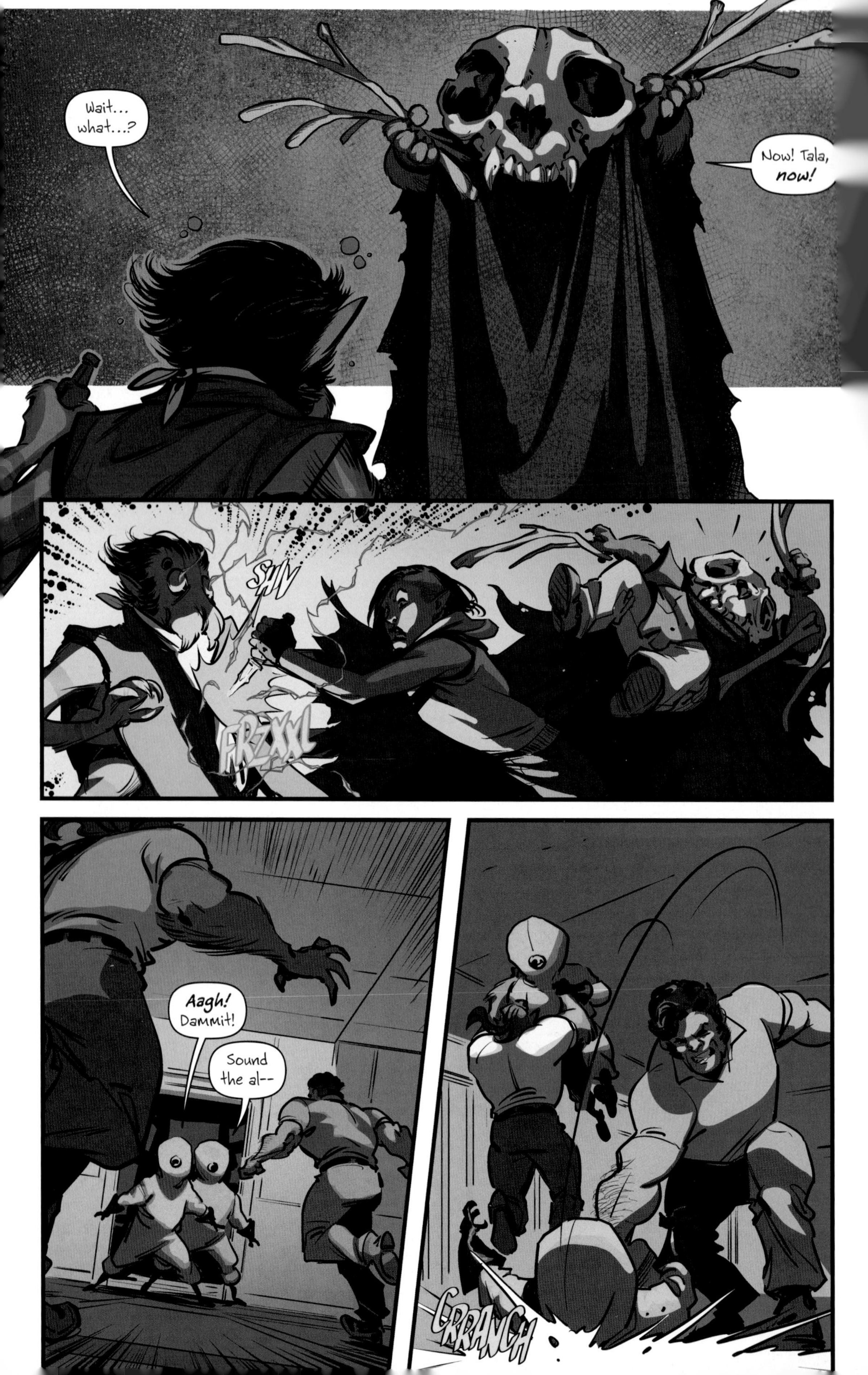
Wait... what...?
Now! Tala, now!
SHV
FRZXXL
Aagh! Dammit!
Sound the al--
CRRANCH

SPLURTCH

...

Heheh.

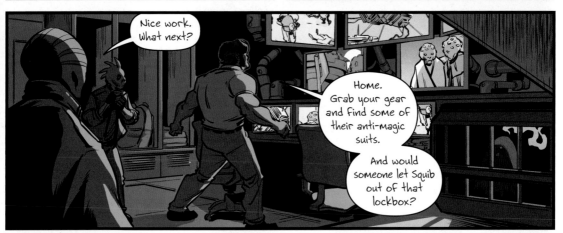

Nice work. What next?

Home. Grab your gear and find some of their anti-magic suits.

And would someone let Squib out of that lockbox?

They're monitoring the gateways in and out. We won't make it past the first jump.

Gotta try. Once the S'Taera arrive--

First place they'll look for us is right here.

We should have this conversation somewhere else.

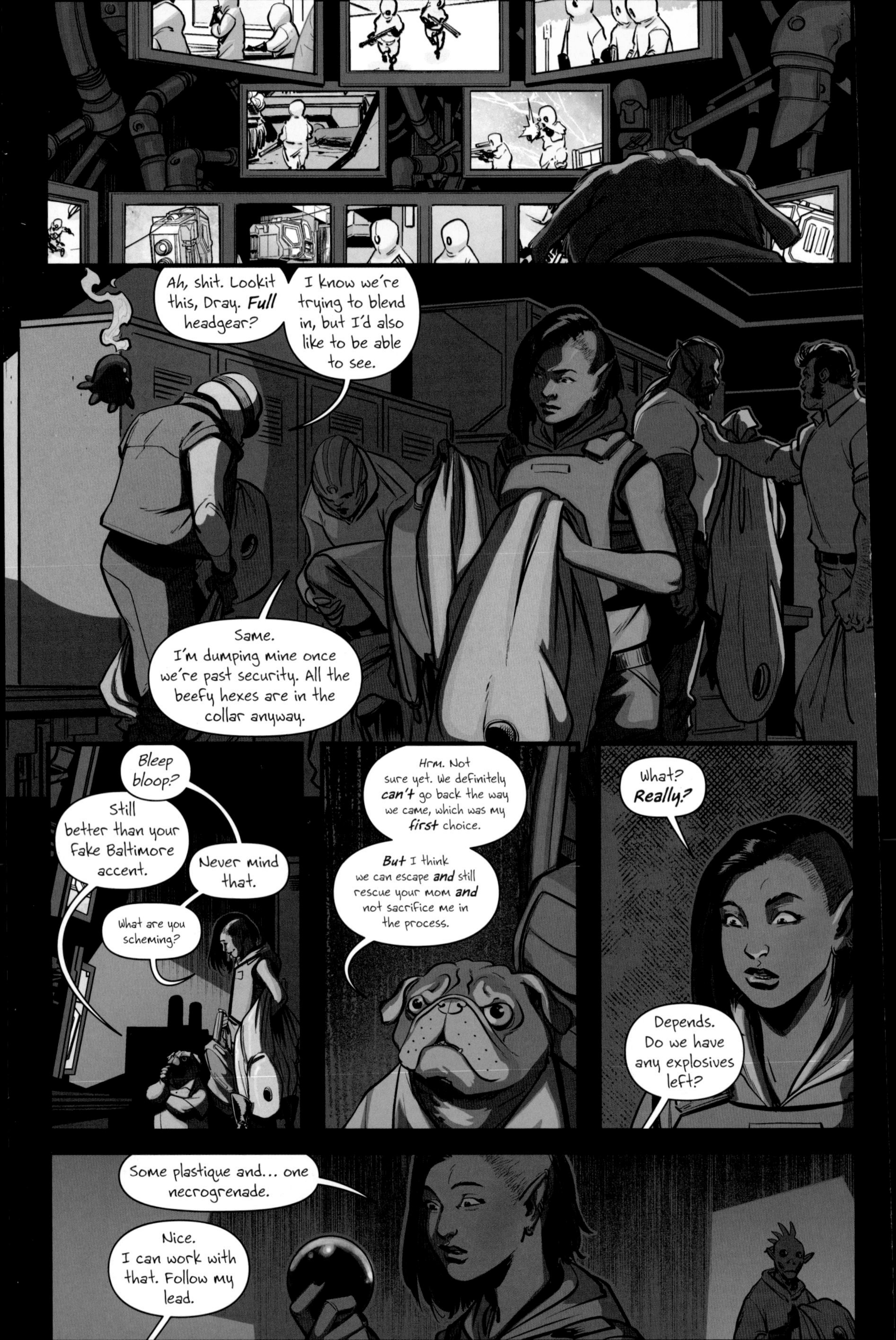
Ah, shit. Lookit this, Dray. Full headgear?
I know we're trying to blend in, but I'd also like to be able to see.
Same. I'm dumping mine once we're past security. All the beefy hexes are in the collar anyway.
Bleep bloop?
Still better than your fake Baltimore accent.
Never mind that.
What are you scheming?
Hrm. Not sure yet. We definitely can't go back the way we came, which was my first choice.
But I think we can escape and still rescue your mom and not sacrifice me in the process.
What? Really?
Depends. Do we have any explosives left?
Some plastique and... one necrogrenade.
Nice. I can work with that. Follow my lead.

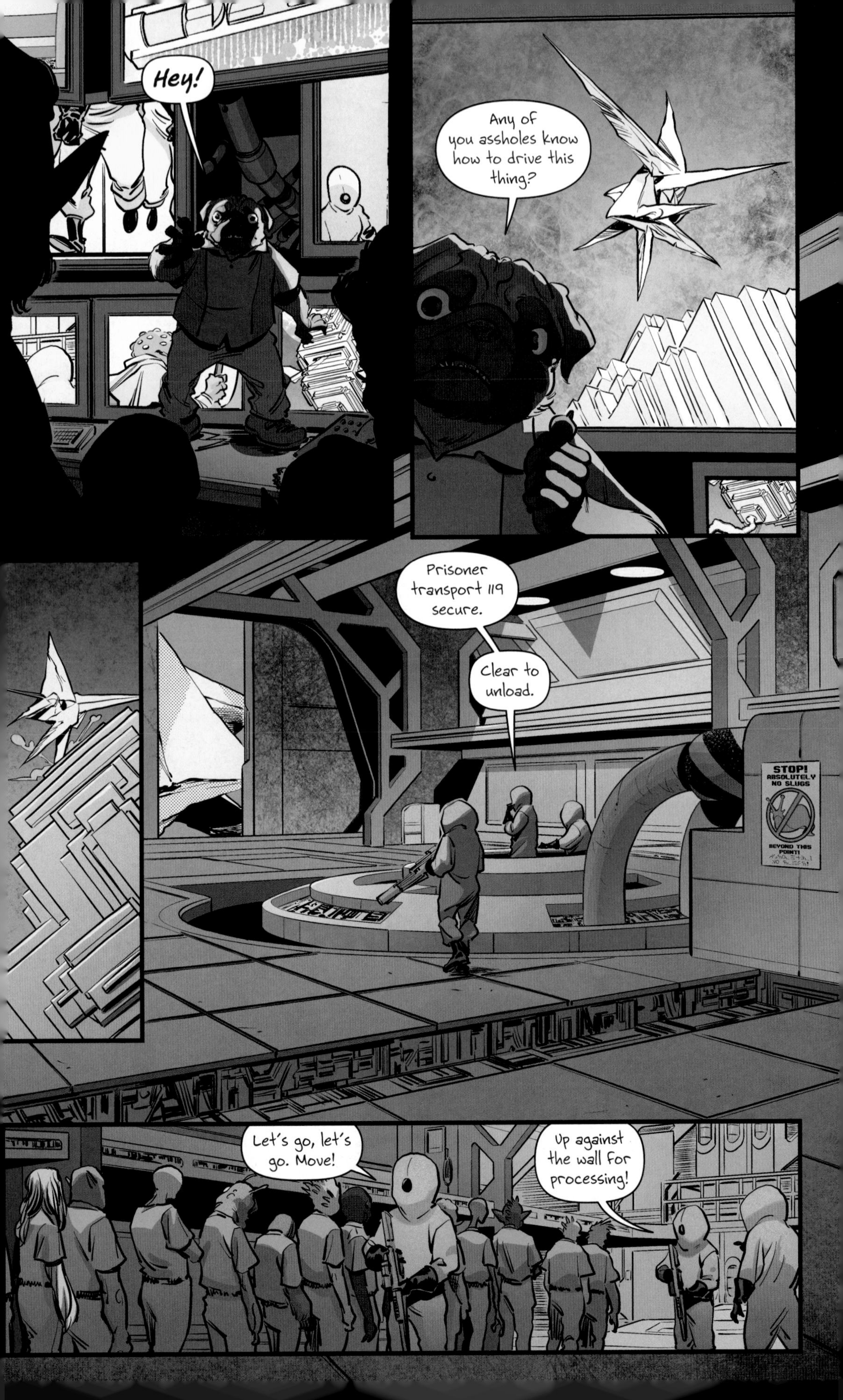
Hey!
Any of you assholes know how to drive this thing?
Prisoner transport 119 secure.
Clear to unload.
STOP!
ABSOLUTELY NO SLUGS
BEYOND THIS POINT!
Let's go, let's go. Move!
Up against the wall for processing!

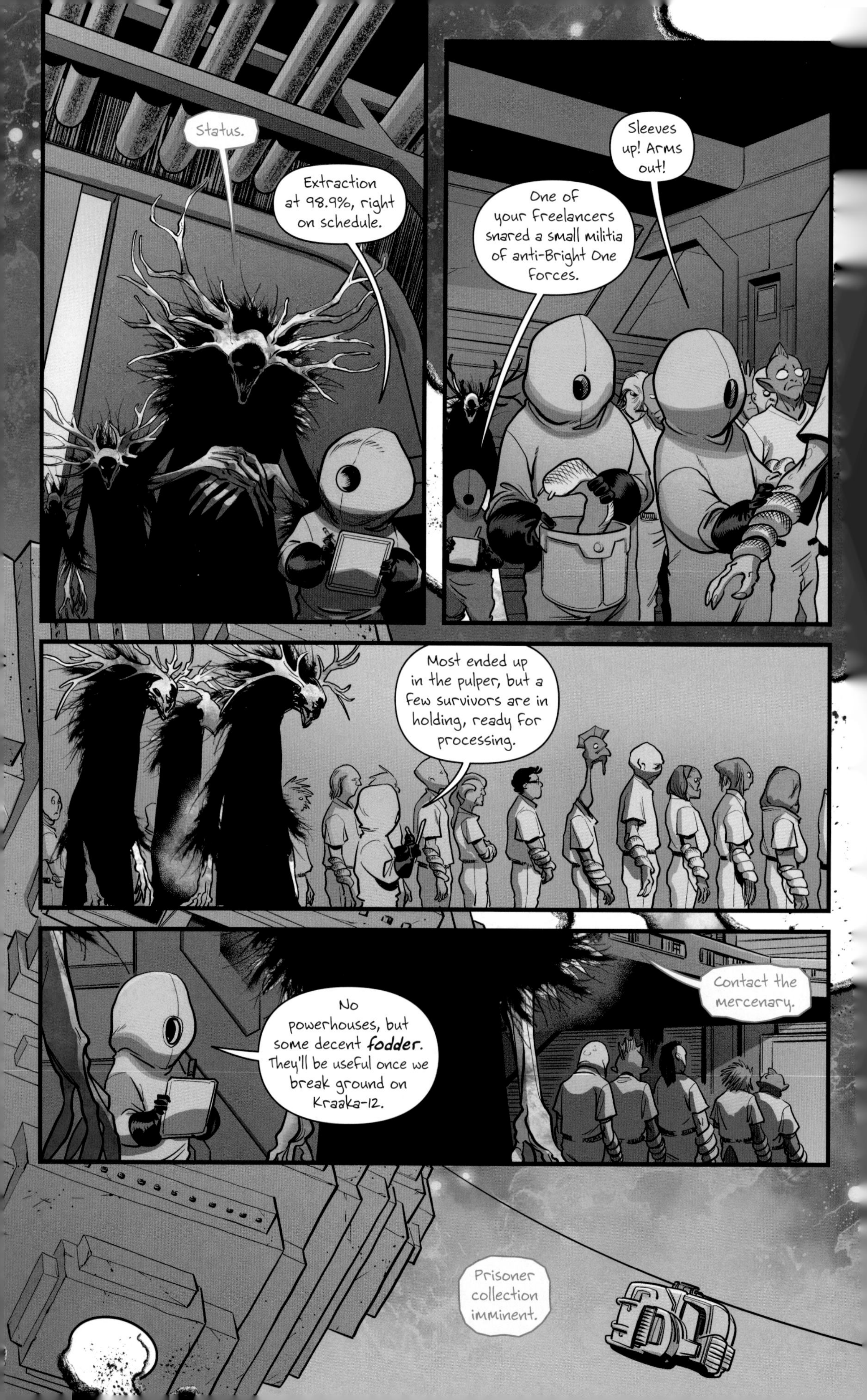
Status.
Extraction at 98.9%, right on schedule.
Sleeves up! Arms out!
One of your freelancers snared a small militia of anti-Bright One forces.
Most ended up in the pulper, but a few survivors are in holding, ready for processing.
No powerhouses, but some decent **fodder**. They'll be useful once we break ground on Kraaka-12.
Contact the mercenary.
Prisoner collection imminent.

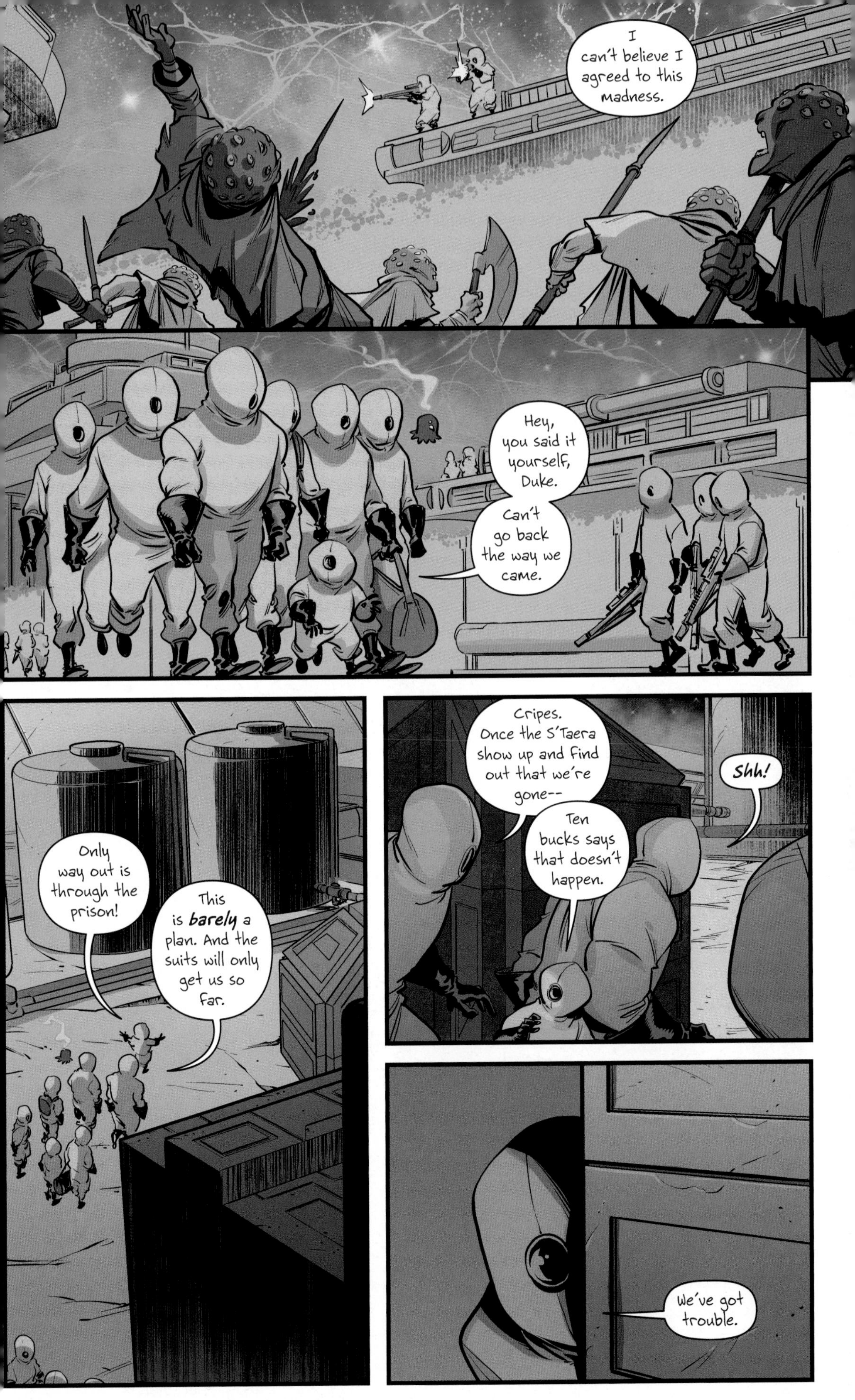
I can't believe I agreed to this madness.
Hey, you said it yourself, Duke.
Can't go back the way we came.
Only way out is through the prison!
This is **barely** a plan. And the suits will only get us so far.
Cripes. Once the S'Taera show up and find out that we're gone--
Ten bucks says that doesn't happen.
Shh!
We've got trouble.

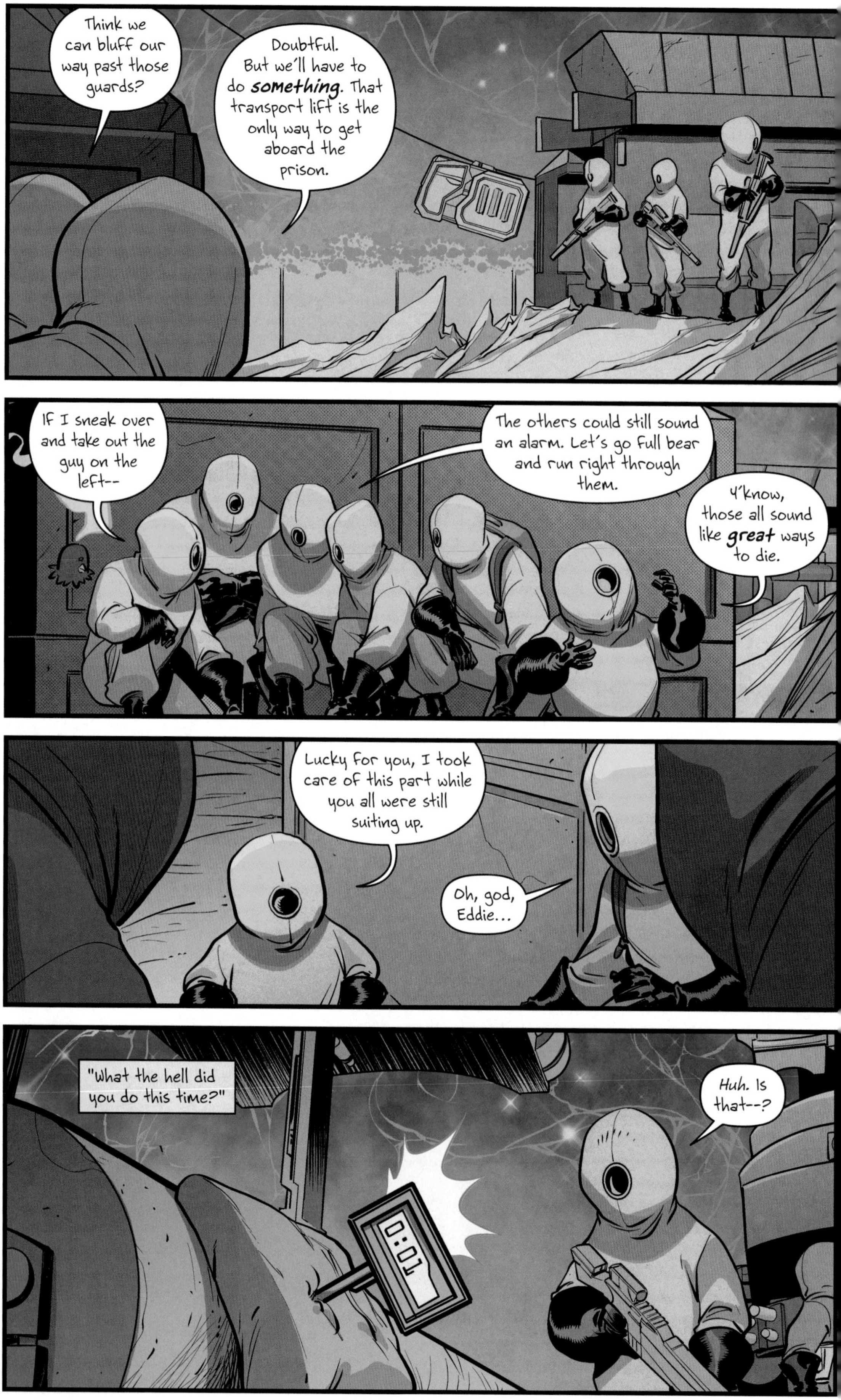
Think we can bluff our way past those guards?
Doubtful. But we'll have to do **something**. That transport lift is the only way to get aboard the prison.
If I sneak over and take out the guy on the left--
The others could still sound an alarm. Let's go full bear and run right through them.
Y'know, those all sound like **great** ways to die.
Lucky for you, I took care of this part while you all were still suiting up.
Oh, god, Eddie...
"What the hell did you do this time?"
Huh. Is that--?
0:01

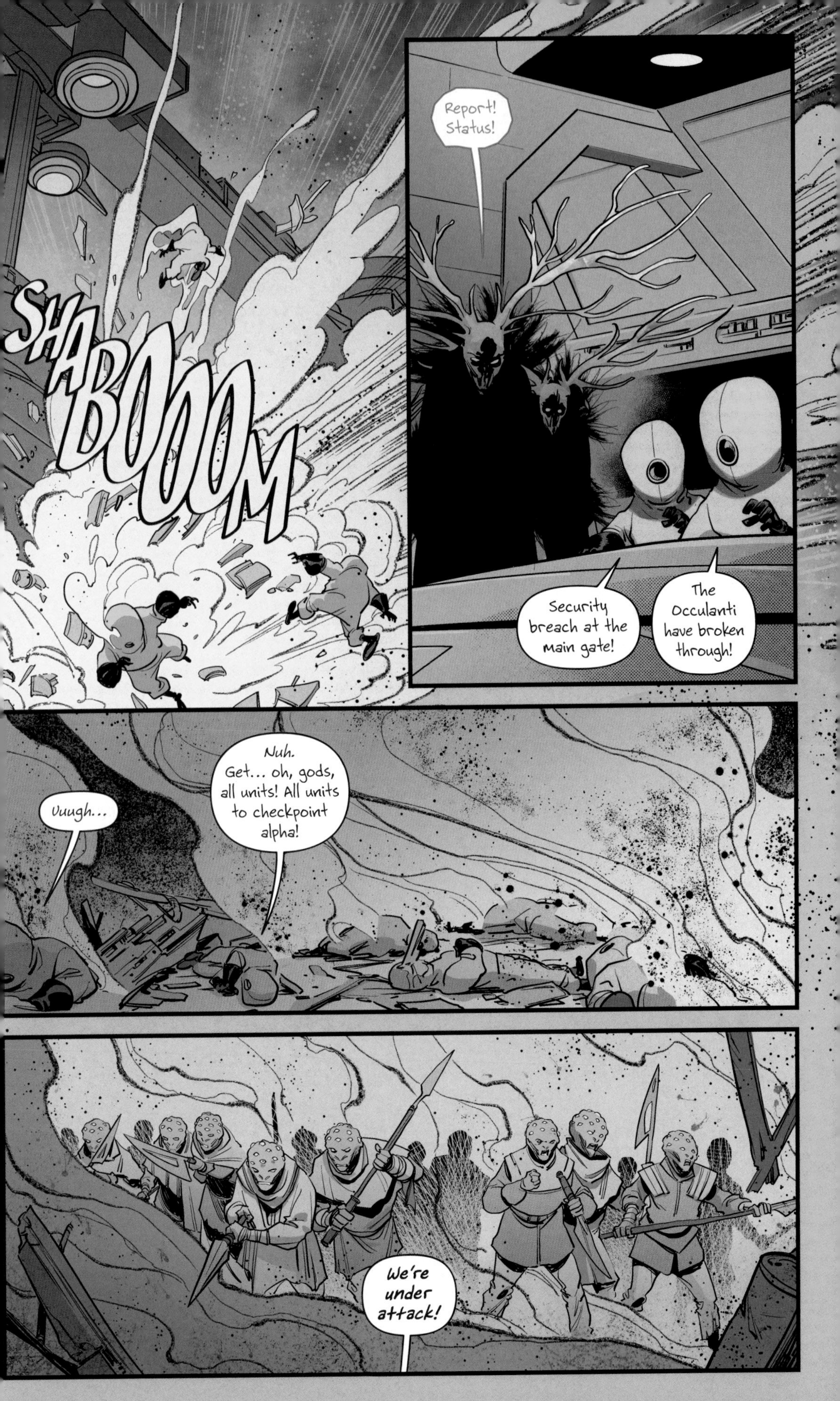
SHABOOOM
Report! Status!
Security breach at the main gate!
The Occulanti have broken through!
Uuugh...
Nuh. Get... oh, gods, all units! All units to checkpoint alpha!
We're under attack!

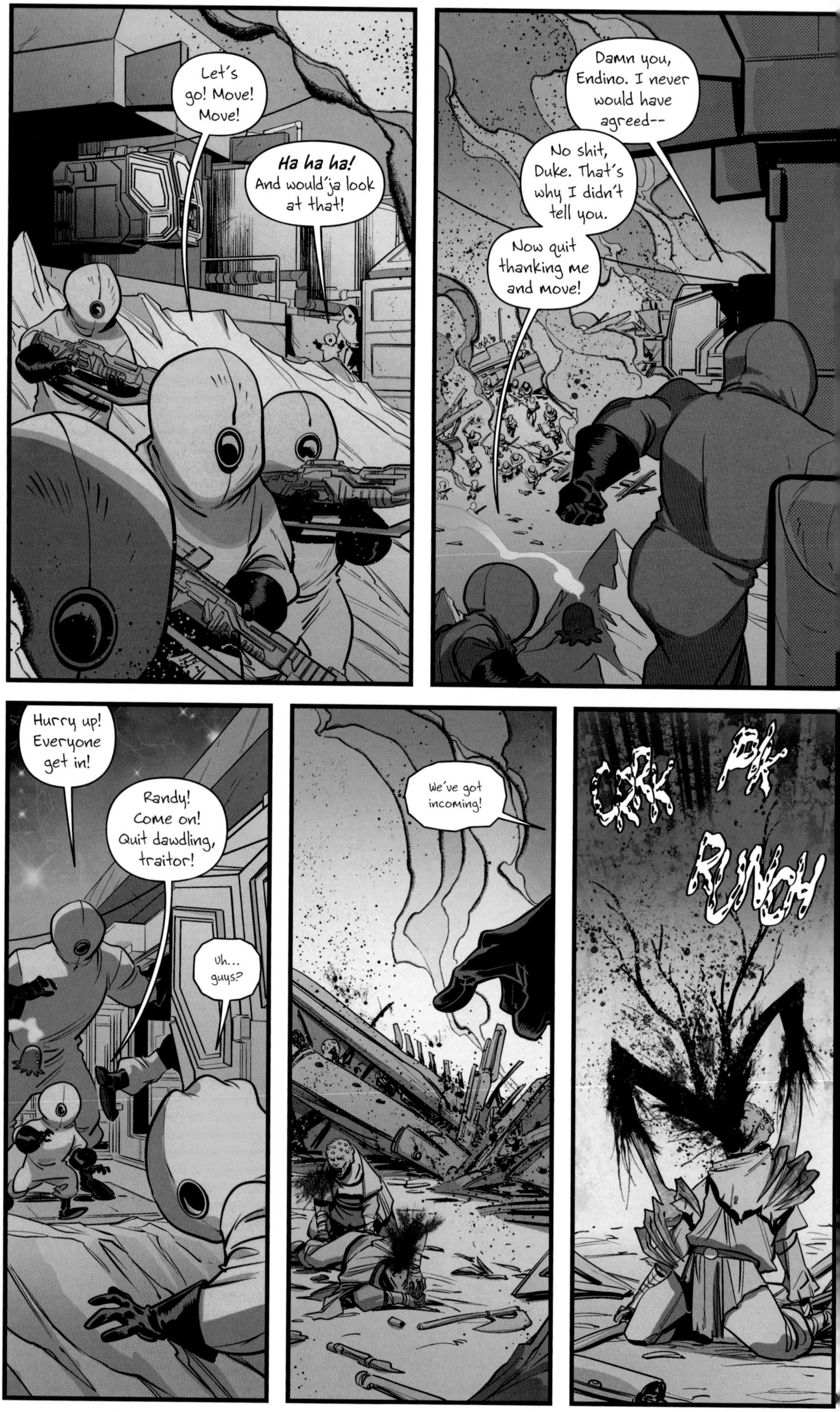

Let's go! Move! Move!
Ha ha ha! And would'ja look at that!
Damn you, Endino. I never would have agreed--
No shit, Duke. That's why I didn't tell you.
Now quit thanking me and move!
Hurry up! Everyone get in!
Randy! Come on! Quit dawdling, traitor!
Uh... guys?
We've got incoming!
CRK
PK
RUNCH

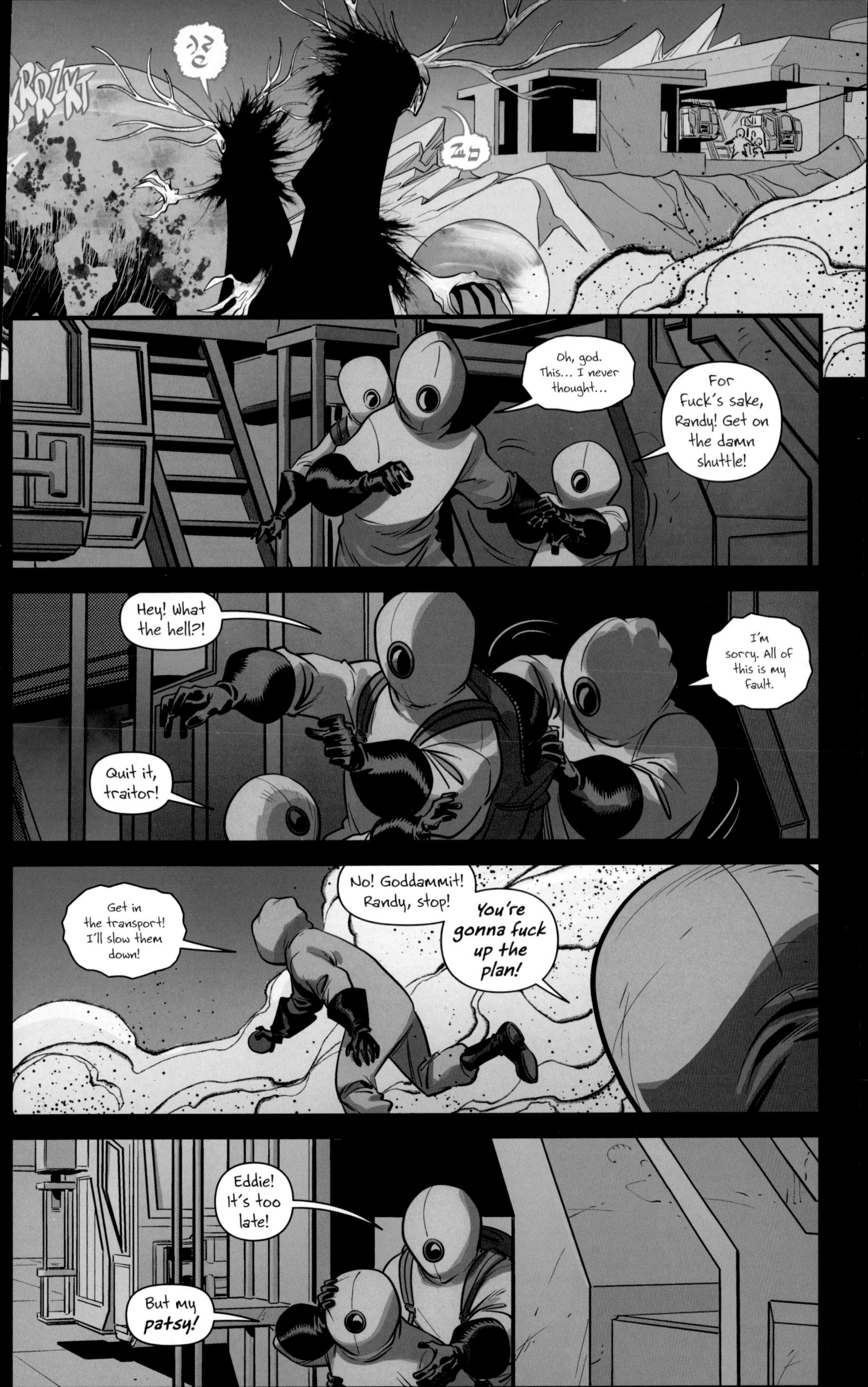

Oh, god. This... I never thought...
For fuck's sake, Randy! Get on the damn shuttle!
Hey! What the hell?!
I'm sorry. All of this is my fault.
Quit it, traitor!
Get in the transport! I'll slow them down!
No! Goddammit! Randy, stop!
You're gonna fuck up the plan!
Eddie! It's too late!
But my *patsy!*

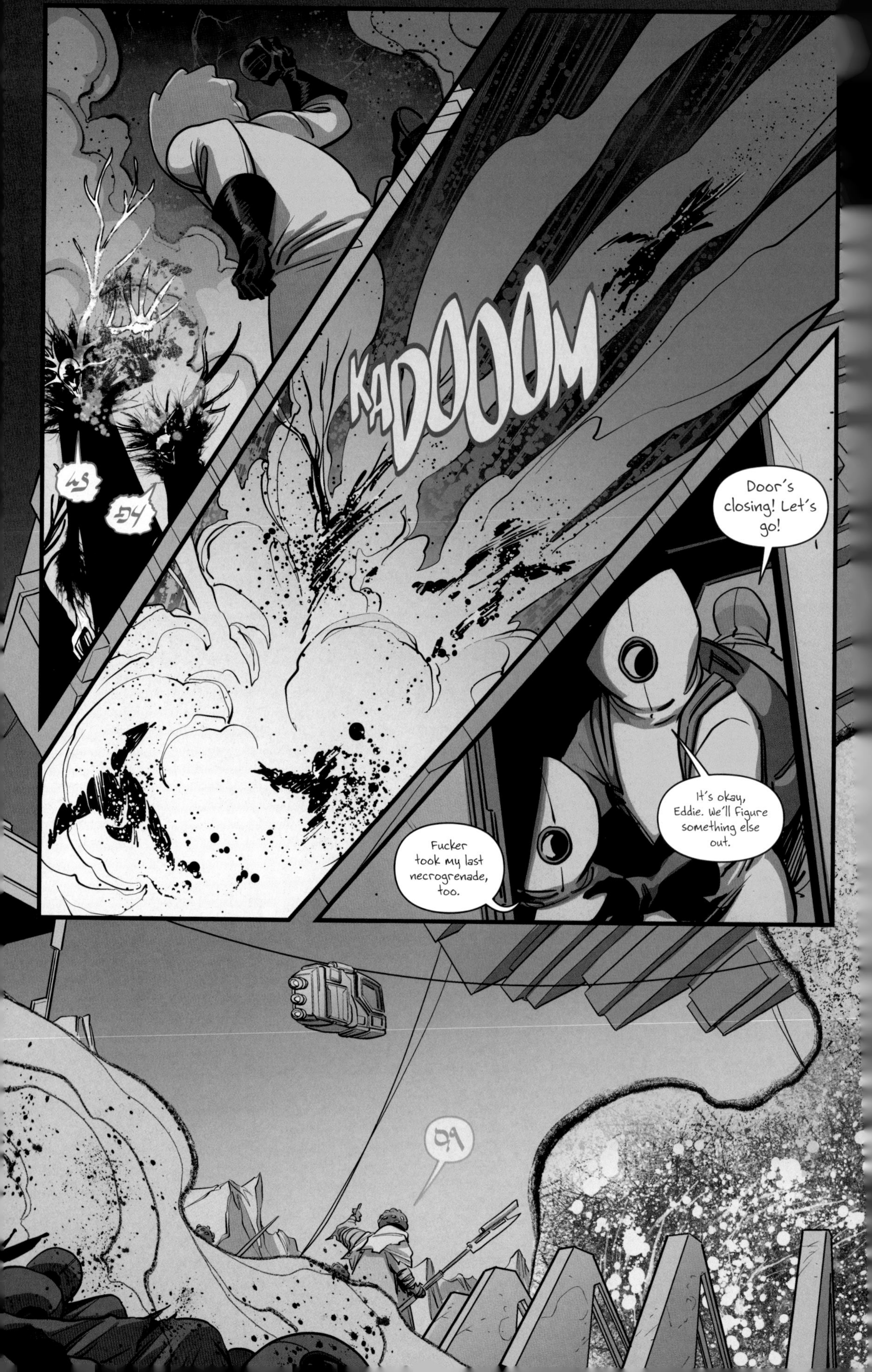
KADOOOM
Door's closing! Let's go!
It's okay, Eddie. We'll figure something else out.
Fucker took my last necrogrenade, too.

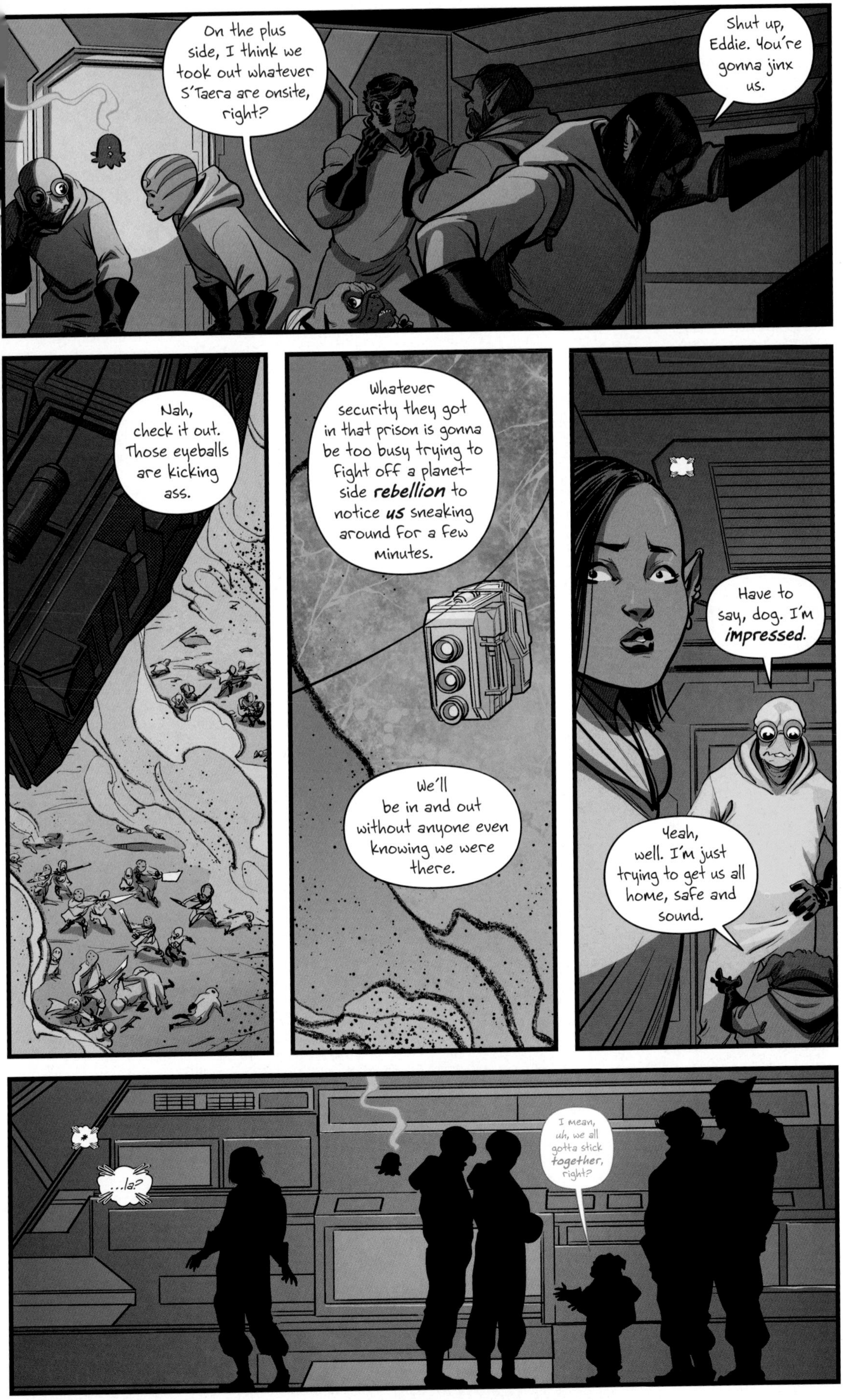
On the plus side, I think we took out whatever S'Taera are onsite, right?
Shut up, Eddie. You're gonna jinx us.
Nah, check it out. Those eyeballs are kicking ass.
Whatever security they got in that prison is gonna be too busy trying to fight off a planet-side **rebellion** to notice ***us*** sneaking around for a few minutes.
We'll be in and out without anyone even knowing we were there.
Have to say, dog. I'm ***impressed***.
Yeah, well. I'm just trying to get us all home, safe and sound.
...la?
I mean, uh, we all gotta stick ***together***, right?

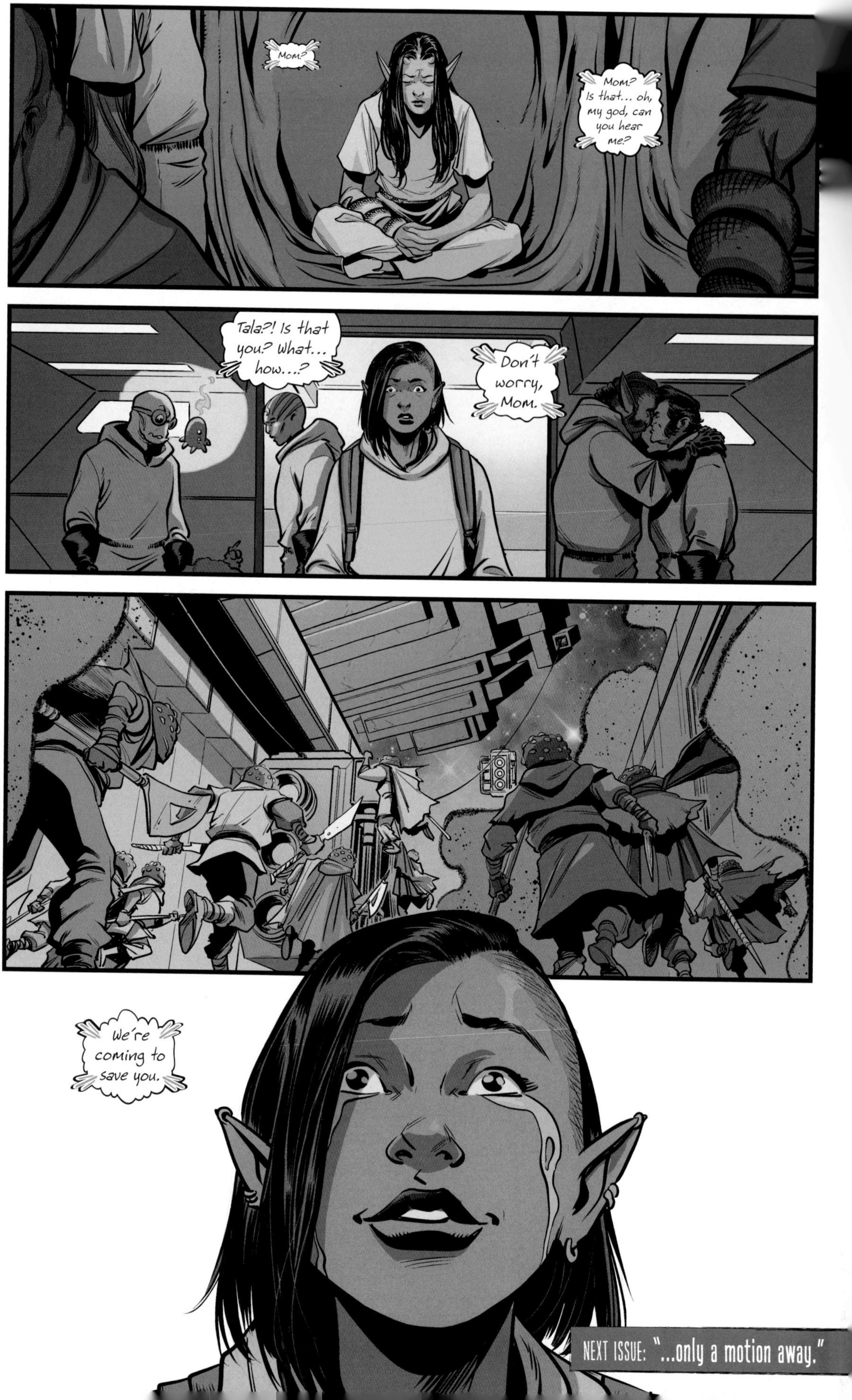
Mom?
Mom? Is that... oh, my god, can you hear me?
Tala?! Is that you? What... how...?
Don't worry, Mom.
We're coming to save you.
NEXT ISSUE: "...only a motion away."

BOOK FOUR

ᏦᎡᏦ ᎯᏞᏕᎧ
ᏫᎯᏕᏞᏴᏦᎡᎯᏦ!
· · · · · · · · · ·
JAILBREAK!

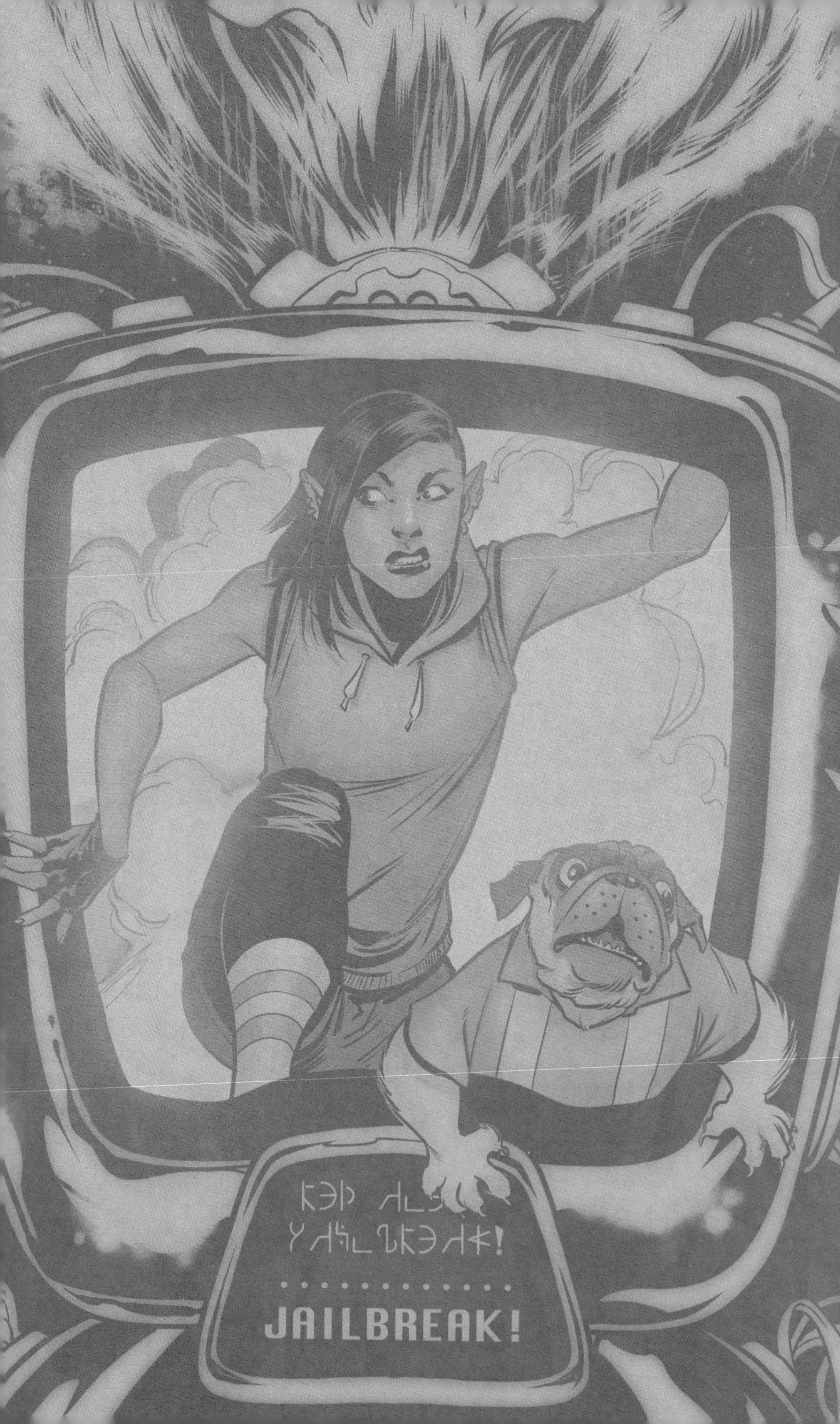
JAILBREAK!

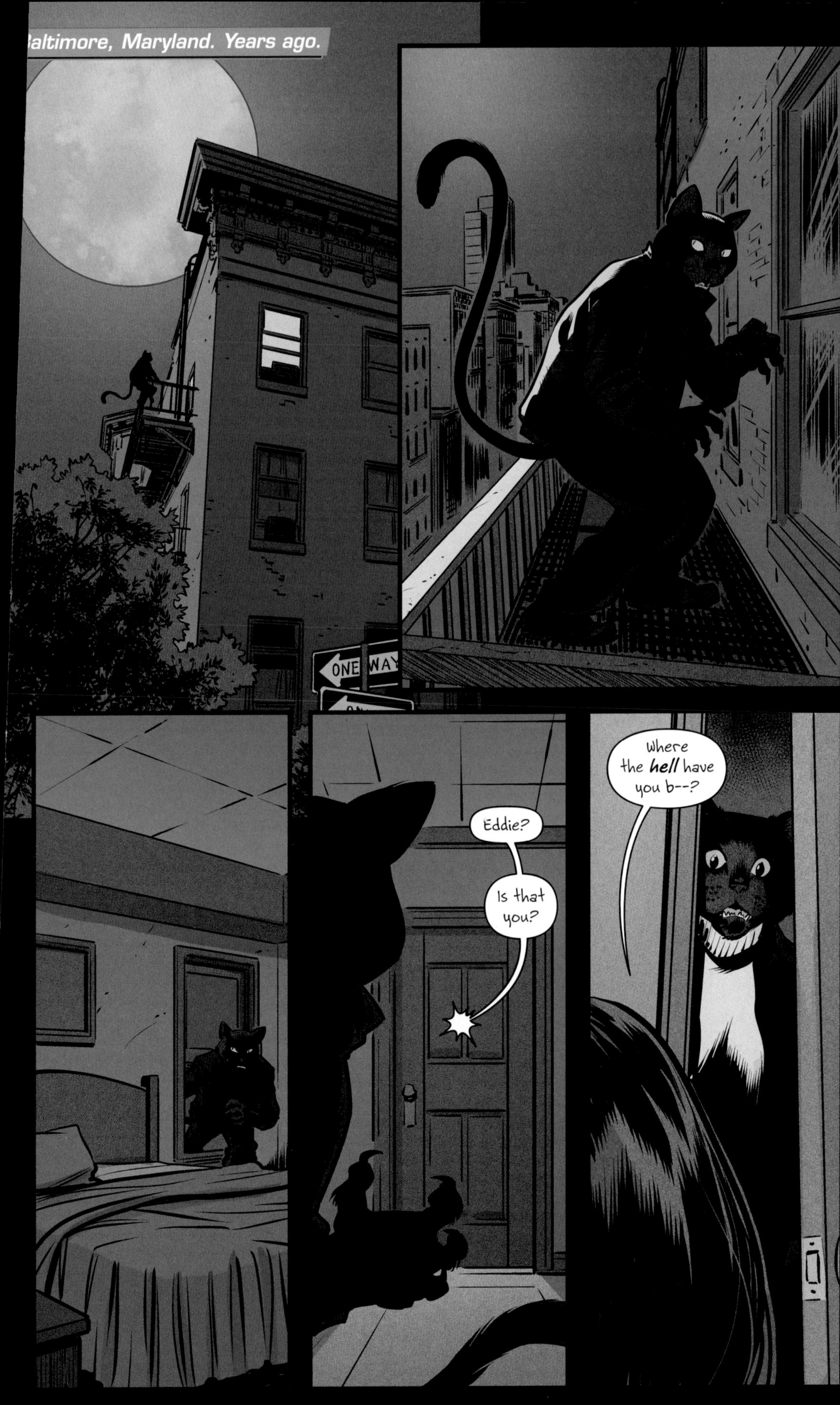
Baltimore, Maryland. Years ago.
ONE WAY
Eddie?
Is that you?
Where the **hell** have you b--?

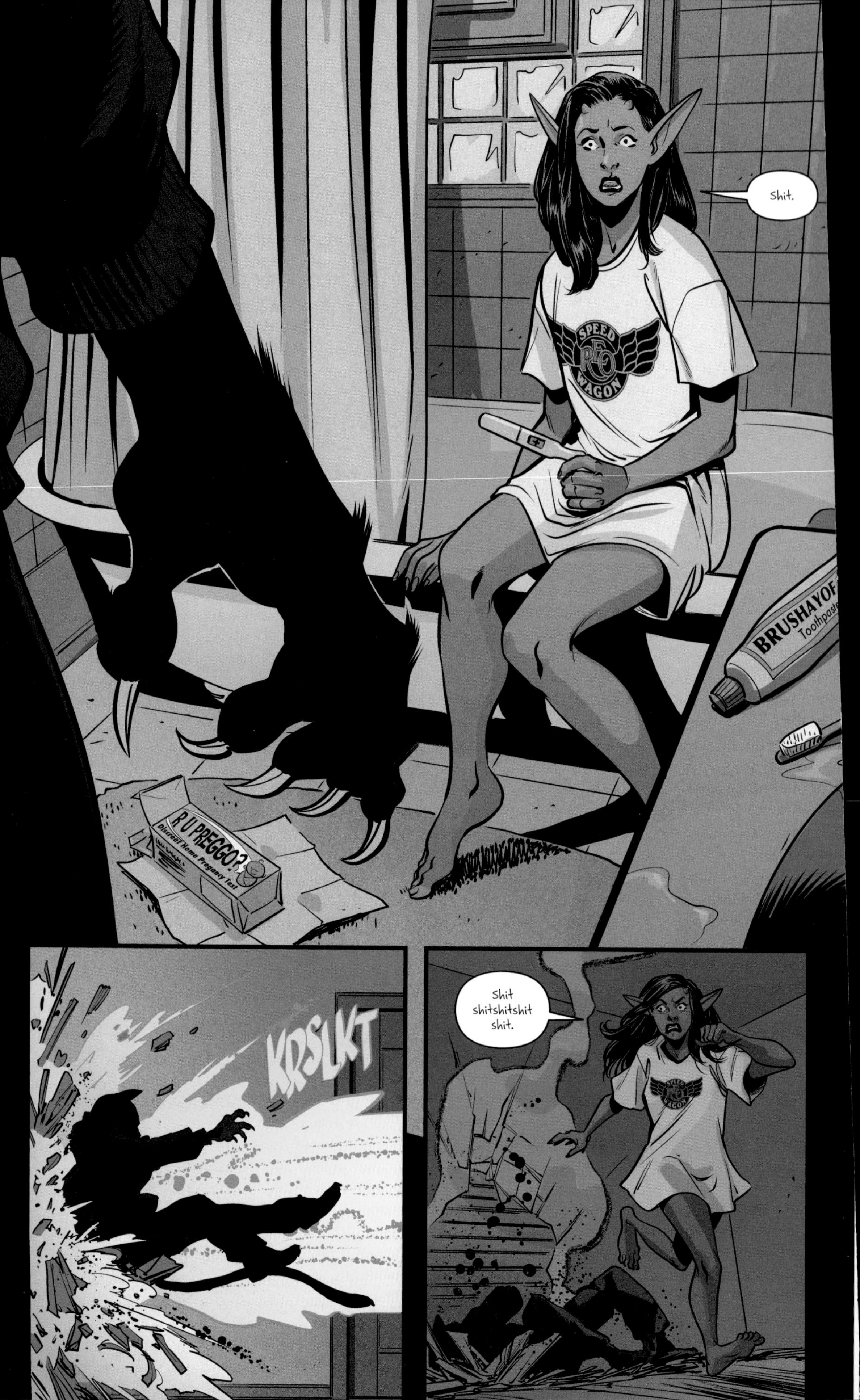
SPEED REO WAGON
Shit.
R U PREGGO?
Discreet Home Pregnancy Test
KRSLKT
Shit shitshitshit shit.

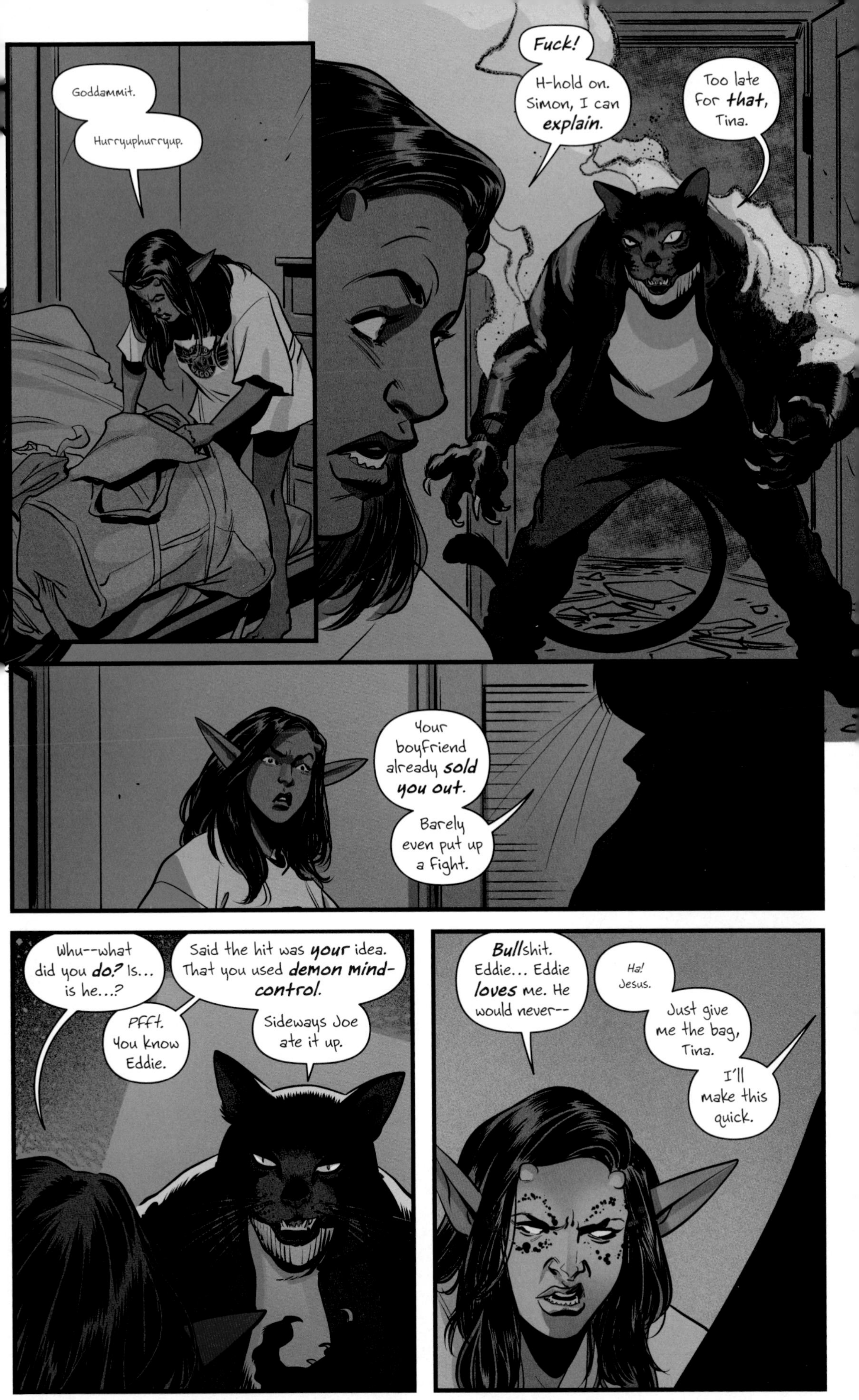
Goddammit.
Hurryuphurryup.
Fuck!
H-hold on. Simon, I can explain.
Too late for that, Tina.
Your boyfriend already sold you out.
Barely even put up a fight.
Whu--what did you do? Is... is he...?
Said the hit was your idea. That you used demon mind-control.
Pfft. You know Eddie.
Sideways Joe ate it up.
Bullshit. Eddie... Eddie loves me. He would never--
Ha! Jesus.
Just give me the bag, Tina.
I'll make this quick.

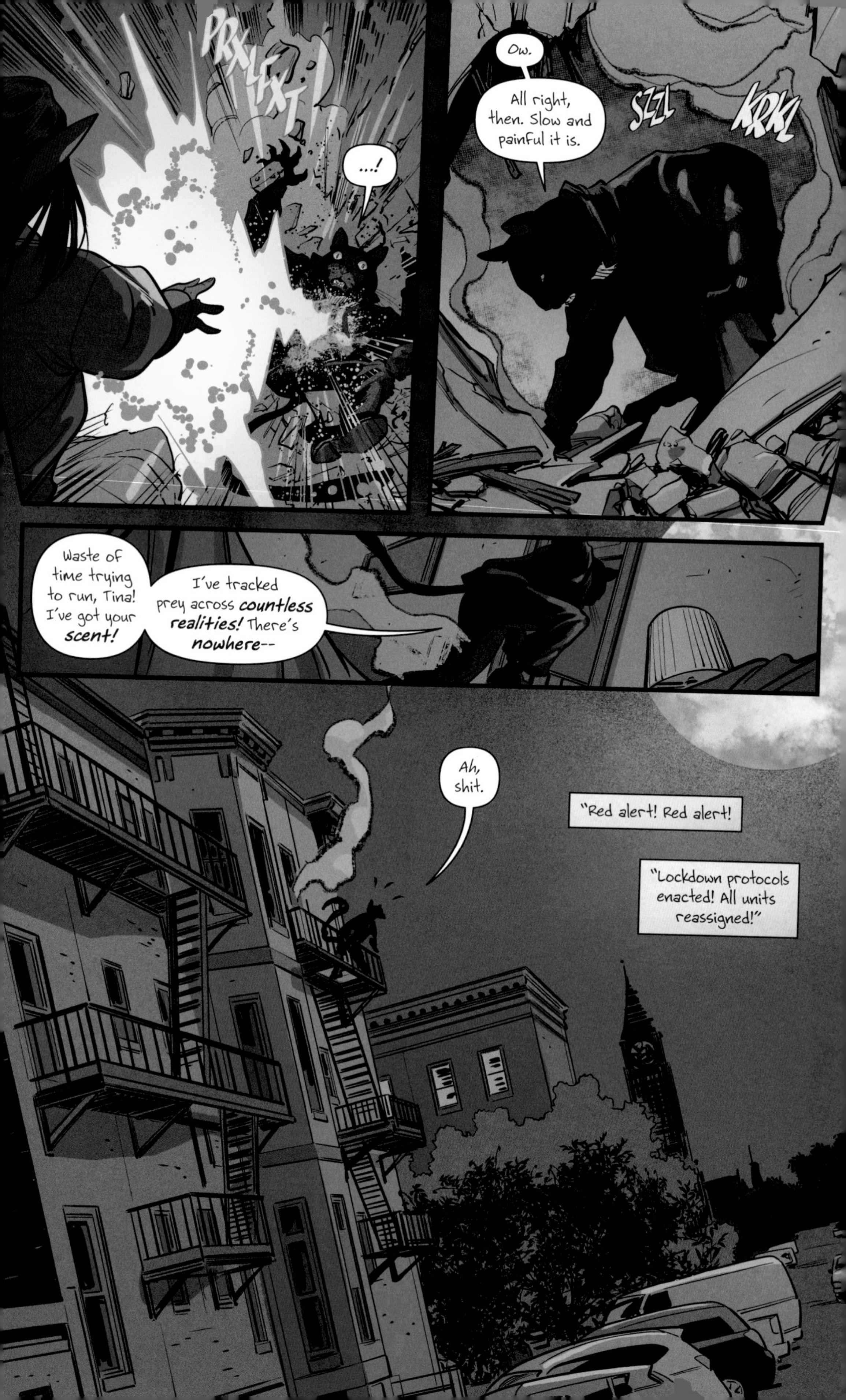
PRXLFXT
...!
Ow.
All right, then. Slow and painful it is.
SZZL
KRKL
Waste of time trying to run, Tina! I've got your **scent!**
I've tracked prey across **countless realities!** There's **nowhere--**
Ah, shit.
"Red alert! Red alert!
"Lockdown protocols enacted! All units reassigned!"

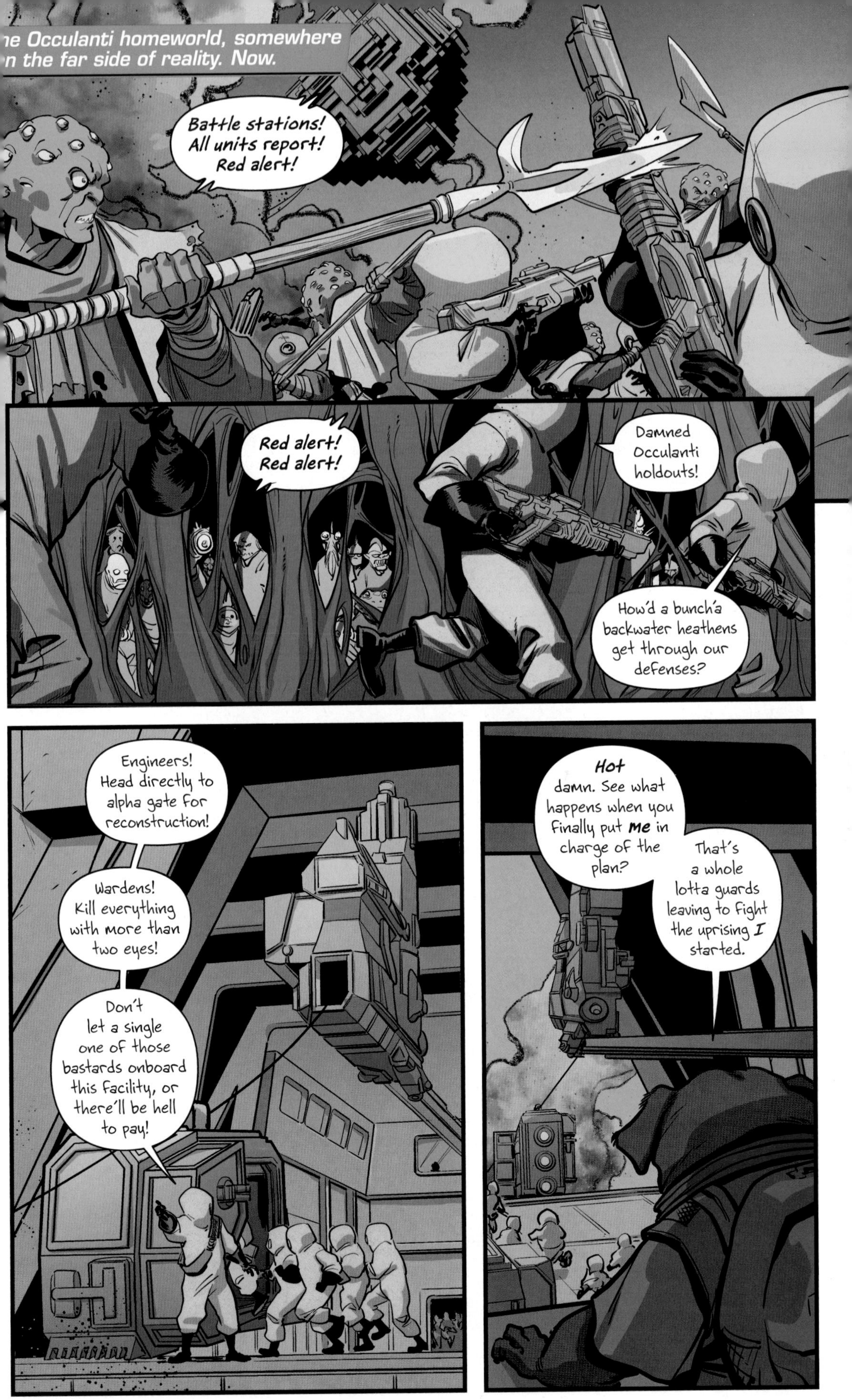
ne Occulanti homeworld, somewhere
n the far side of reality. Now.
Battle stations! All units report! Red alert!
Red alert! Red alert!
Damned Occulanti holdouts!
How'd a bunch'a backwater heathens get through our defenses?
Engineers! Head directly to alpha gate for reconstruction!
Wardens! Kill everything with more than two eyes!
Don't let a single one of those bastards onboard this facility, or there'll be hell to pay!
Hot damn. See what happens when you finally put me in charge of the plan?
That's a whole lotta guards leaving to fight the uprising I started.

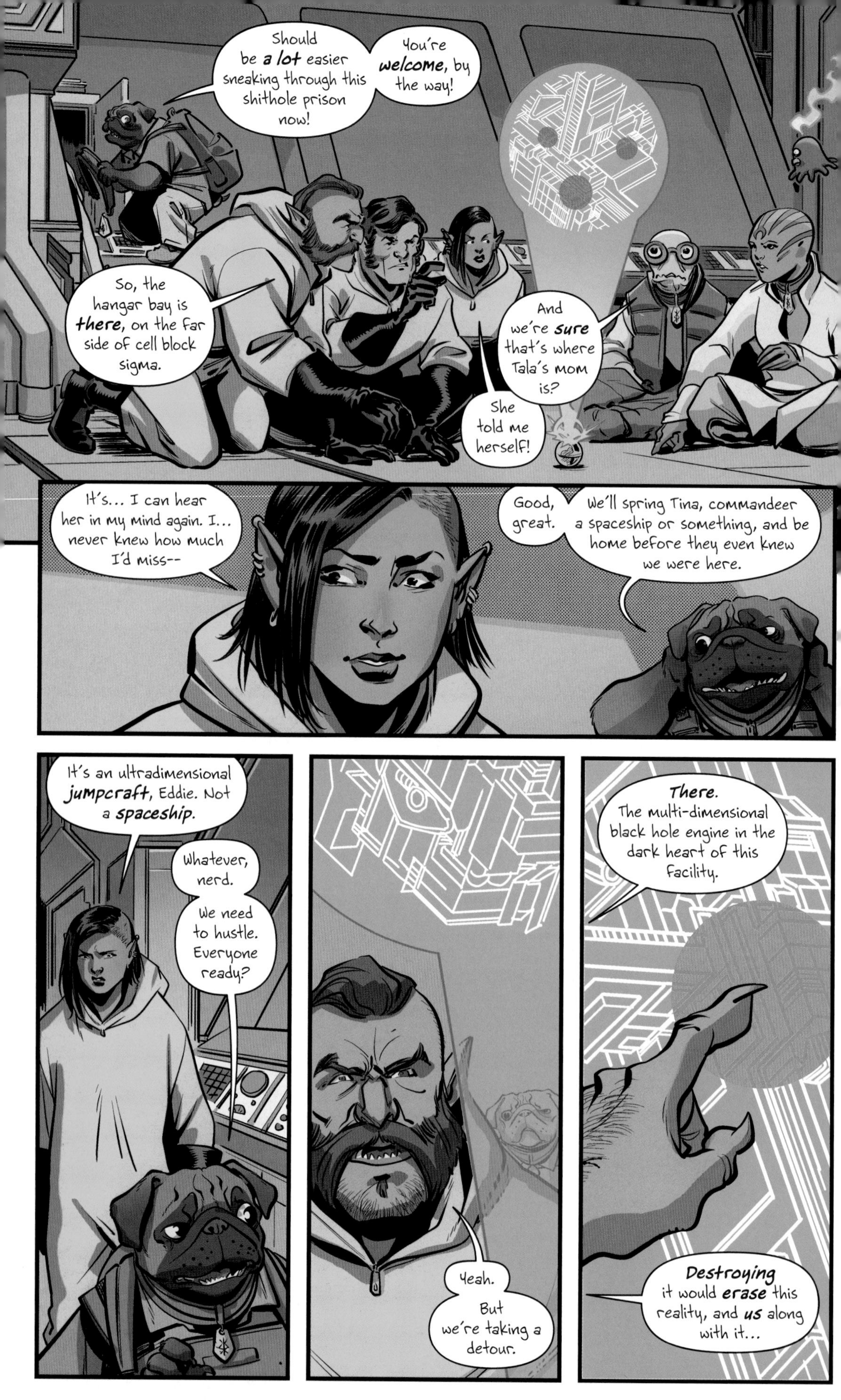
Should be a lot easier sneaking through this shithole prison now!
You're welcome, by the way!
So, the hangar bay is there, on the far side of cell block sigma.
And we're sure that's where Tala's mom is?
She told me herself!
It's... I can hear her in my mind again. I... never knew how much I'd miss--
Good, great.
We'll spring Tina, commandeer a spaceship or something, and be home before they even knew we were here.
It's an ultradimensional jumpcraft, Eddie. Not a spaceship.
Whatever, nerd.
We need to hustle. Everyone ready?
Yeah.
But we're taking a detour.
There. The multi-dimensional black hole engine in the dark heart of this facility.
Destroying it would erase this reality, and us along with it...

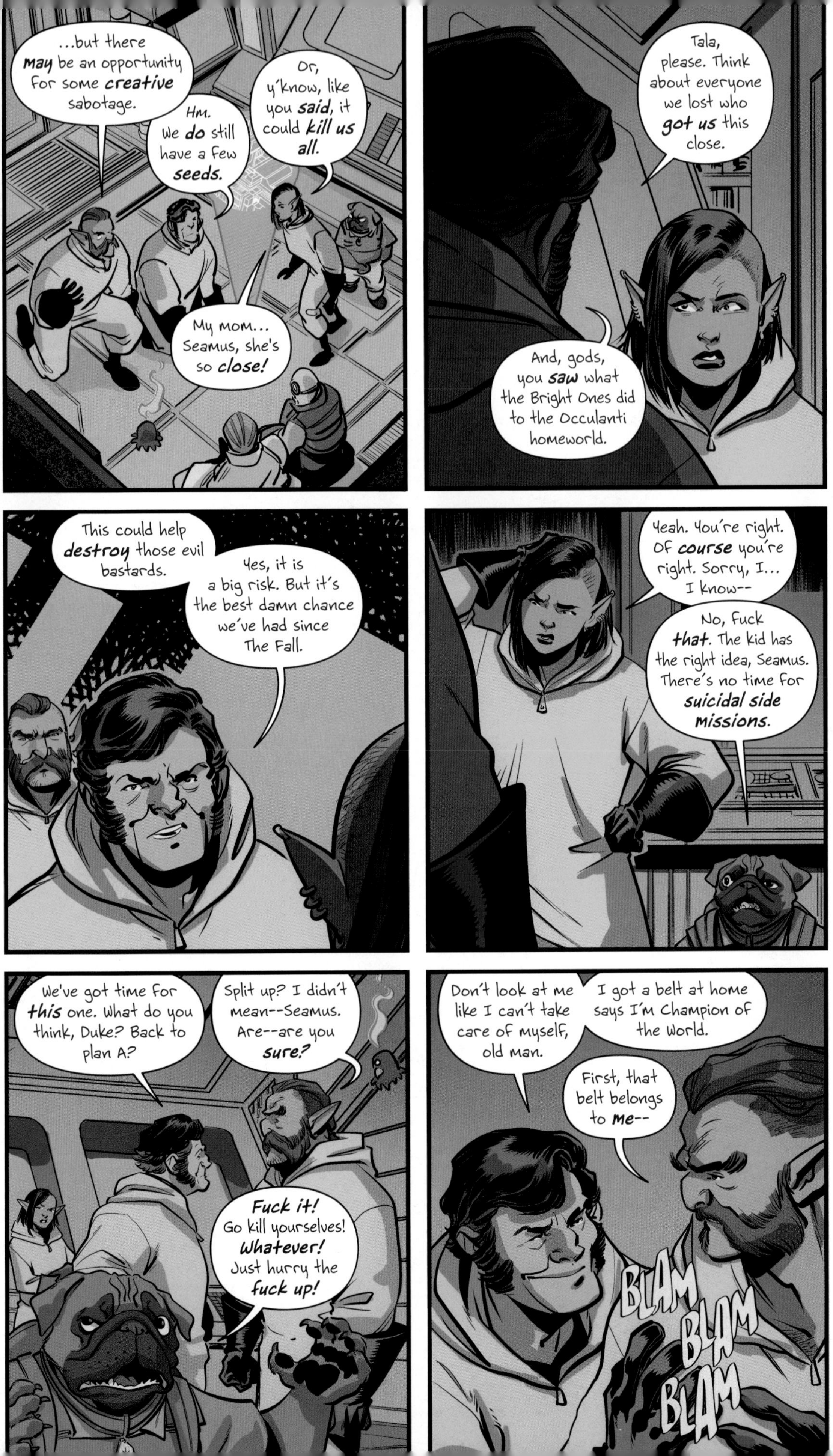
...but there may be an opportunity for some creative sabotage.
Hm. We do still have a few seeds.
Or, y'know, like you said, it could kill us all.
My mom... Seamus, she's so close!
Tala, please. Think about everyone we lost who got us this close.
And, gods, you saw what the Bright Ones did to the Occulanti homeworld.
This could help destroy those evil bastards.
Yes, it is a big risk. But it's the best damn chance we've had since The Fall.
Yeah. You're right. Of course you're right. Sorry, I... I know--
No, fuck that. The kid has the right idea, Seamus. There's no time for suicidal side missions.
We've got time for this one. What do you think, Duke? Back to plan A?
Split up? I didn't mean--Seamus. Are--are you sure?
Fuck it! Go kill yourselves! Whatever! Just hurry the fuck up!
Don't look at me like I can't take care of myself, old man.
I got a belt at home says I'm Champion of the World.
First, that belt belongs to me--
BLAM
BLAM
BLAM

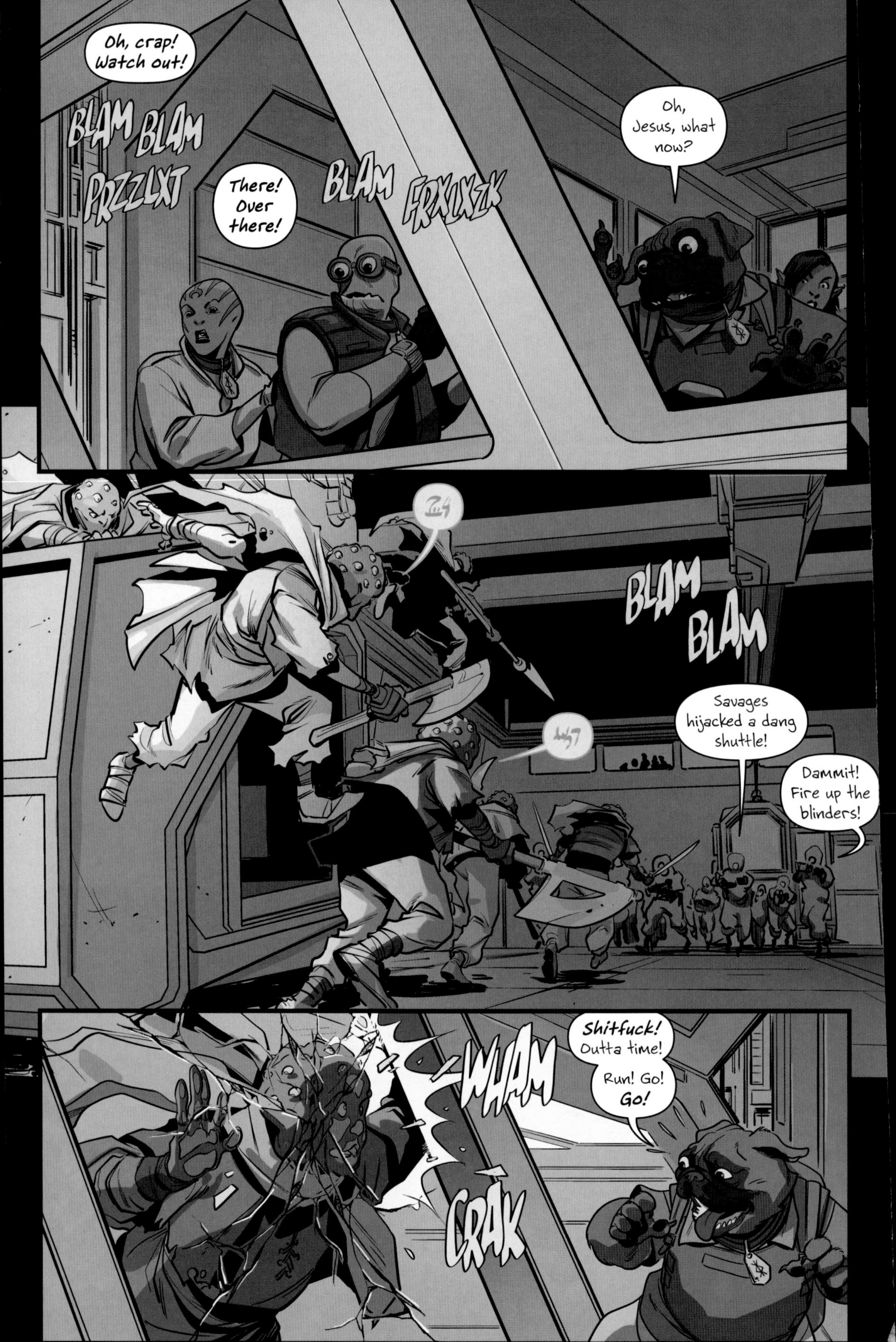
Oh, crap! Watch out!
BLAM BLAM
PRZZLXT
There! Over there!
BLAM
FRXLXZK
Oh, Jesus, what now?
BLAM
BLAM
Savages hijacked a dang shuttle!
Dammit! Fire up the blinders!
WHAM
CRAK
Shitfuck! Outta time!
Run! Go! Go!

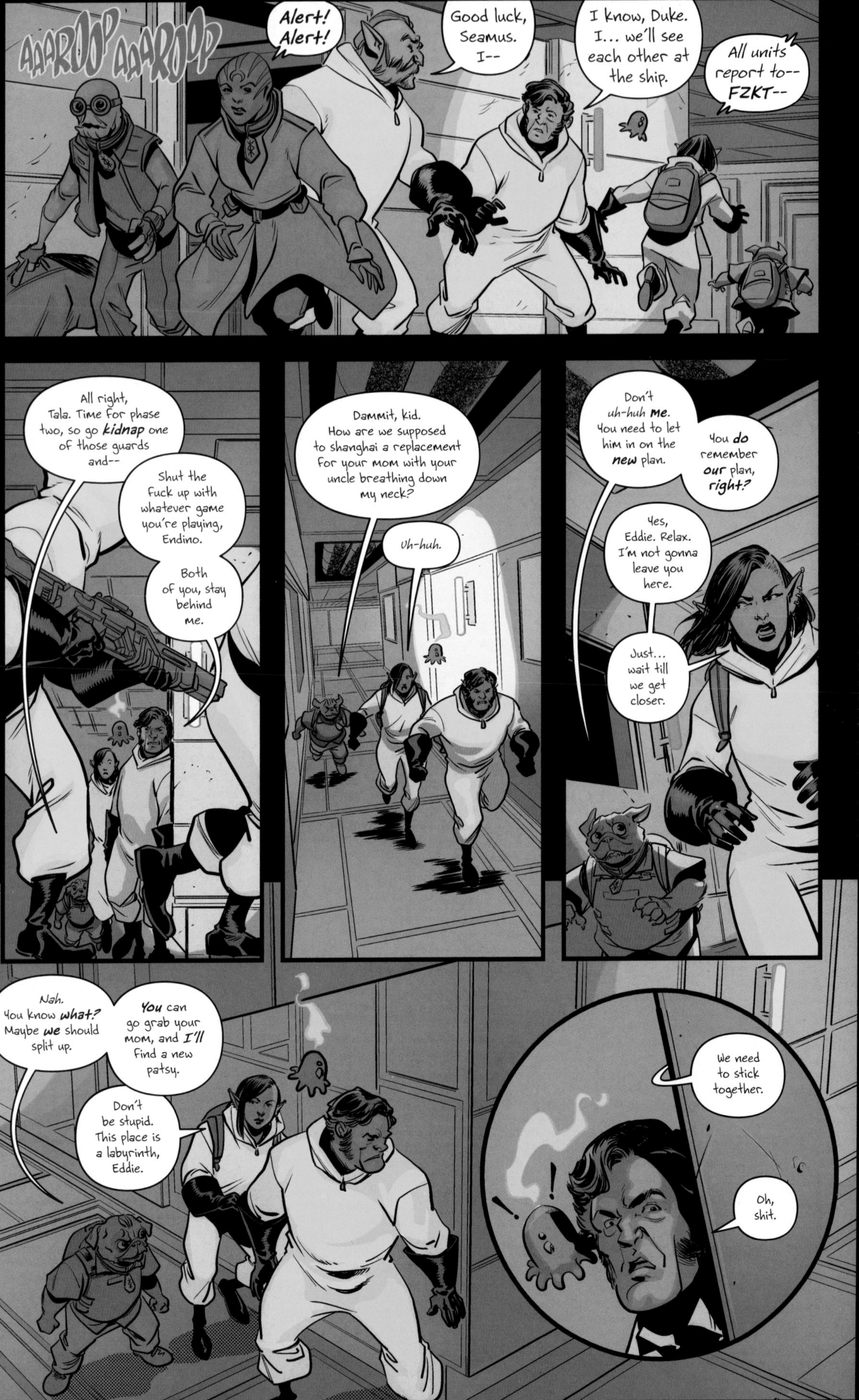
AAAROOP AAAROOP
Alert! Alert!
Good luck, Seamus. I--
I know, Duke. I... we'll see each other at the ship.
All units report to-- FZKT--
All right, Tala. Time for phase two, so go kidnap one of those guards and--
Shut the fuck up with whatever game you're playing, Endino.
Both of you, stay behind me.
Dammit, kid. How are we supposed to shanghai a replacement for your mom with your uncle breathing down my neck?
Uh-huh.
Don't uh-huh me. You need to let him in on the new plan.
You do remember our plan, right?
Yes, Eddie. Relax. I'm not gonna leave you here.
Just... wait till we get closer.
Nah. You know what? Maybe we should split up.
You can go grab your mom, and I'll find a new patsy.
Don't be stupid. This place is a labyrinth, Eddie.
We need to stick together.
!
!
Oh, shit.

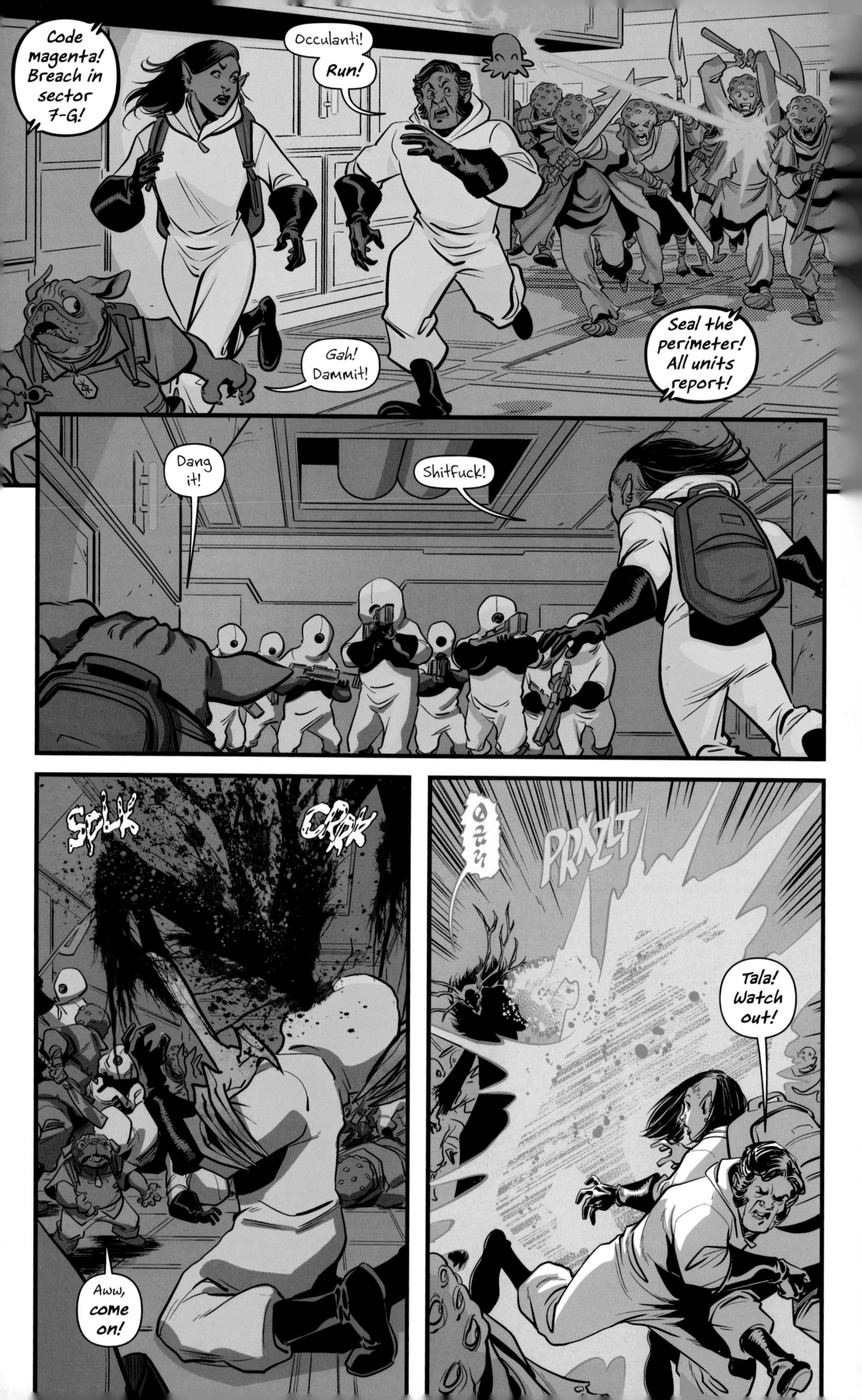
Code magenta! Breach in sector 7-G!
Occulanti!
Run!
Gah! Dammit!
Seal the perimeter! All units report!
Dang it!
Shitfuck!
SPLK
CRAK
Aww, come on!
PRXZLT
Tala! Watch out!

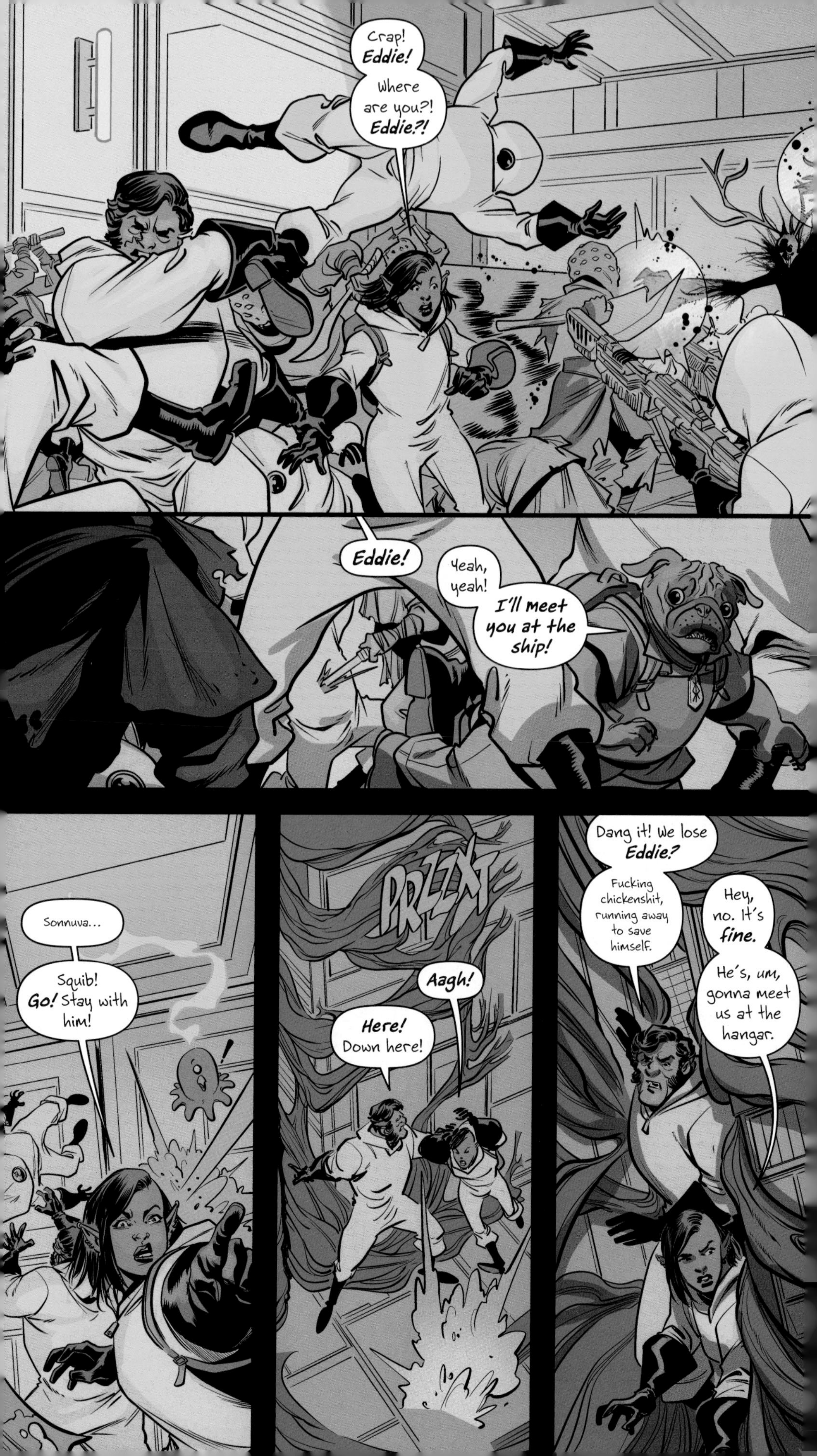
Crap!
Eddie!
Where are you?!
Eddie?!
Eddie!
Yeah, yeah!
I'll meet you at the ship!
Sonnuva...
Squib! Go! Stay with him!
PRZZXT
Aagh!
Here! Down here!
Dang it! We lose Eddie?
Fucking chickenshit, running away to save himself.
Hey, no. It's fine.
He's, um, gonna meet us at the hangar.

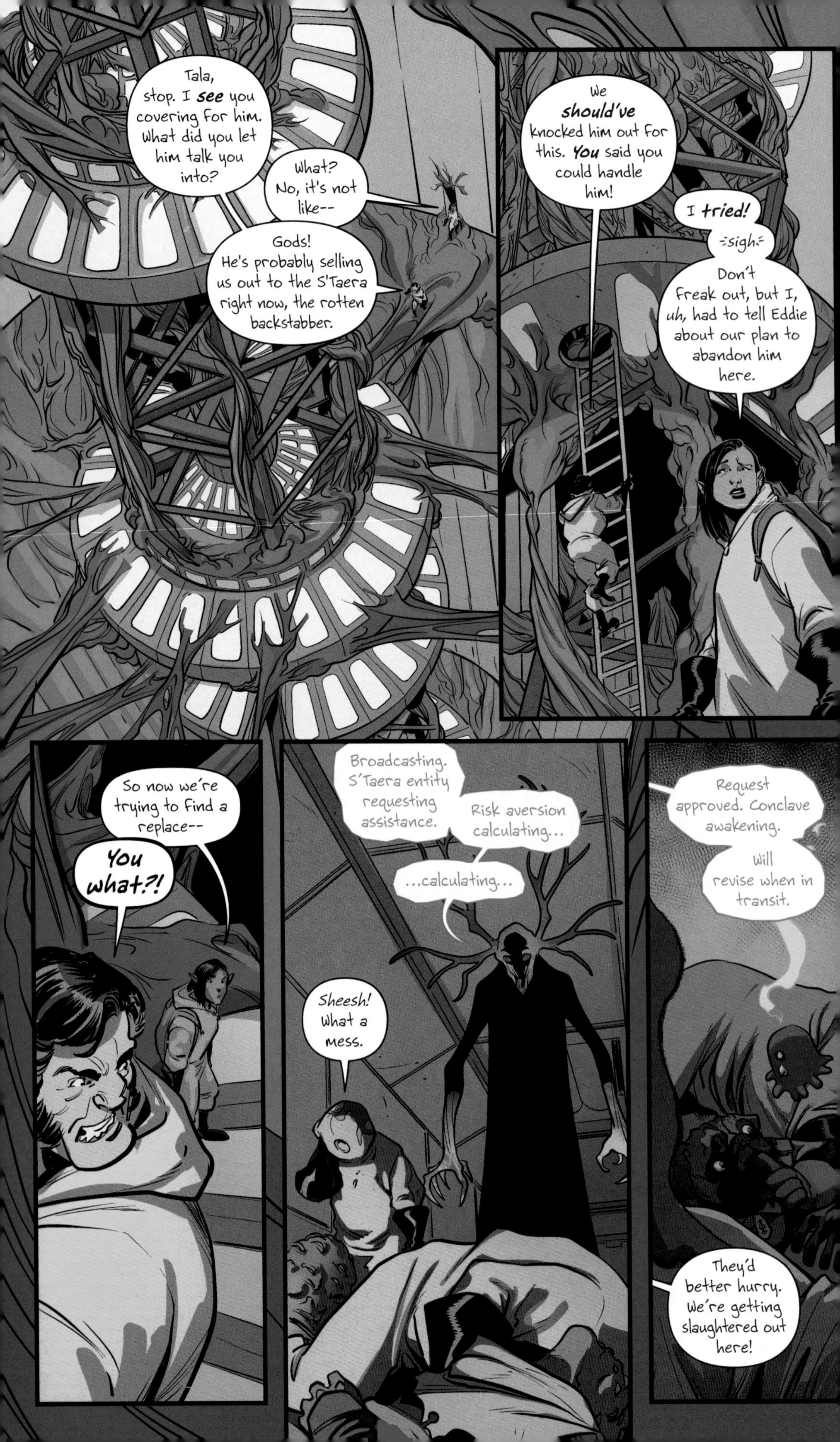

Tala, stop. I **see** you covering for him. What did you let him talk you into?
What? No, it's not like--
Gods! He's probably selling us out to the S'Taera right now, the rotten backstabber.
We **should've** knocked him out for this. **You** said you could handle him!
I **tried!**
sigh
Don't freak out, but I, *uh,* had to tell Eddie about our plan to abandon him here.
So now we're trying to find a replace--
You what?!
Broadcasting. S'Taera entity requesting assistance.
Risk aversion calculating...
...calculating...
Sheesh! What a mess.
Request approved. Conclave awakening.
Will revise when in transit.
They'd better hurry. We're getting slaughtered out here!

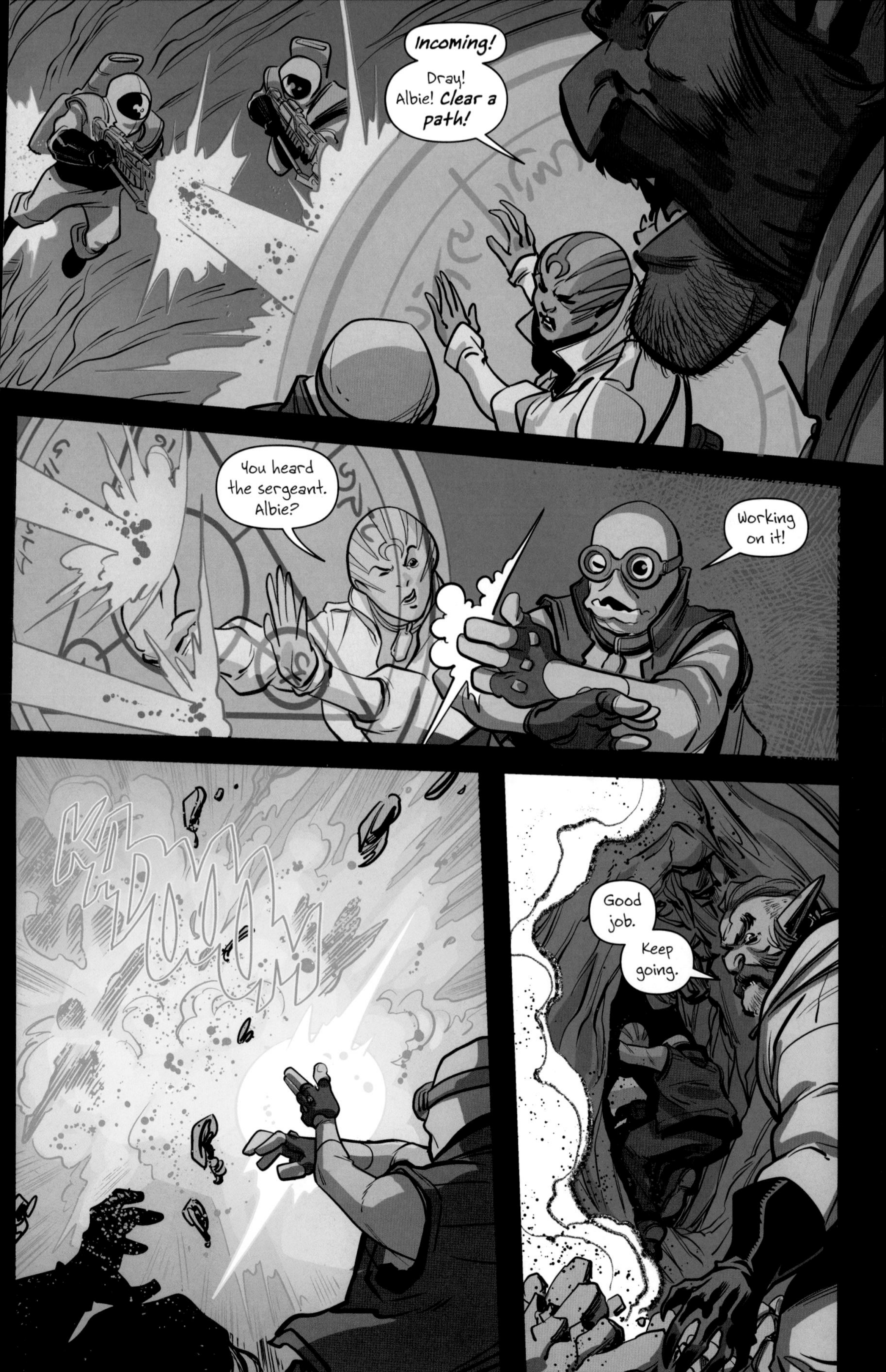
Incoming!
Dray! Albie! Clear a path!
You heard the sergeant. Albie?
Working on it!
Good job.
Keep going.

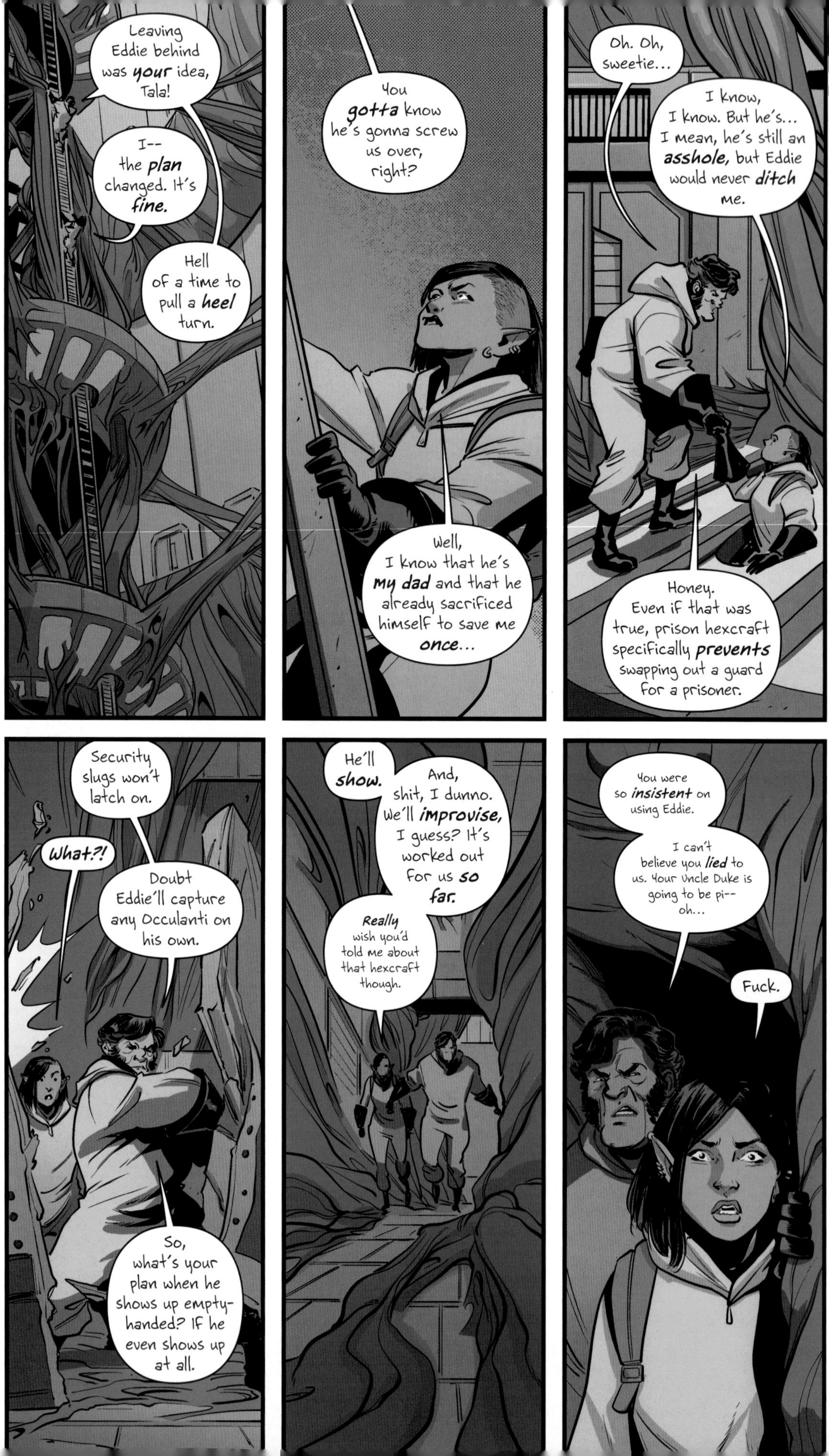
Leaving Eddie behind was your idea, Tala!
I-- the plan changed. It's fine.
Hell of a time to pull a heel turn.
You gotta know he's gonna screw us over, right?
Well, I know that he's my dad and that he already sacrificed himself to save me once...
Oh. Oh, sweetie...
I know, I know. But he's... I mean, he's still an asshole, but Eddie would never ditch me.
Honey. Even if that was true, prison hexcraft specifically prevents swapping out a guard for a prisoner.
Security slugs won't latch on.
What?!
Doubt Eddie'll capture any Occulanti on his own.
So, what's your plan when he shows up empty-handed? If he even shows up at all.
He'll show.
And, shit, I dunno. We'll improvise, I guess? It's worked out for us so far.
Really wish you'd told me about that hexcraft though.
You were so insistent on using Eddie.
I can't believe you lied to us. Your Uncle Duke is going to be pi-- oh...
Fuck.

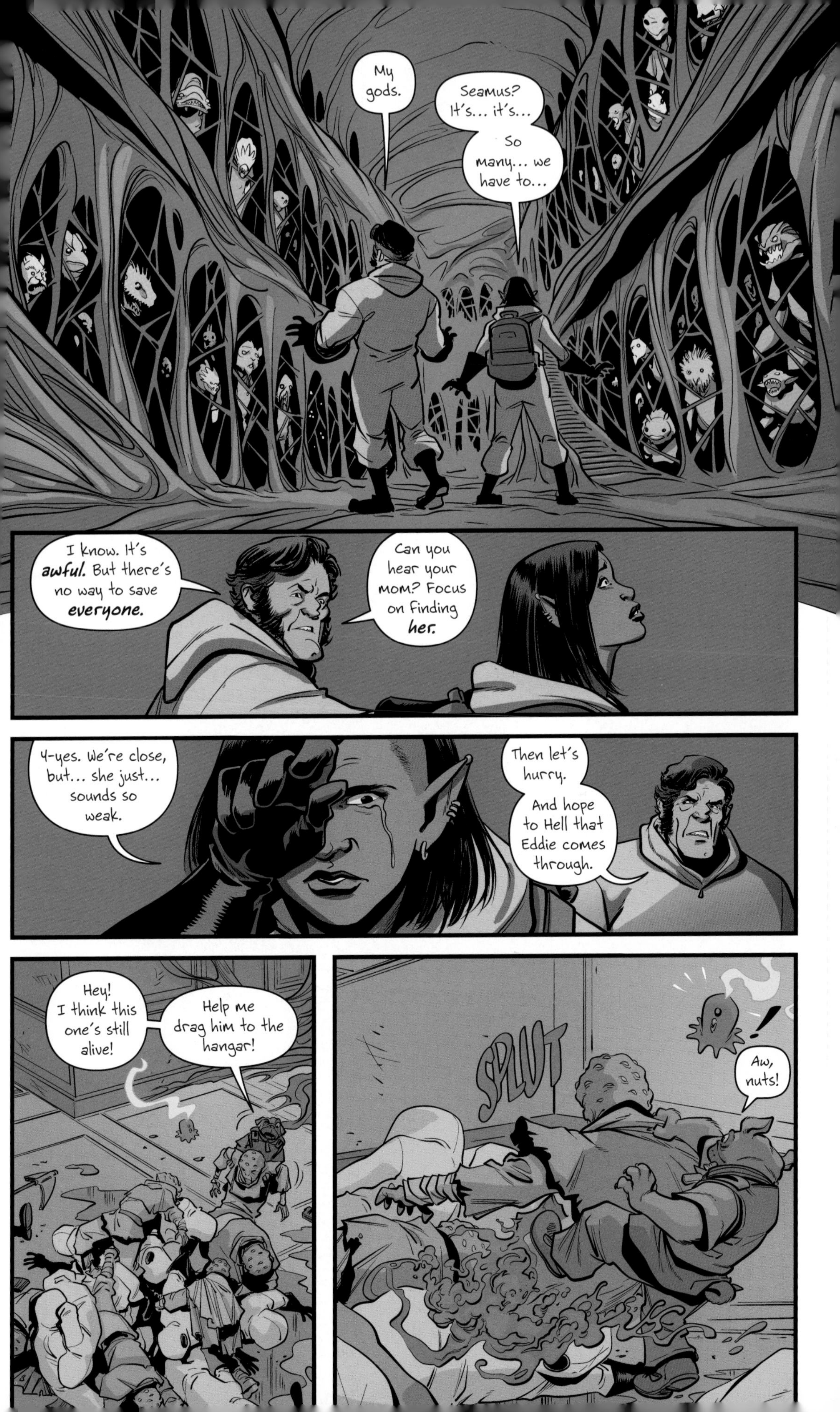
My gods.
Seamus? It's... it's...
So many... we have to...
I know. It's **awful.** But there's no way to save **everyone.**
Can you hear your mom? Focus on finding **her.**
Y-yes. We're close, but... she just... sounds so weak.
Then let's hurry.
And hope to Hell that Eddie comes through.
Hey! I think this one's still alive!
Help me drag him to the hangar!
SPLUT
Aw, nuts!

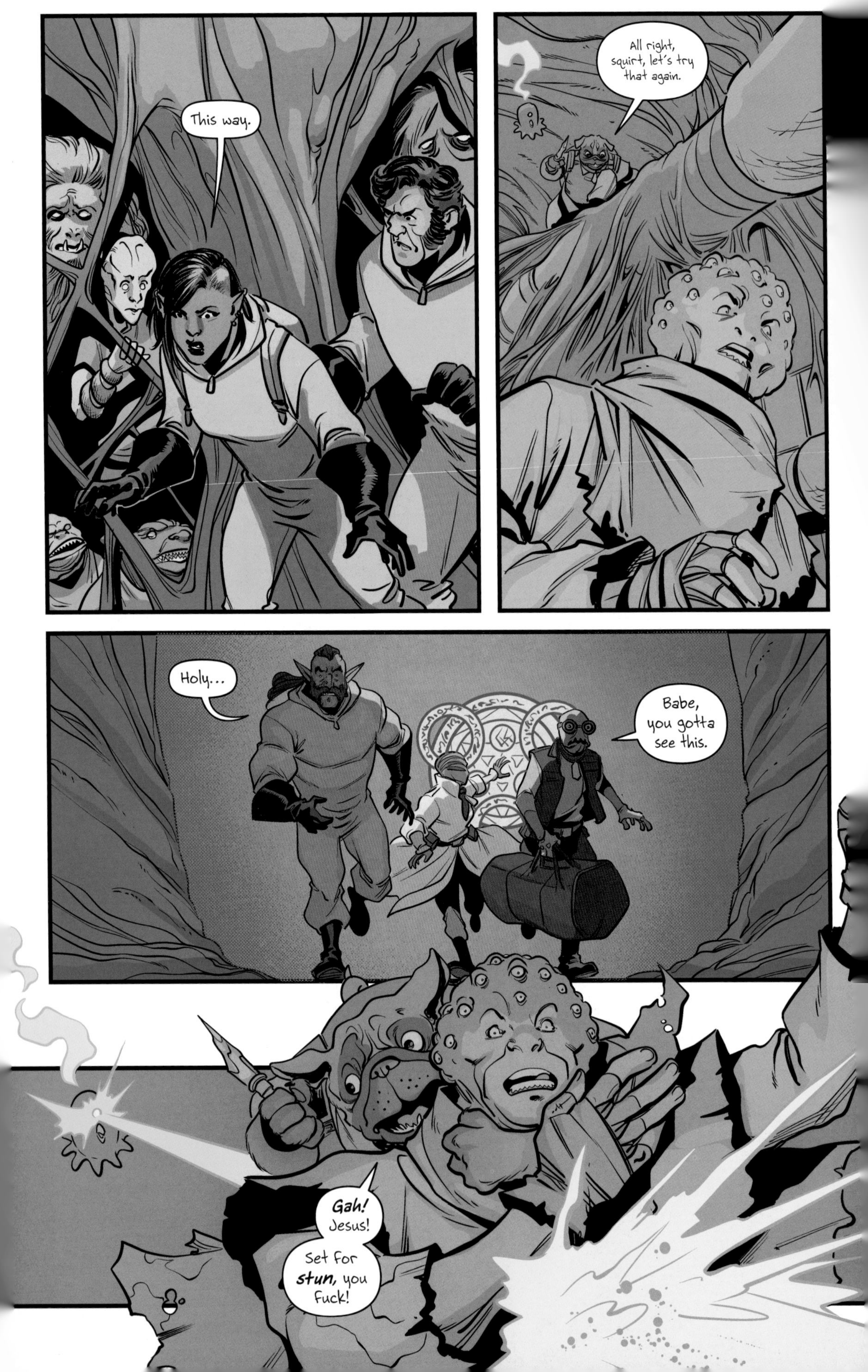
This way.
All right, squirt, let's try that again.
Holy...
Babe, you gotta see this.
Gah! Jesus!
Set for stun, you Fuck!

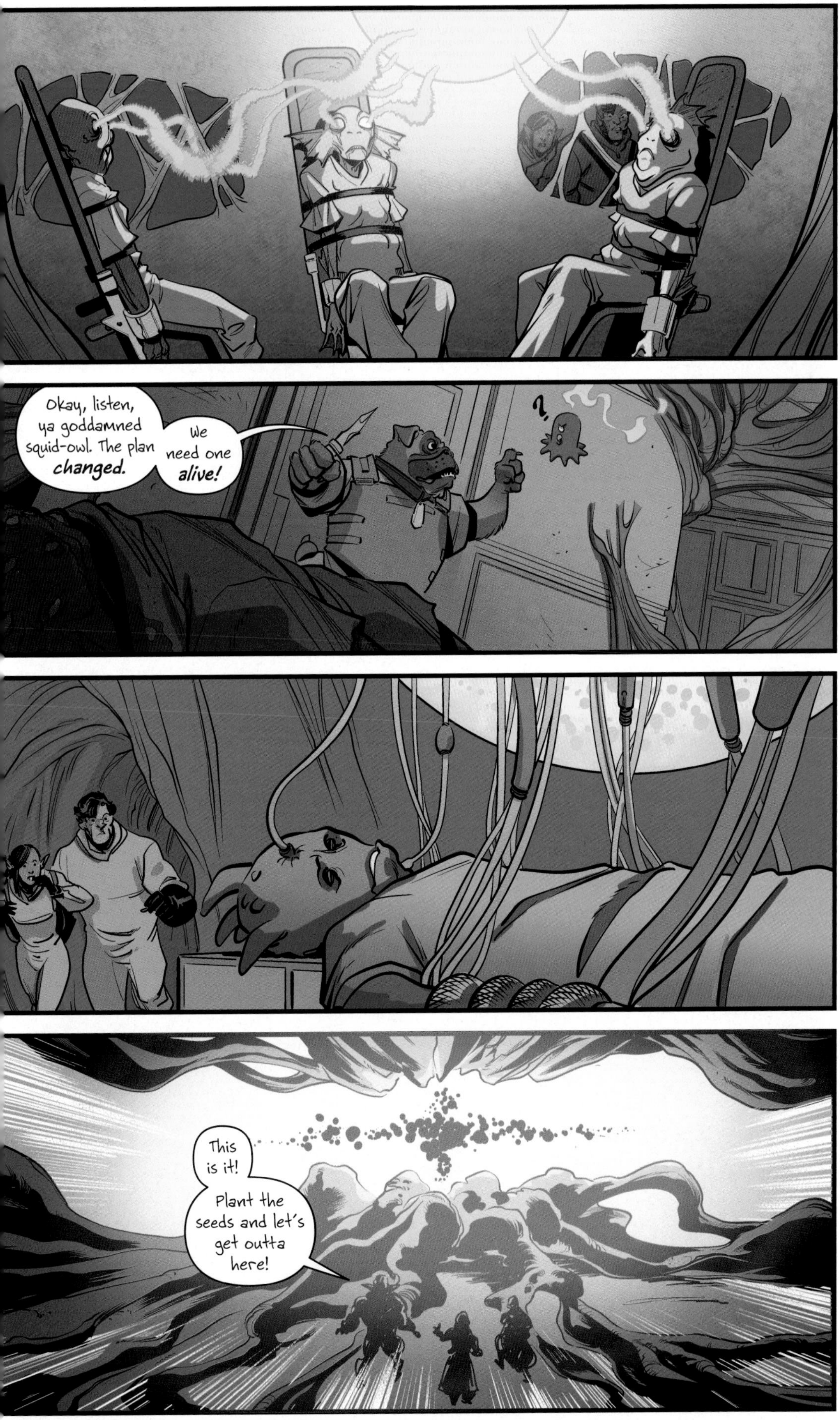
Okay, listen, ya goddamned squid-owl. The plan *changed.*
We need one *alive!*
?
This is it!
Plant the seeds and let's get outta here!

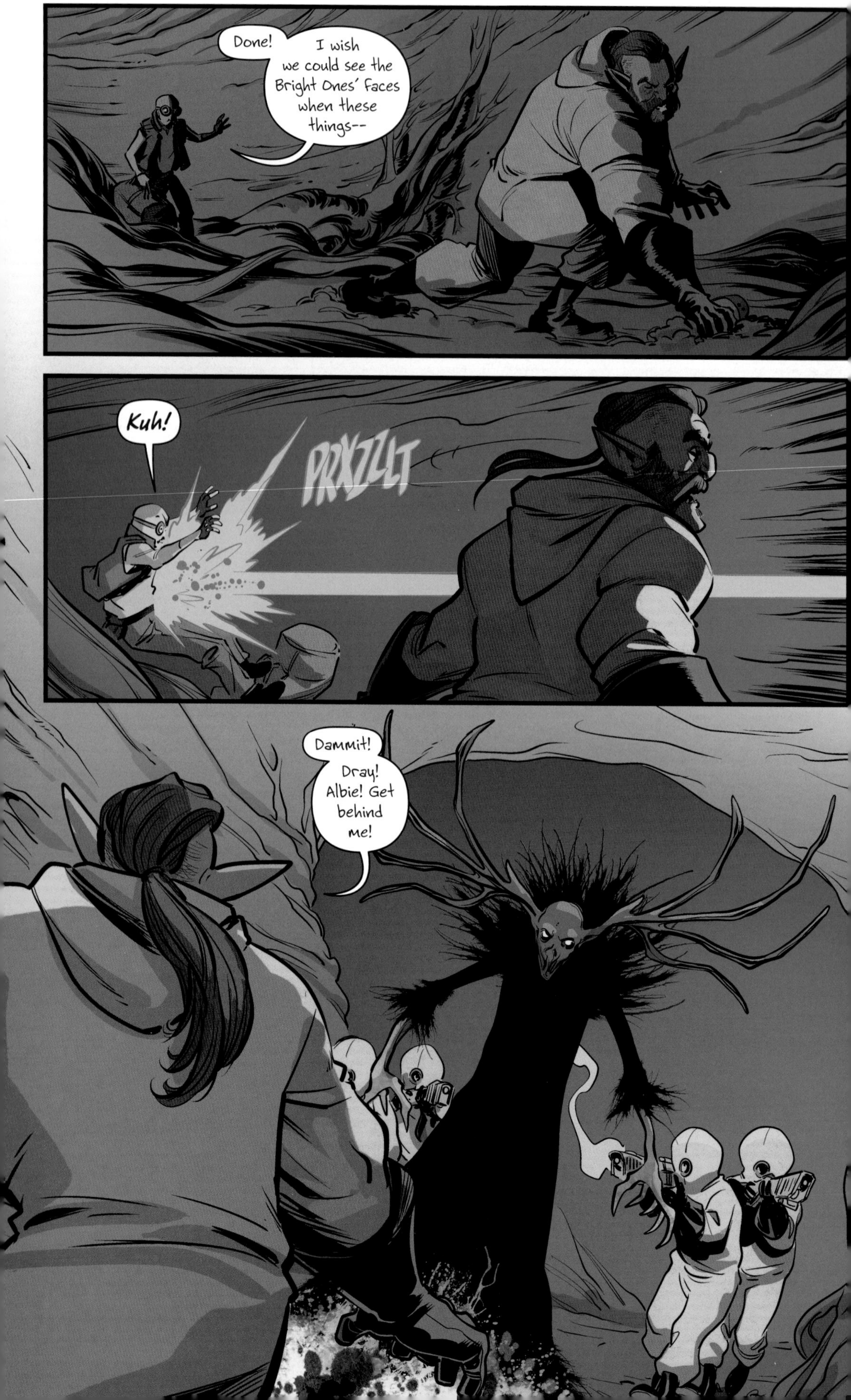
Done!
I wish we could see the Bright Ones' faces when these things--
Kuh!
PRXZZLT
Dammit! Dray! Albie! Get behind me!

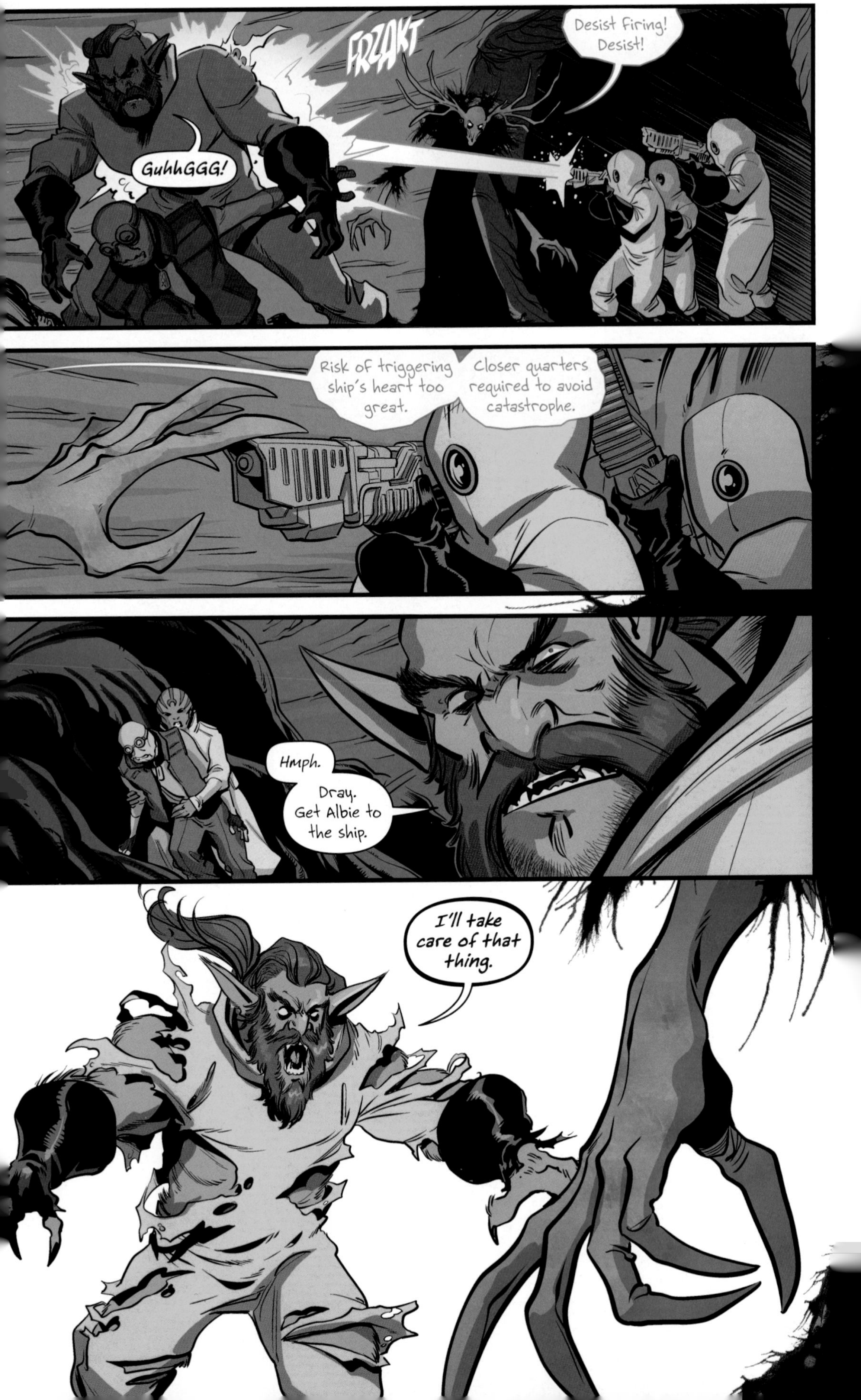
FRZAKT
Desist Firing! Desist!
GuhhGGG!
Risk of triggering ship's heart too great.
Closer quarters required to avoid catastrophe.
Hmph.
Dray. Get Albie to the ship.
I'll take care of that thing.

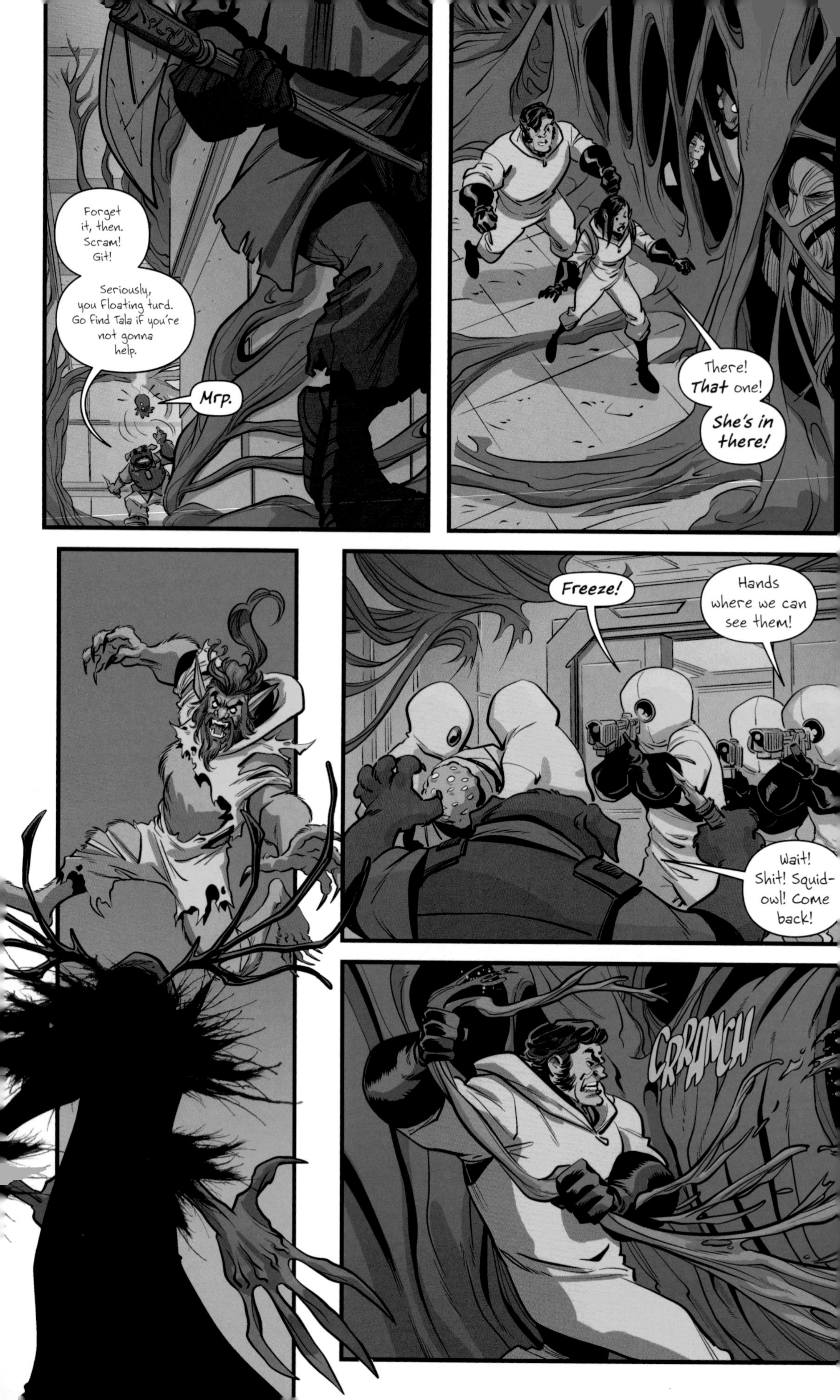

Forget it, then. Scram! Git!
Seriously, you floating turd. Go find Tala if you're not gonna help.
Mrp.
There! That one!
She's in there!
Freeze!
Hands where we can see them!
Wait! Shit! Squid-owl! Come back!
CRRUNCH

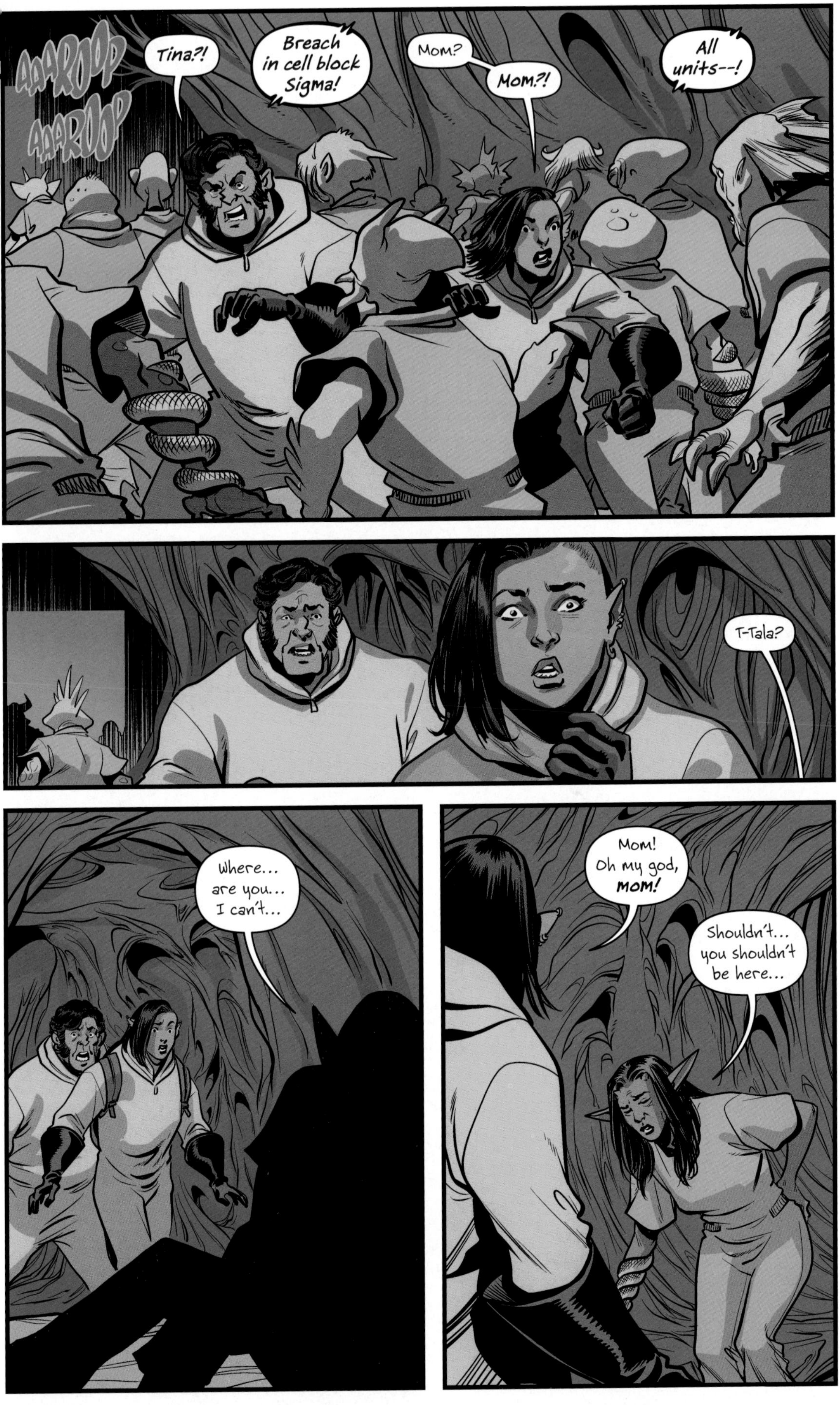
AAAROOP
AAAROOP
Tina?!
Breach in cell block Sigma!
Mom?
Mom?!
All units--!
T-Tala?
Where... are you... I can't...
Mom! Oh my god, MOM!
Shouldn't... you shouldn't be here...

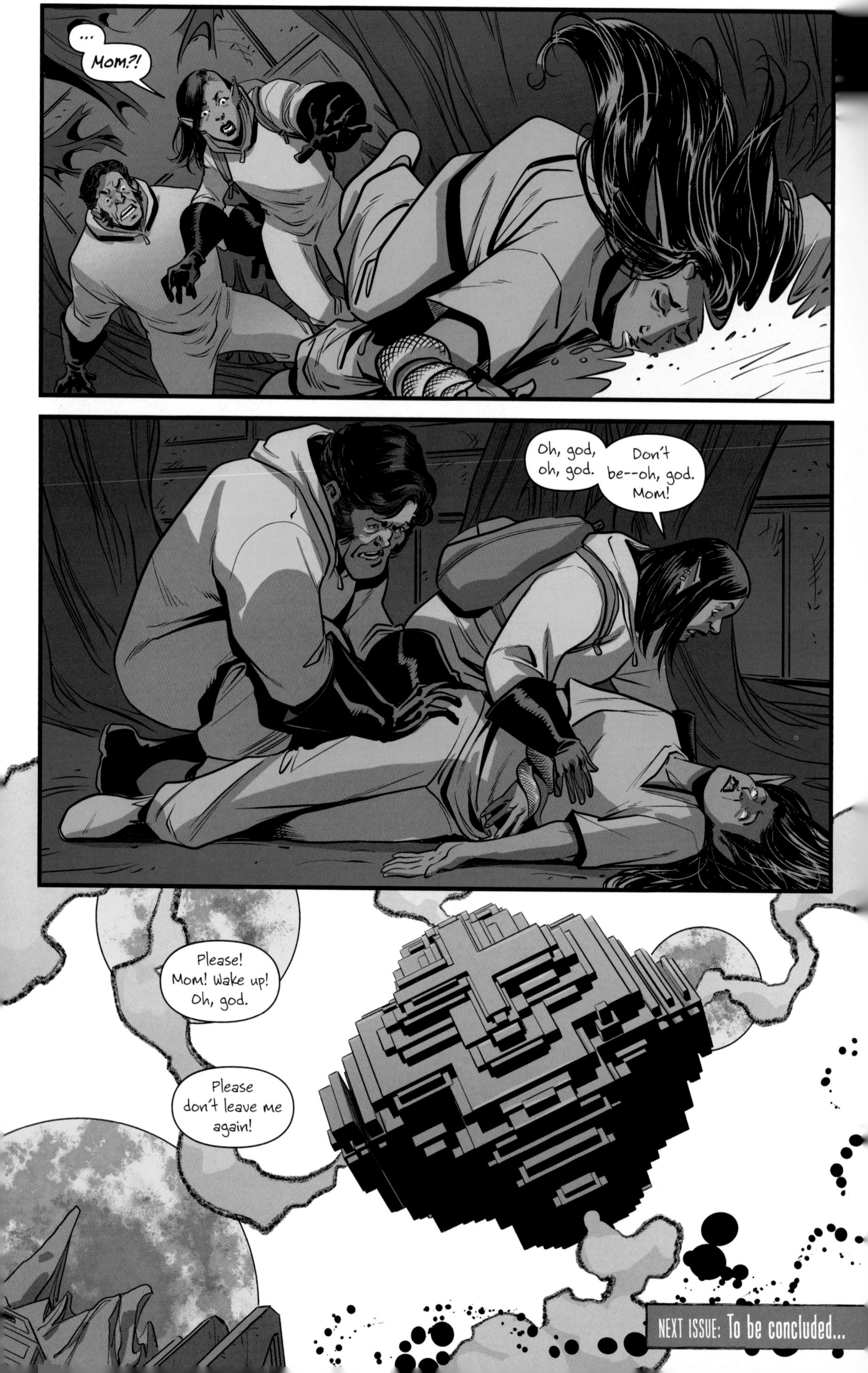
...
Mom?!
Oh, god, oh, god.
Don't be--oh, god. Mom!
Please! Mom! Wake up! Oh, god.
Please don't leave me again!
NEXT ISSUE: To be concluded...

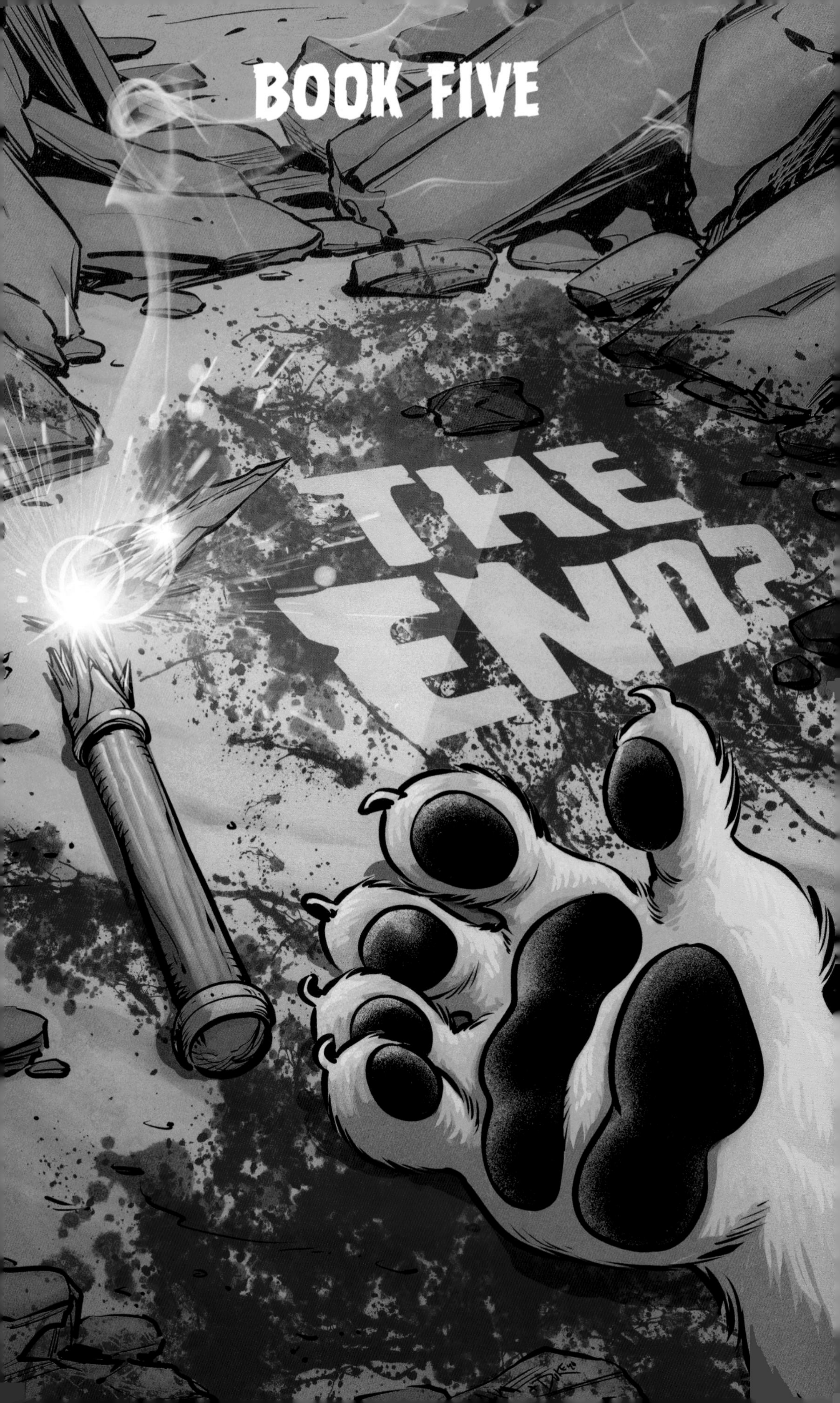
BOOK FIVE
THE END?

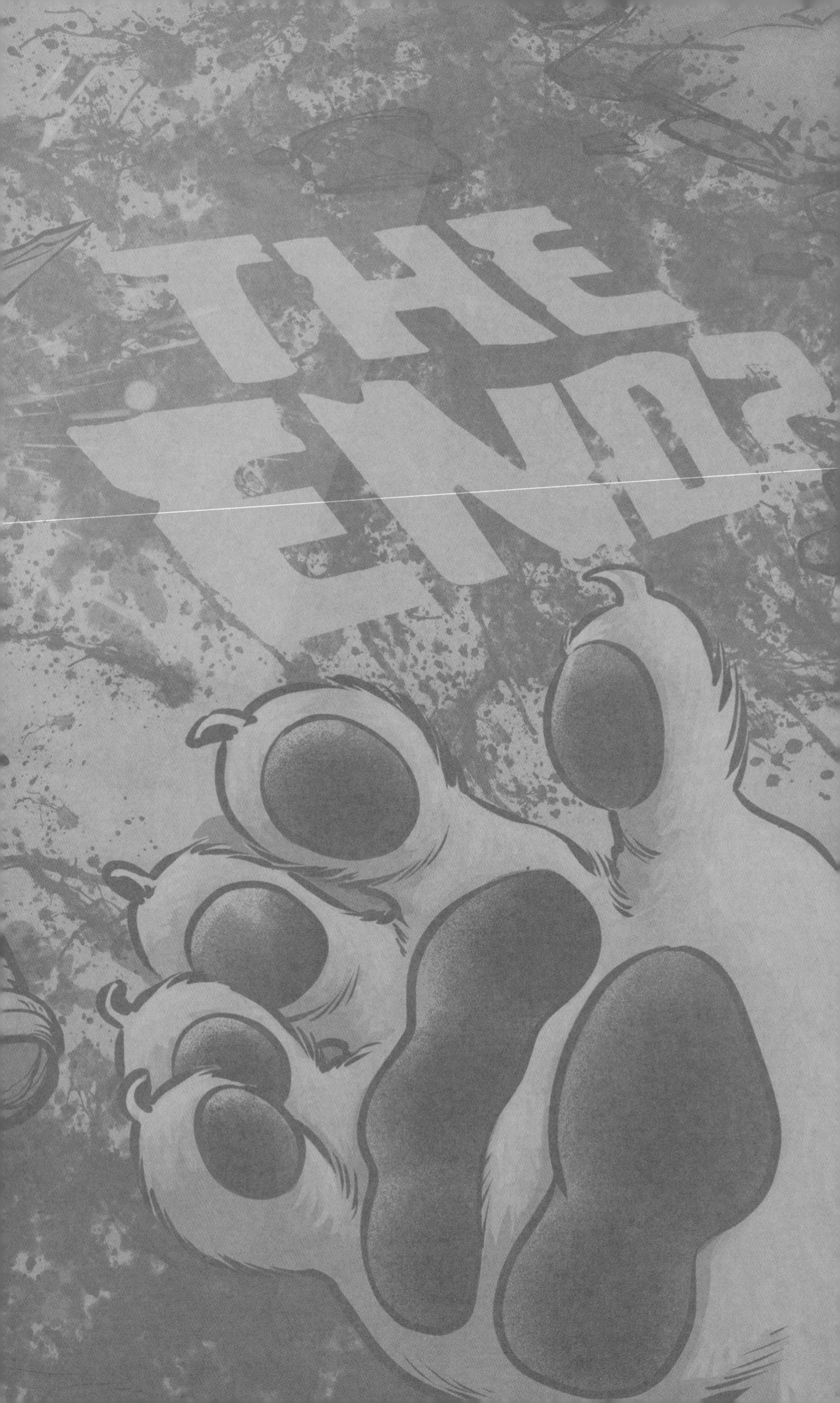
THE END?

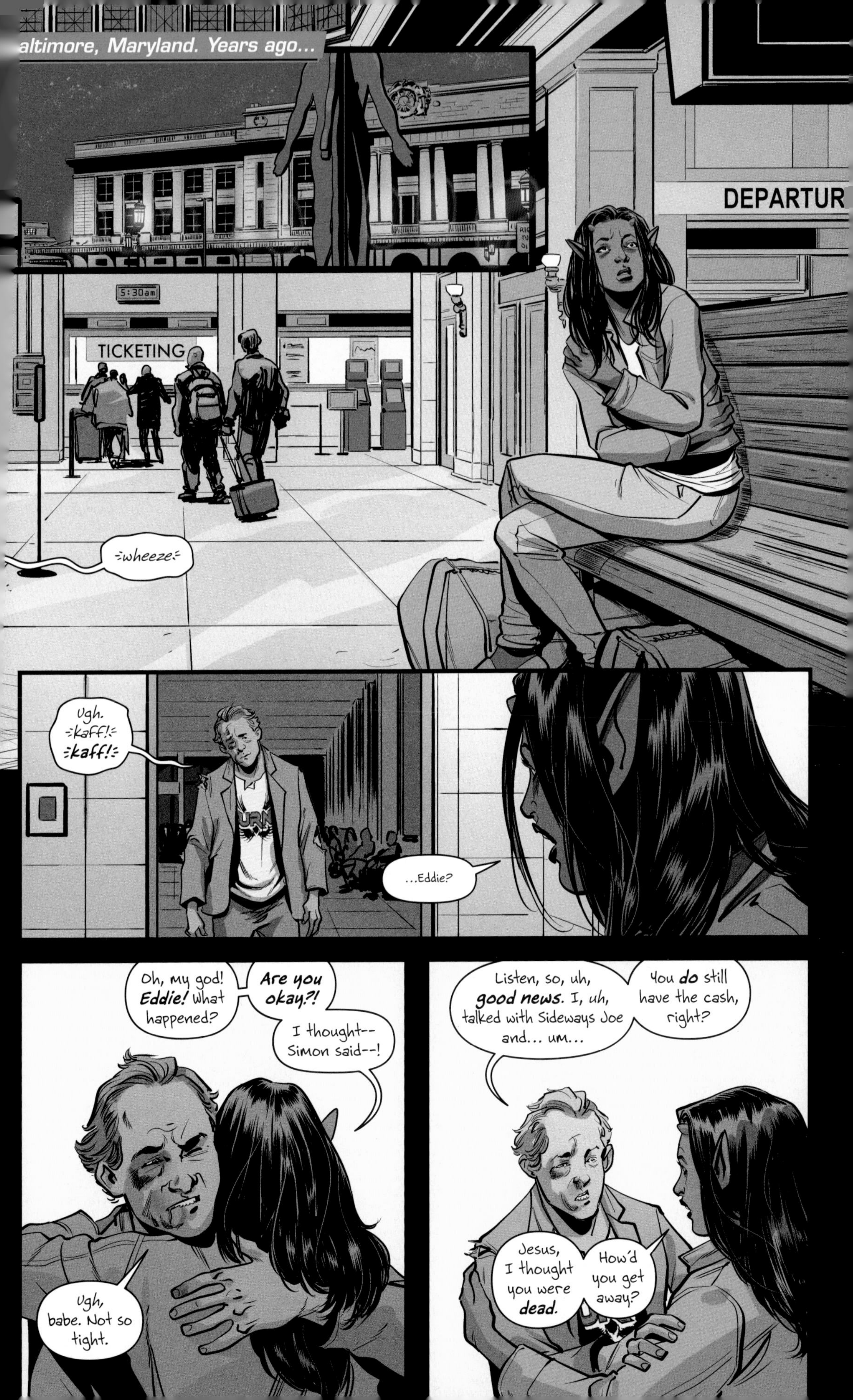
altimore, Maryland. Years ago...
5:30am
TICKETING
DEPARTUR
-wheeze-
Ugh.
-kaff!-
-kaff!-
...Eddie?
Oh, my god! Eddie! What happened?
Are you okay?!
I thought-- Simon said--!
Ugh, babe. Not so tight.
Listen, so, uh, good news. I, uh, talked with Sideways Joe and... um...
You do still have the cash, right?
Jesus, I thought you were dead.
How'd you get away?

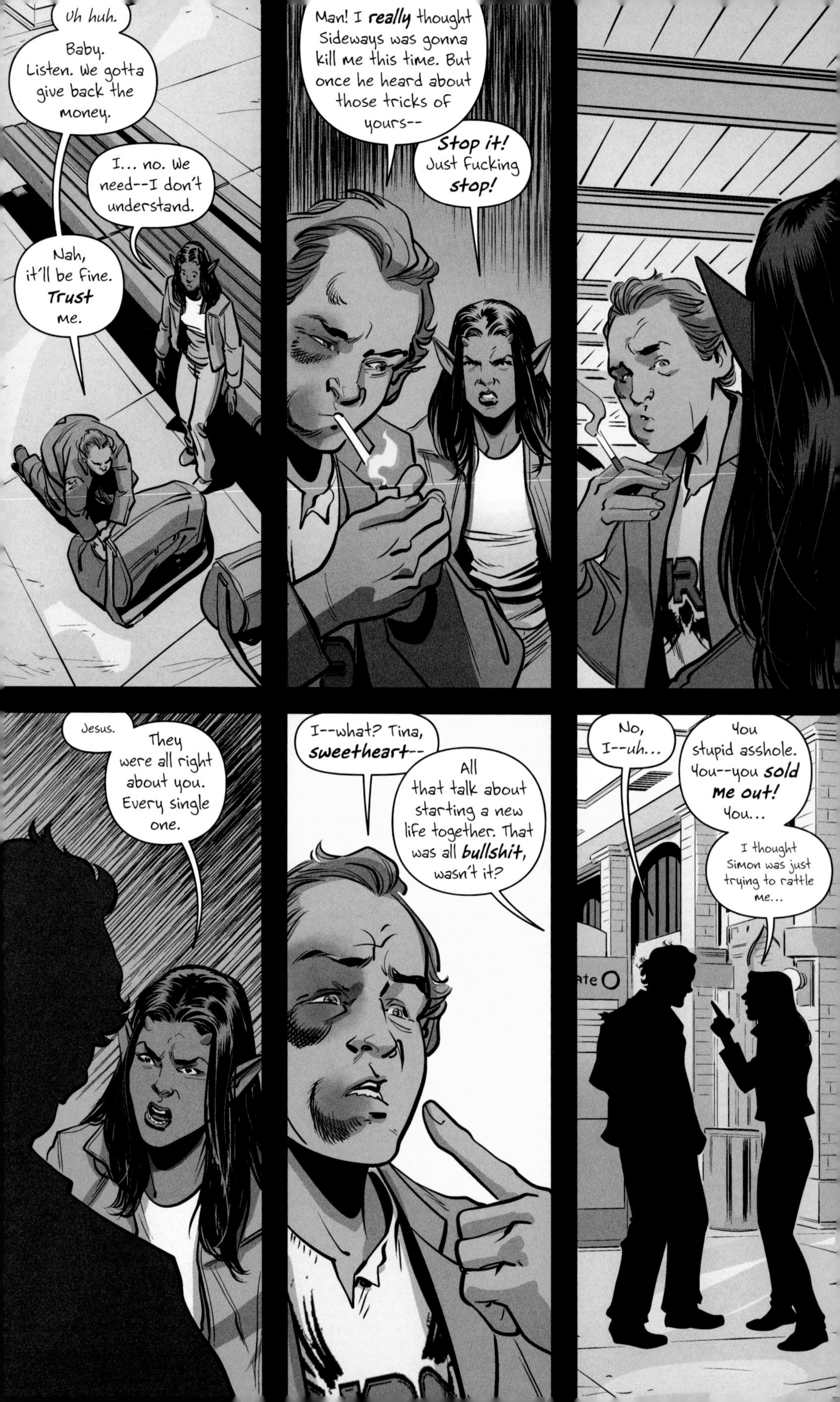

Uh huh.
Baby. Listen. We gotta give back the money.
I... no. We need--I don't understand.
Nah, it'll be fine. **Trust** me.
Man! I **really** thought Sideways was gonna kill me this time. But once he heard about those tricks of yours--
Stop it! Just fucking **stop!**
Jesus.
They were all right about you. Every single one.
I--what? Tina, **sweetheart**--
All that talk about starting a new life together. That was all **bullshit**, wasn't it?
No, I--uh...
You stupid asshole. You--you **sold me out!** You...
I thought Simon was just trying to rattle me...

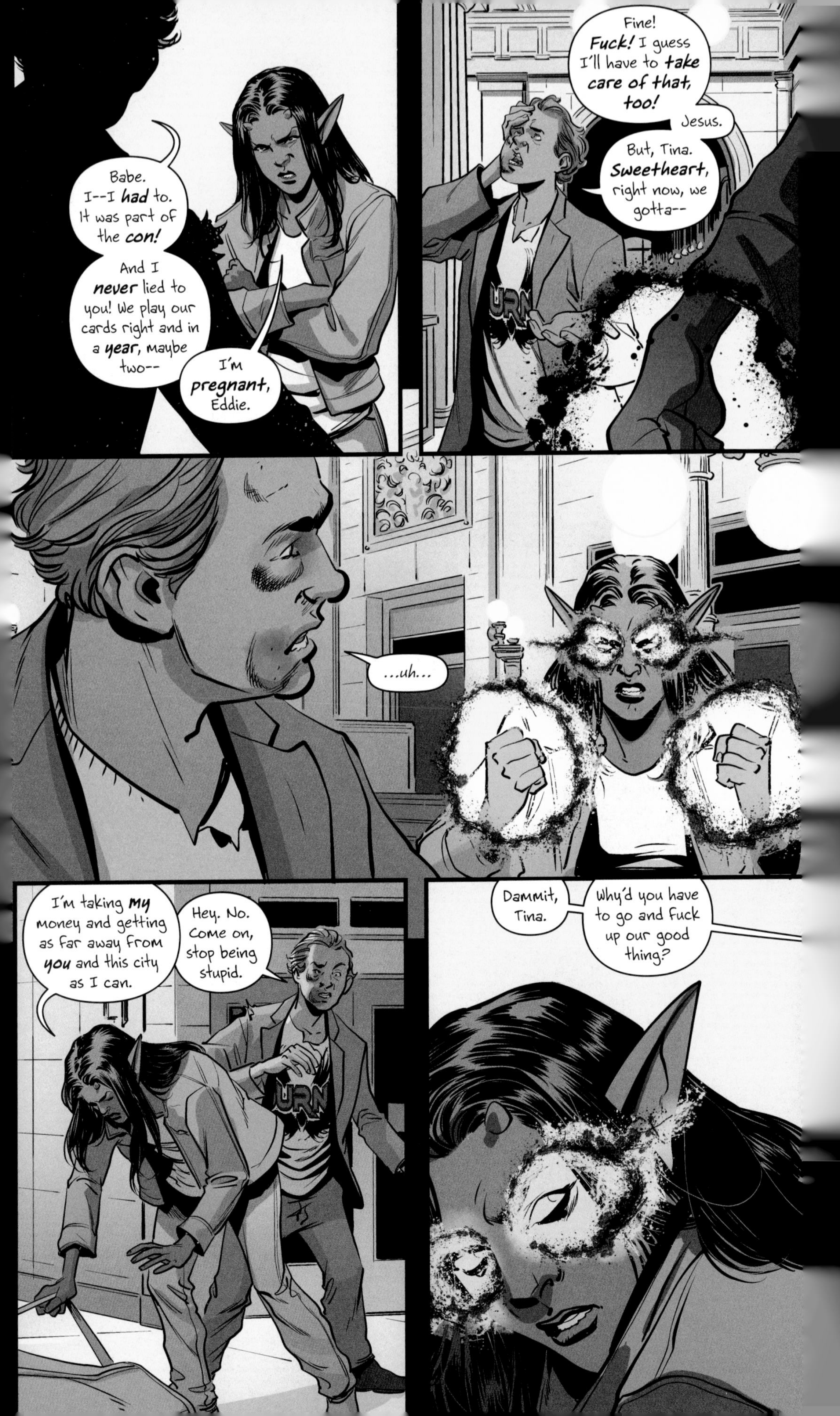
Babe. I--I had to. It was part of the con!
And I never lied to you! We play our cards right and in a year, maybe two--
I'm pregnant, Eddie.
Fine! Fuck! I guess I'll have to take care of that, too!
Jesus.
But, Tina. Sweetheart, right now, we gotta--
...uh...
I'm taking my money and getting as far away from you and this city as I can.
Hey. No. Come on, stop being stupid.
Dammit, Tina.
Why'd you have to go and fuck up our good thing?

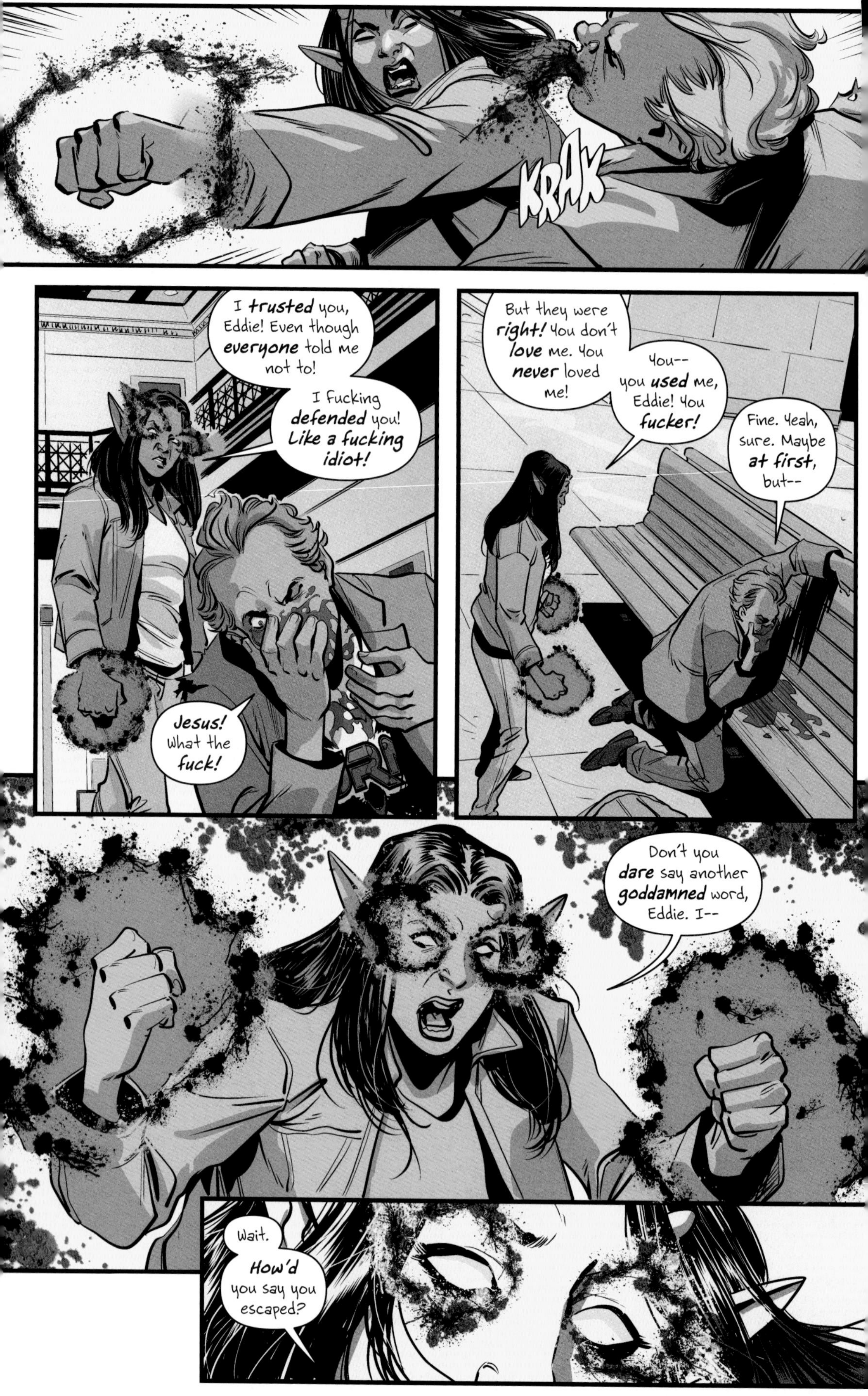
KRAK
I trusted you, Eddie! Even though everyone told me not to!
I fucking defended you! Like a fucking idiot!
Jesus! What the fuck!
But they were right! You don't love me. You never loved me!
You-- you used me, Eddie! You fucker!
Fine. Yeah, sure. Maybe at first, but--
Don't you dare say another goddamned word, Eddie. I--
Wait.
How'd you say you escaped?

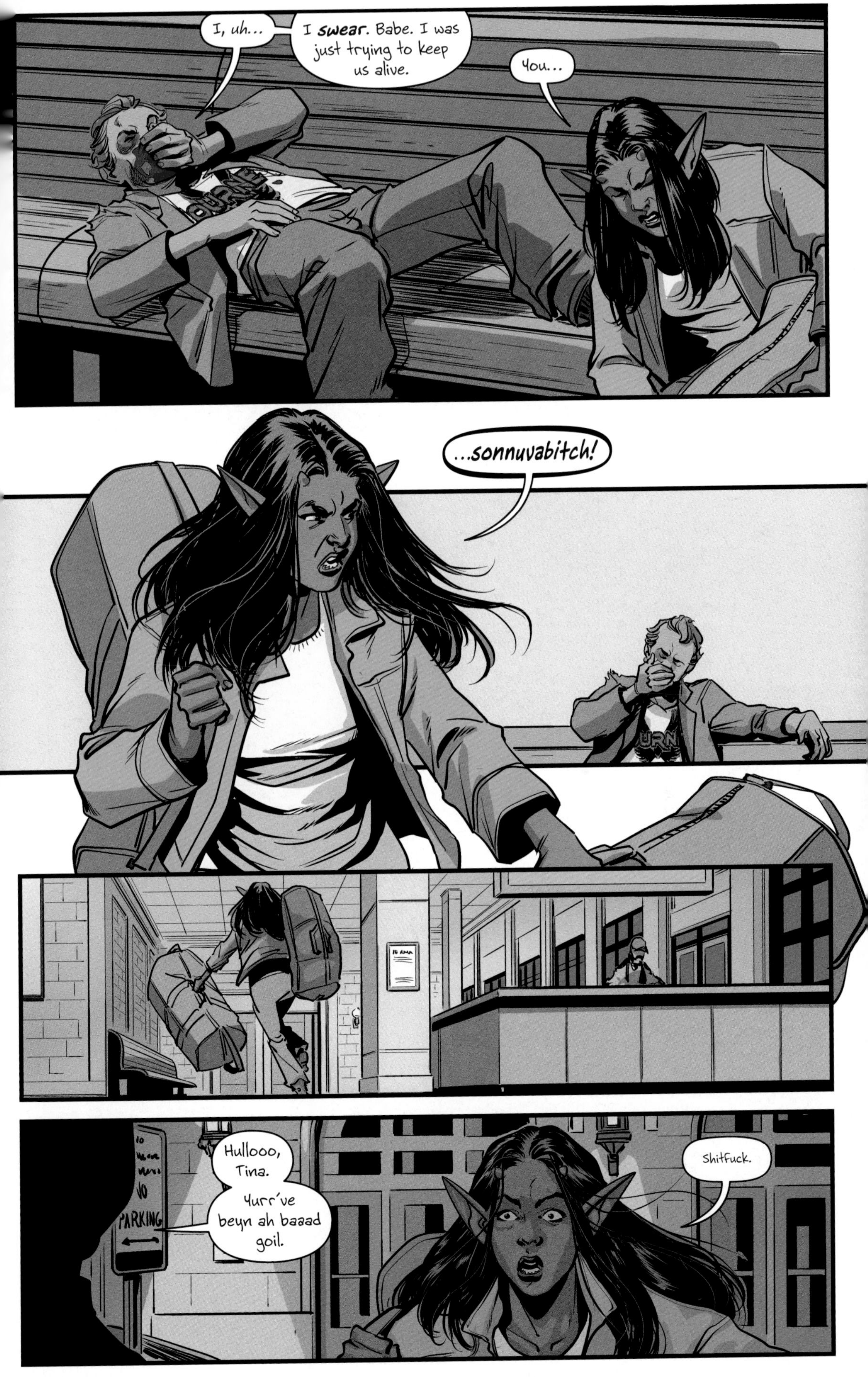

I, uh...
I swear. Babe. I was just trying to keep us alive.
You...
...sonnuvabitch!
Hullooo, Tina.
Yurr've beyn ah baaad goil.
Shitfuck.

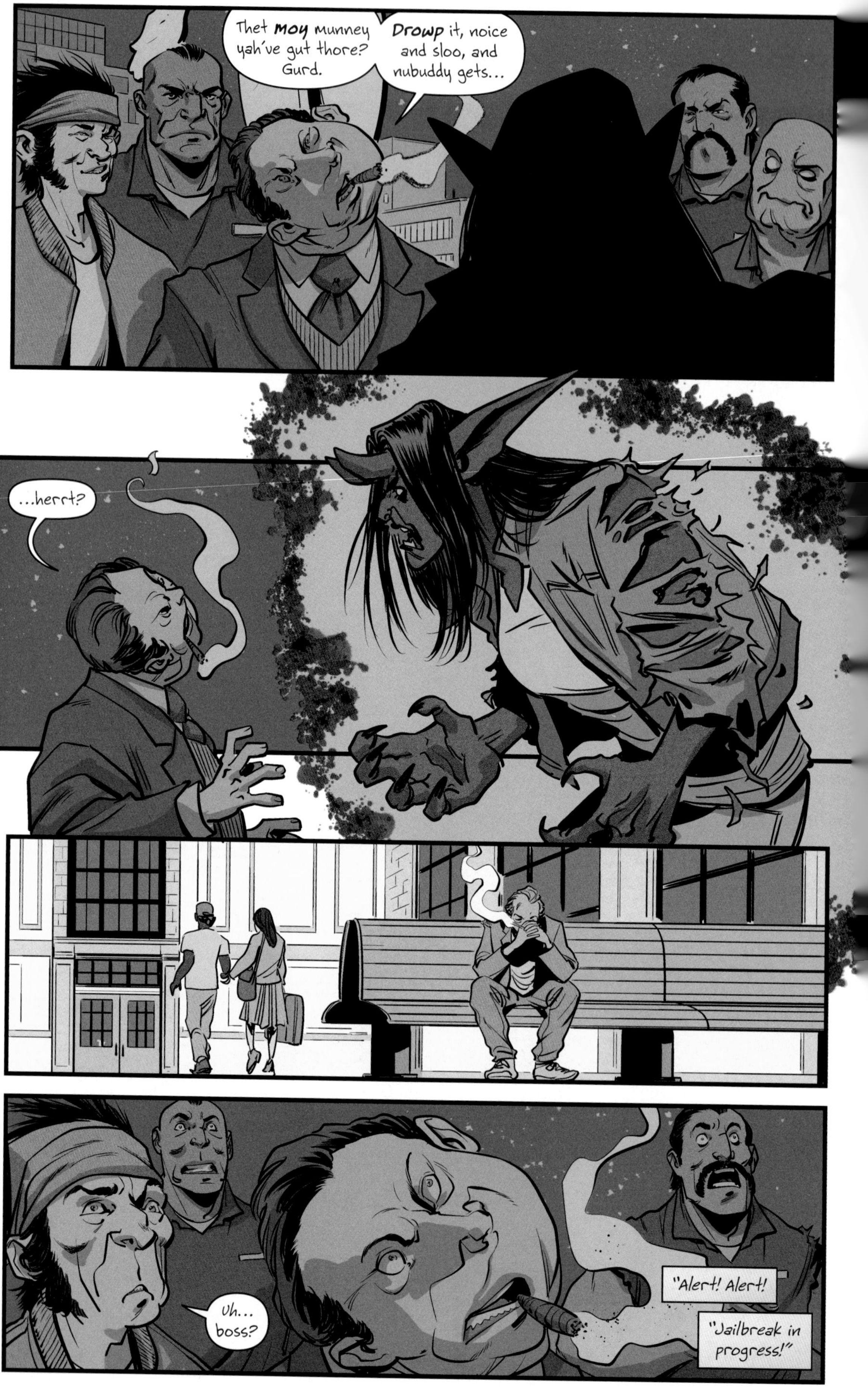
Thet MOY munney yah´ve gut thore? Gurd.
Drowp it, noice and sloo, and nubuddy gets...
...herrt?
Uh... boss?
"Alert! Alert!
"Jailbreak in progress!"

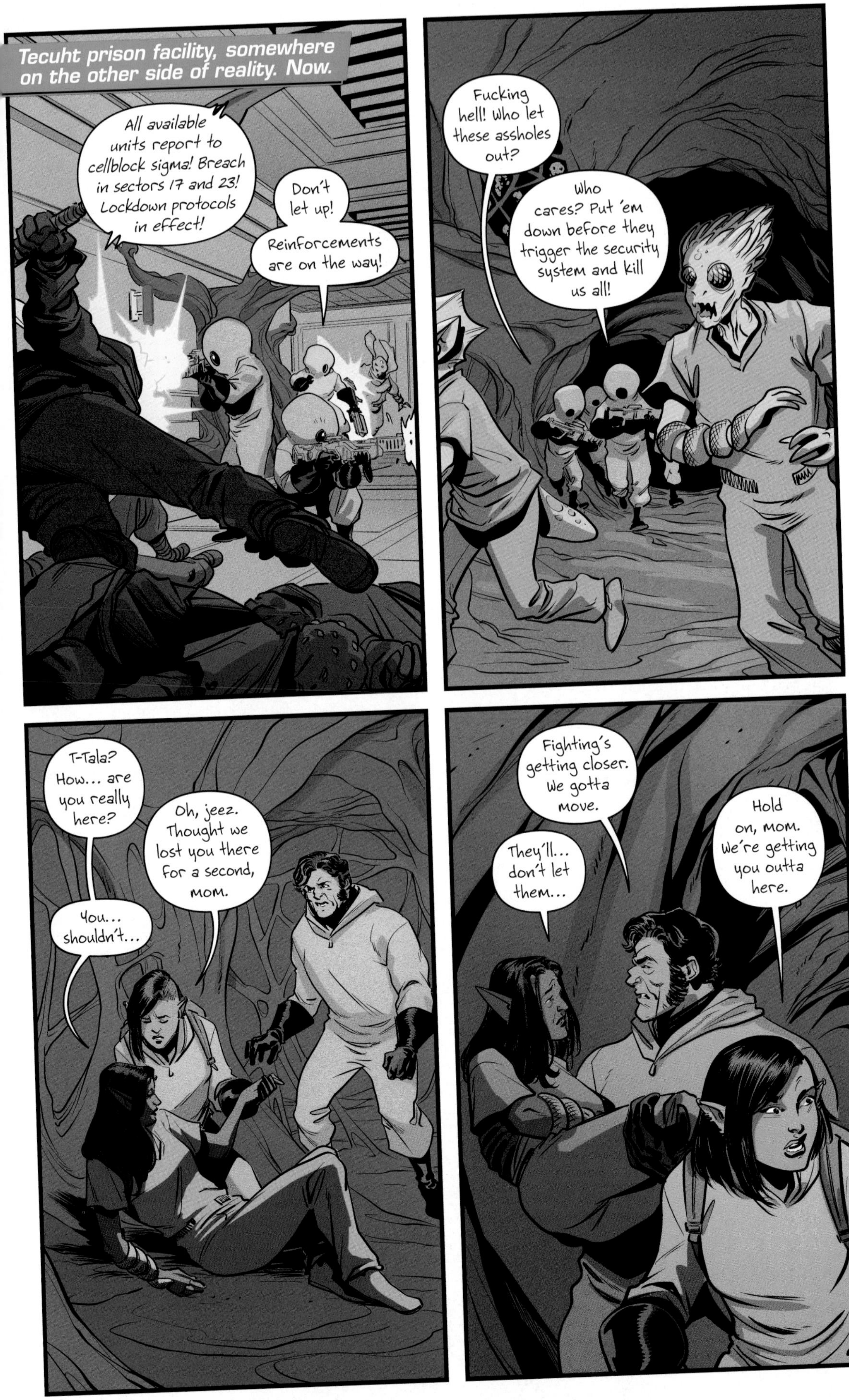
Tecuht prison facility, somewhere on the other side of reality. Now.
All available units report to cellblock sigma! Breach in sectors 17 and 23! Lockdown protocols in effect!
Don't let up!
Reinforcements are on the way!
Fucking hell! Who let these assholes out?
Who cares? Put 'em down before they trigger the security system and kill us all!
T-Tala? How... are you really here?
You... shouldn't...
Oh, jeez. Thought we lost you there for a second, mom.
Fighting's getting closer. We gotta move.
They'll... don't let them...
Hold on, mom. We're getting you outta here.

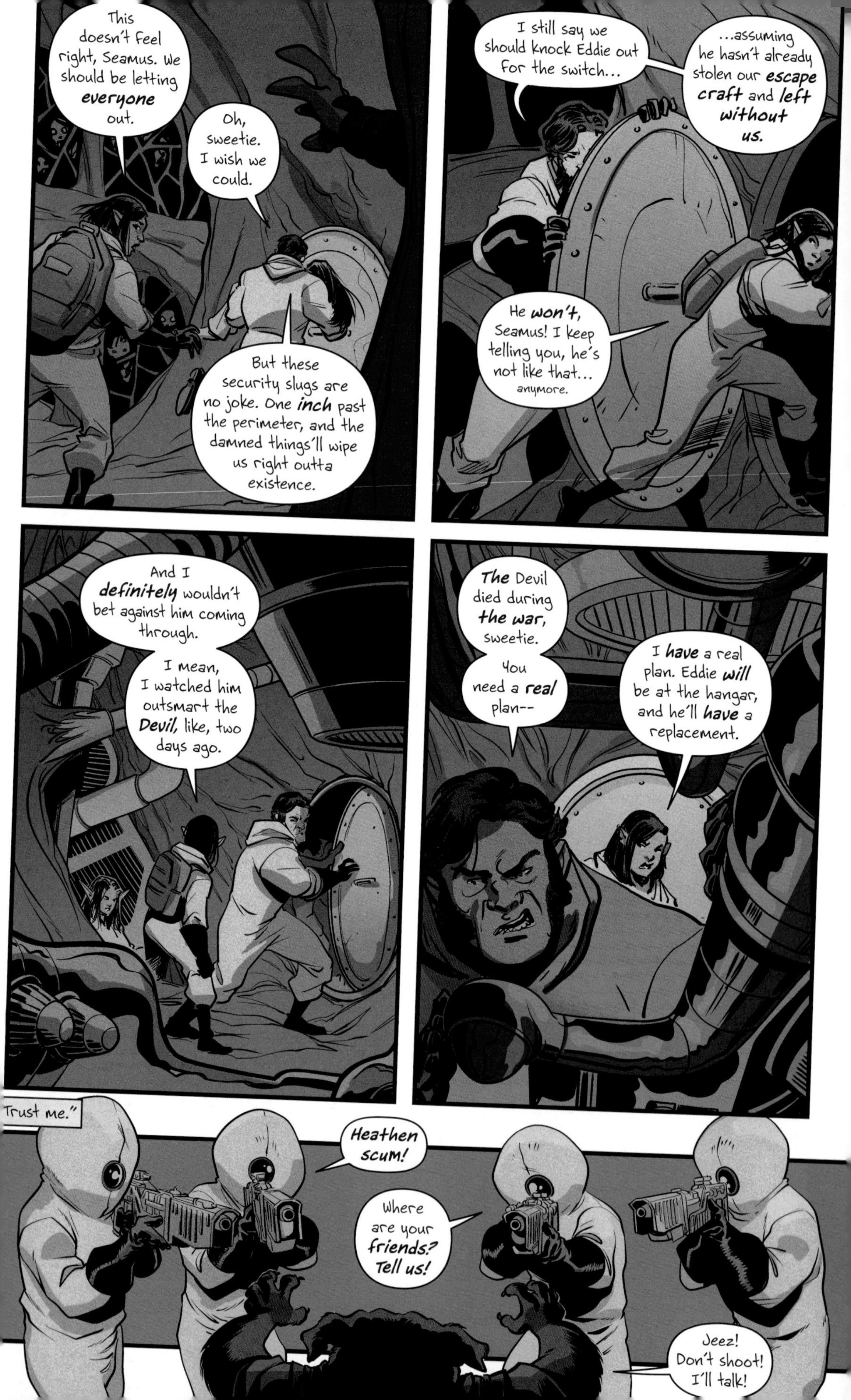
This doesn't feel right, Seamus. We should be letting everyone out.
Oh, sweetie. I wish we could.
But these security slugs are no joke. One inch past the perimeter, and the damned things'll wipe us right outta existence.
I still say we should knock Eddie out for the switch...
...assuming he hasn't already stolen our escape craft and left without us.
He won't, Seamus! I keep telling you, he's not like that... anymore.
And I definitely wouldn't bet against him coming through.
I mean, I watched him outsmart the Devil, like, two days ago.
The Devil died during the war, sweetie.
You need a real plan--
I have a real plan. Eddie will be at the hangar, and he'll have a replacement.
Trust me."
Heathen scum!
Where are your friends? Tell us!
Jeez! Don't shoot! I'll talk!

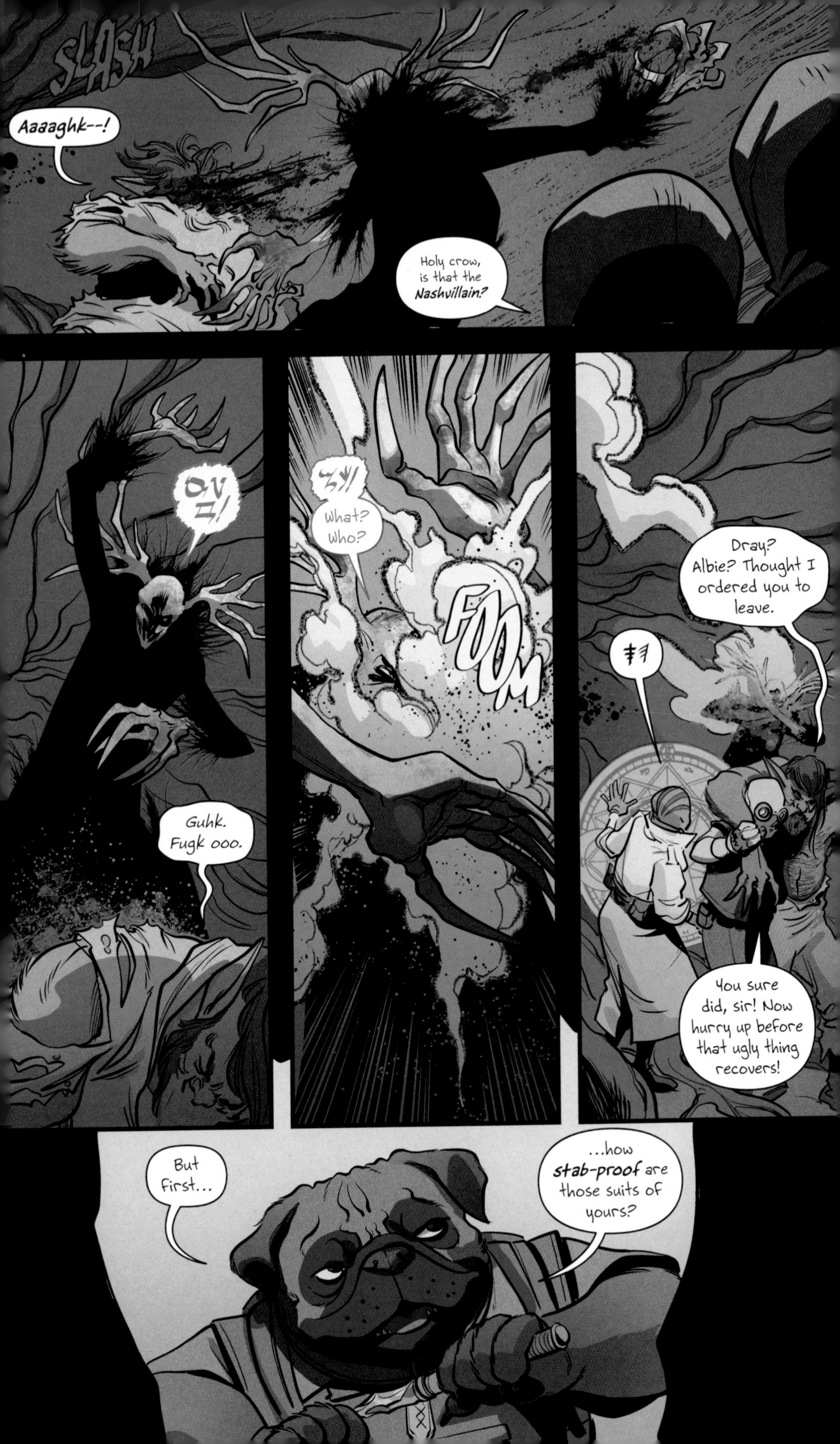
SLASH
Aaaaghk--!
Holy crow, is that the Nashvillain?
Guhk. Fugk ooo.
What? Who?
FOOM
Dray? Albie? Thought I ordered you to leave.
You sure did, sir! Now hurry up before that ugly thing recovers!
But first...
...how stab-proof are those suits of yours?

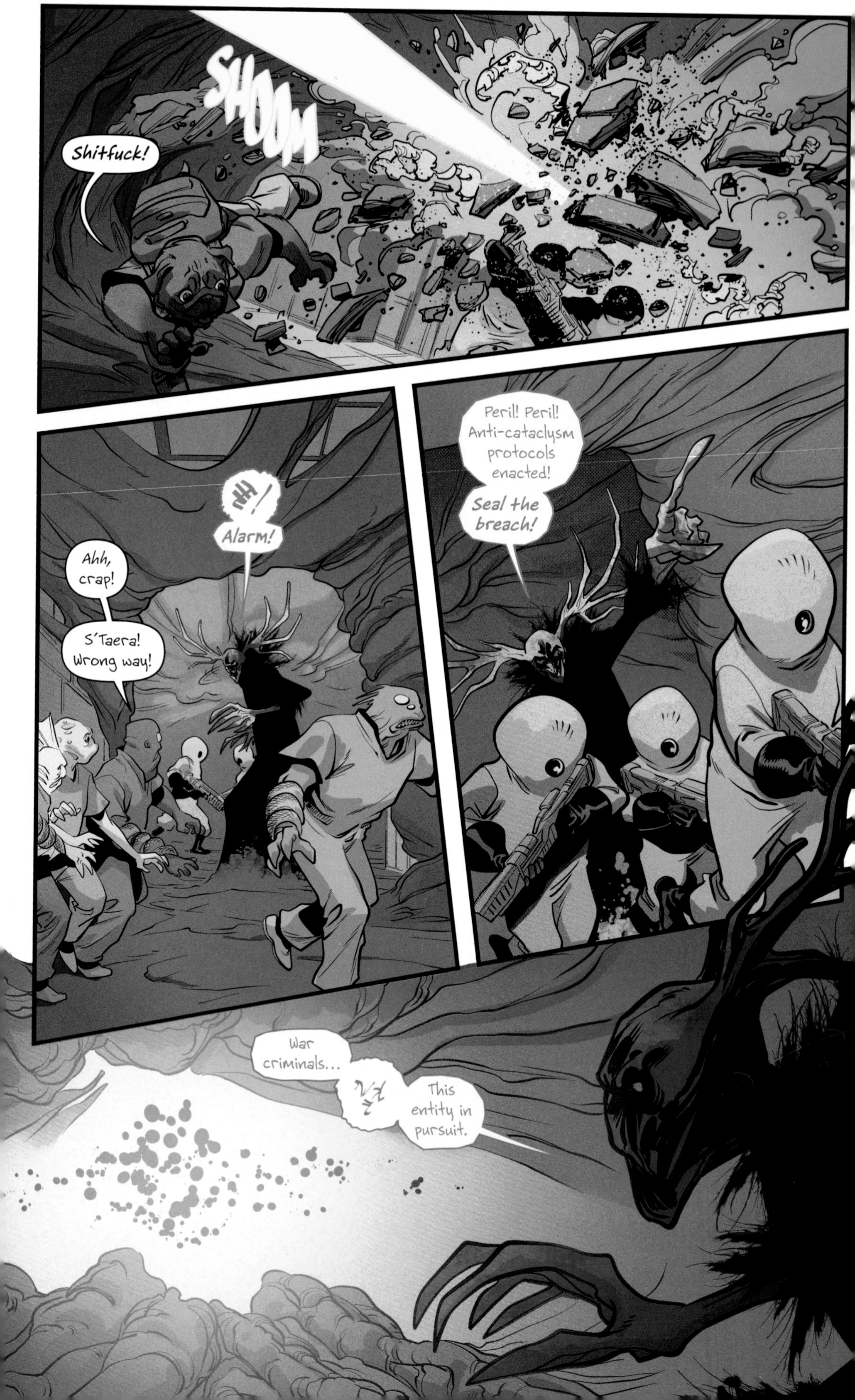
SHOOM
Shitfuck!
Ahh, crap!
S'Taera! Wrong way!
Alarm!
Peril! Peril! Anti-cataclysm protocols enacted!
Seal the breach!
War criminals...
This entity in pursuit.

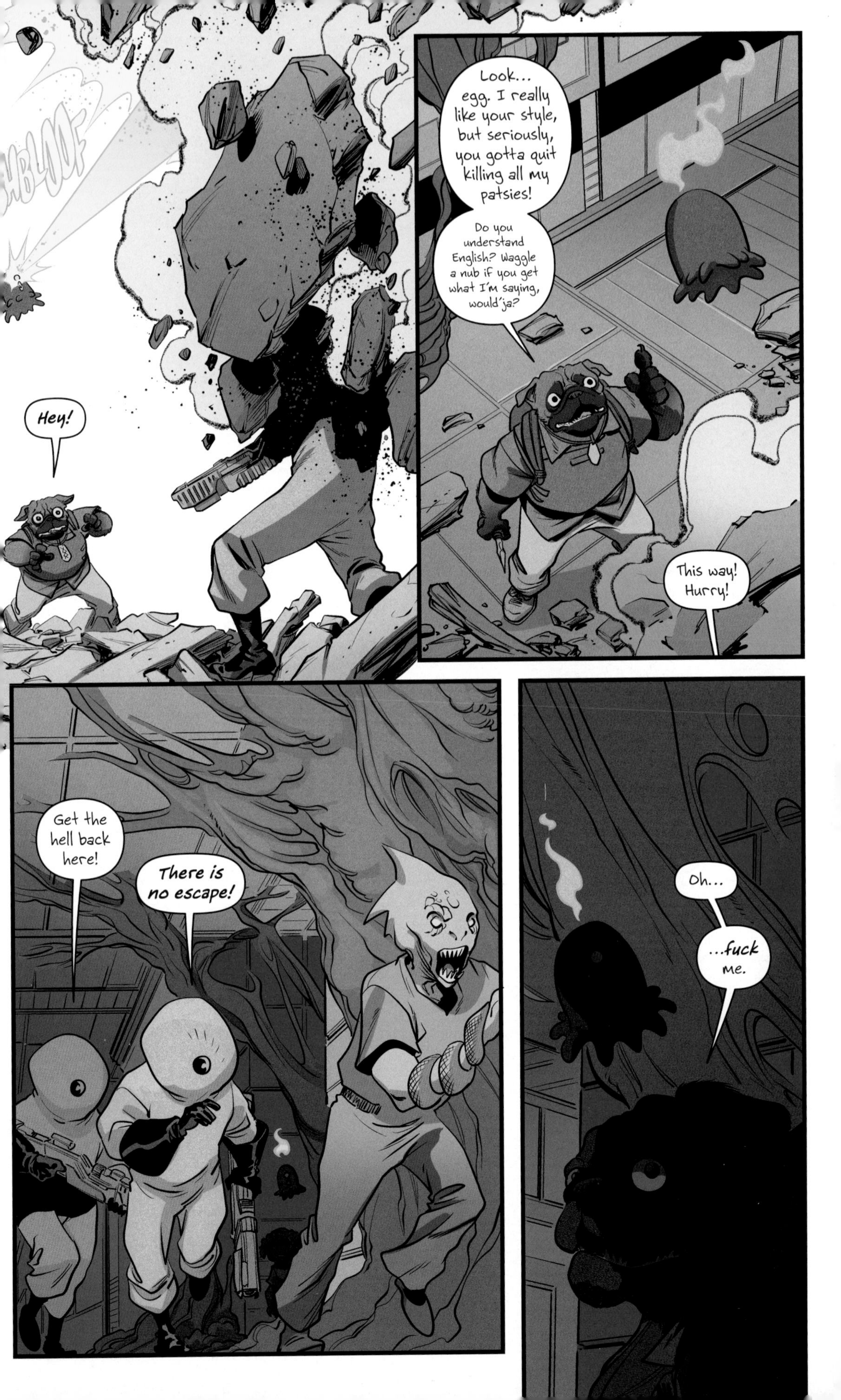
SHBLOOF
Hey!
Look... egg. I really like your style, but seriously, you gotta quit killing all my patsies!
Do you understand English? Waggle a nub if you get what I'm saying, would'ja?
This way! Hurry!
Get the hell back here!
There is no escape!
Oh...
...fuck me.

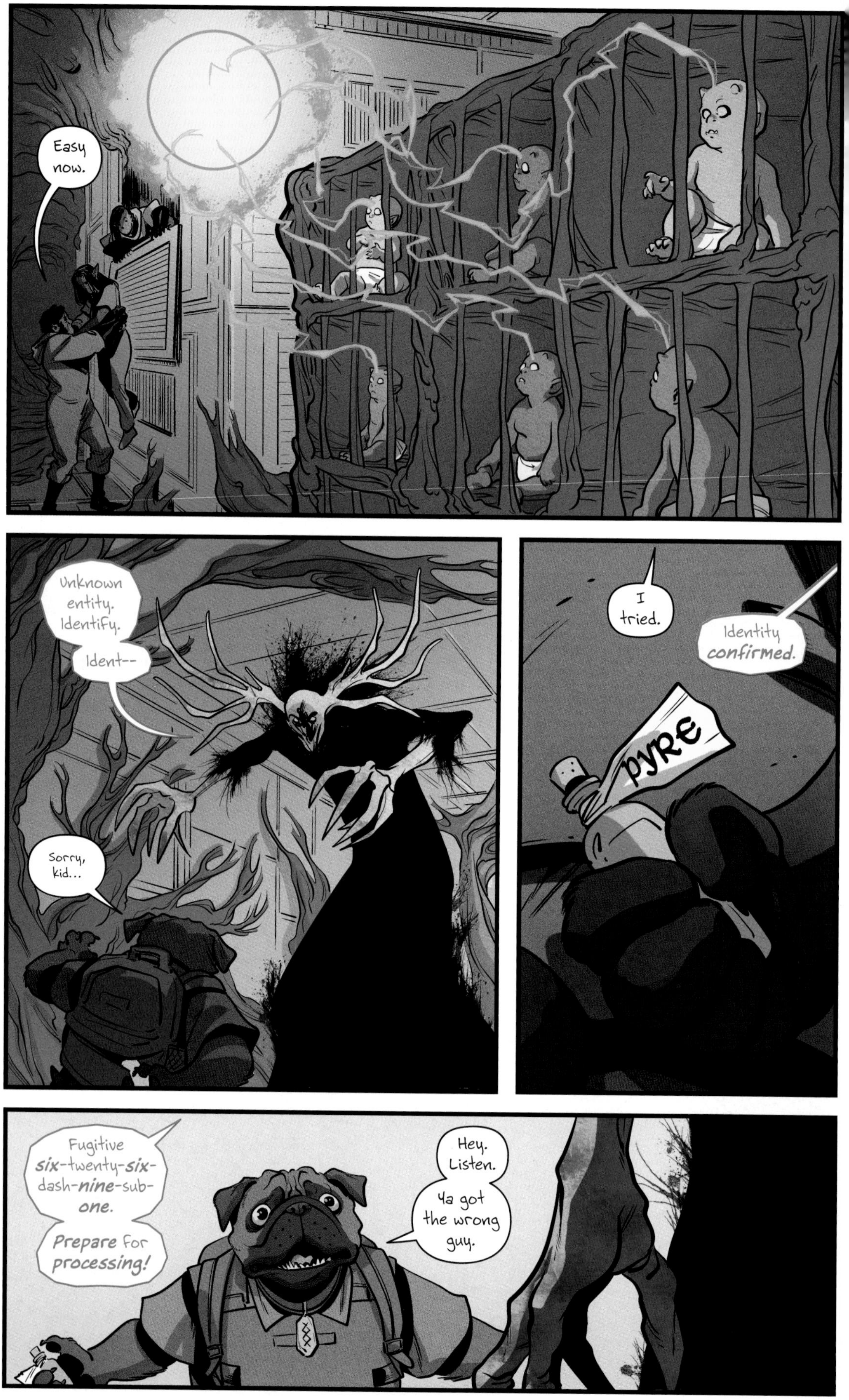
Easy now.
Unknown entity. Identify.
Ident--
Sorry, kid...
I tried.
Identity confirmed.
PYRE
Fugitive six-twenty-six-dash-nine-sub-one.
Prepare for processing!
Hey. Listen.
Ya got the wrong guy.

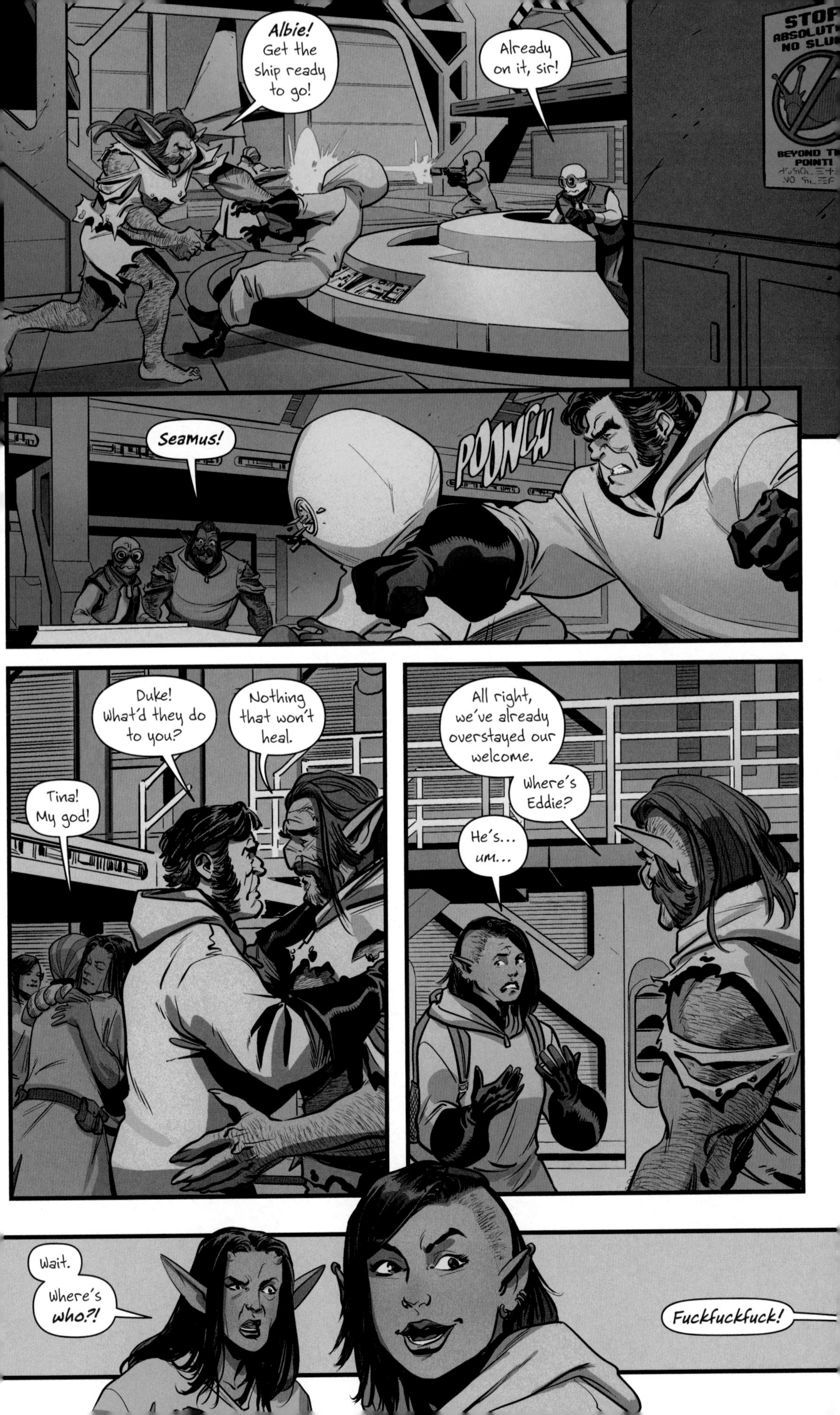
Albie! Get the ship ready to go!
Already on it, sir!
Seamus!
POONCH
Duke! What'd they do to you?
Nothing that won't heal.
Tina! My god!
All right, we've already overstayed our welcome.
Where's Eddie?
He's... um...
Wait.
Where's who?!
Fuckfuckfuck!

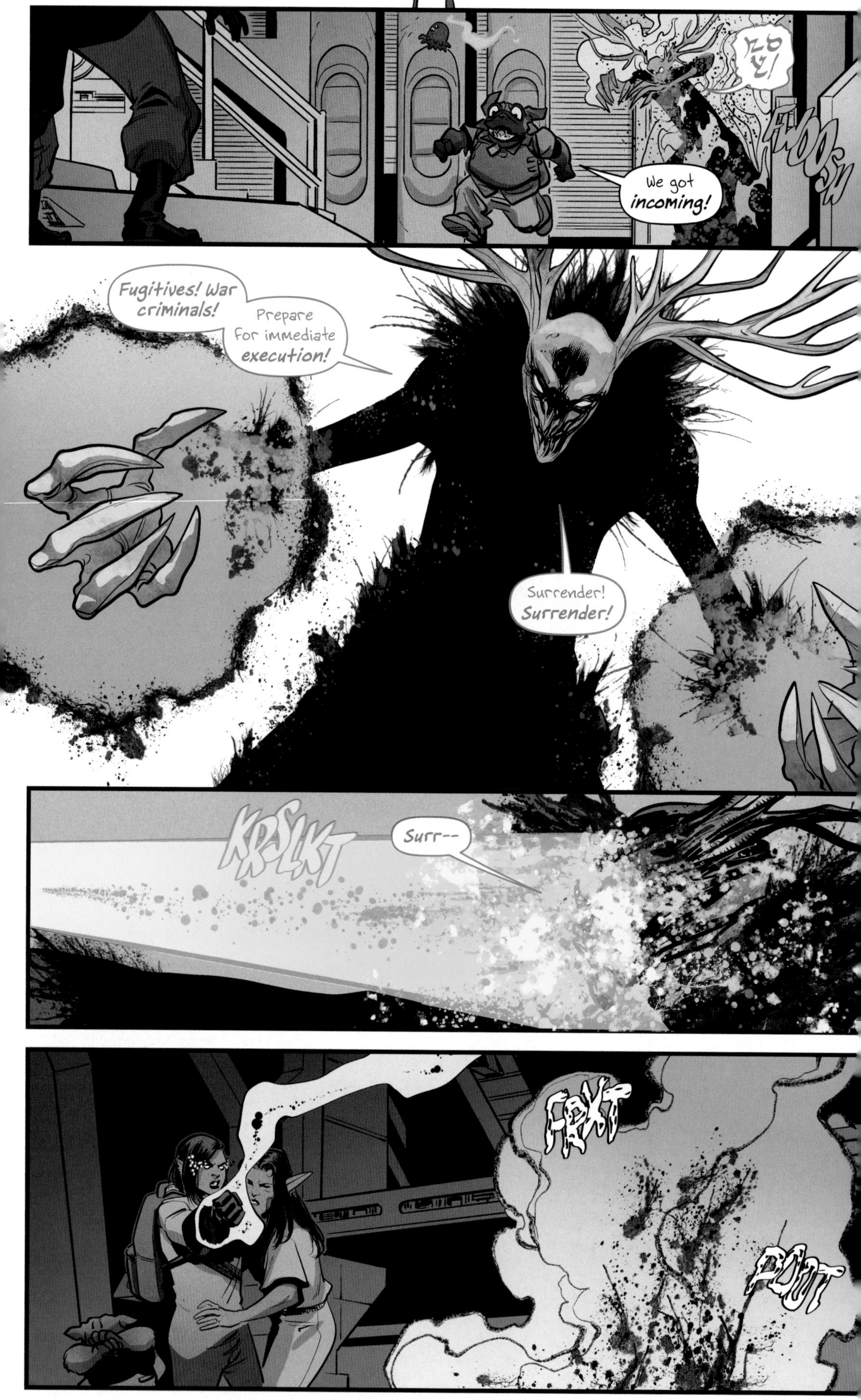FWOOSH
We got incoming!
Fugitives! War criminals!
Prepare for immediate execution!
Surrender! Surrender!
KRSLKT
Surr--
FRXT
POOT

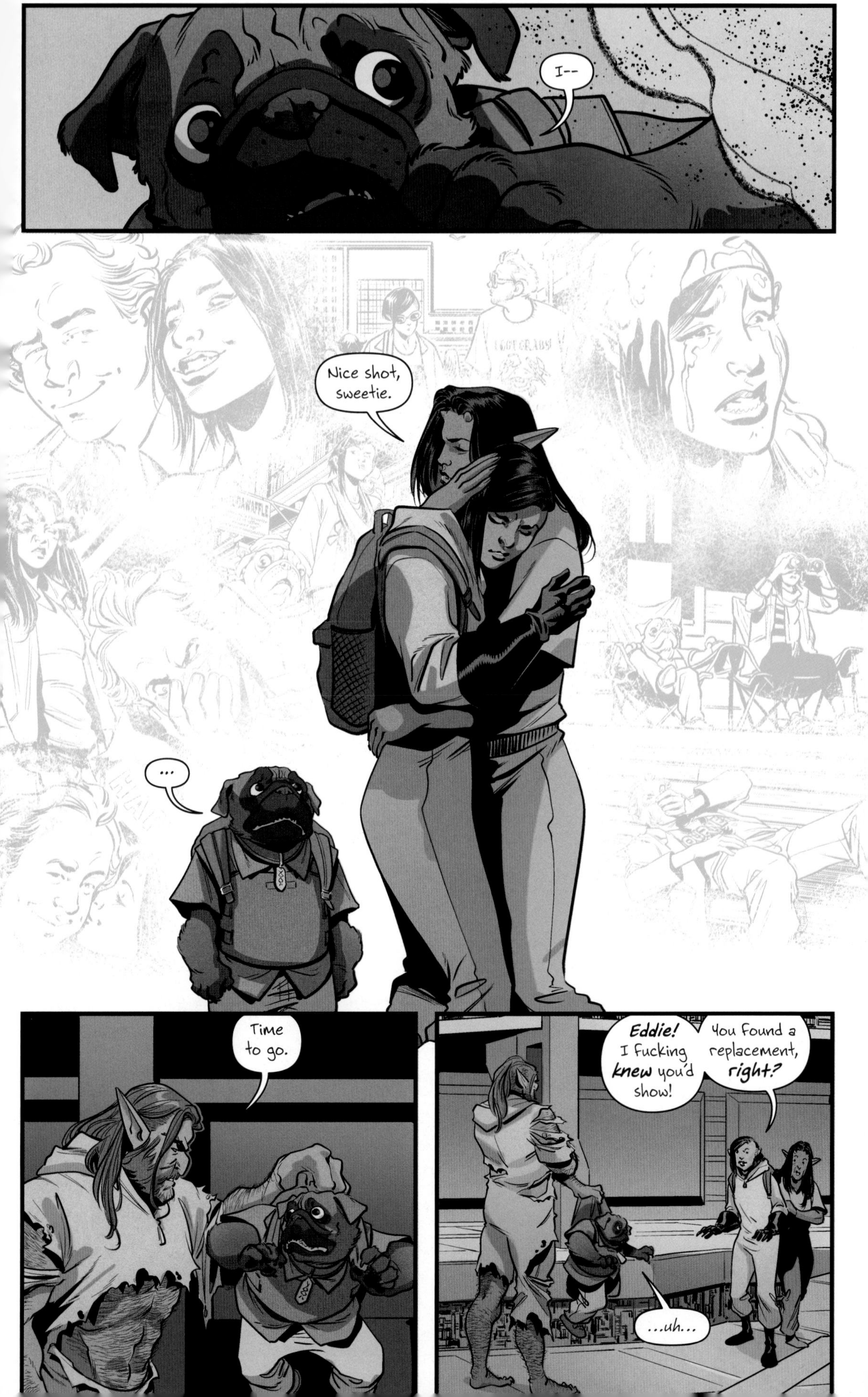
I--
Nice shot, sweetie.
...
Time to go.
Eddie! I fucking knew you'd show!
You found a replacement, right?
...uh...

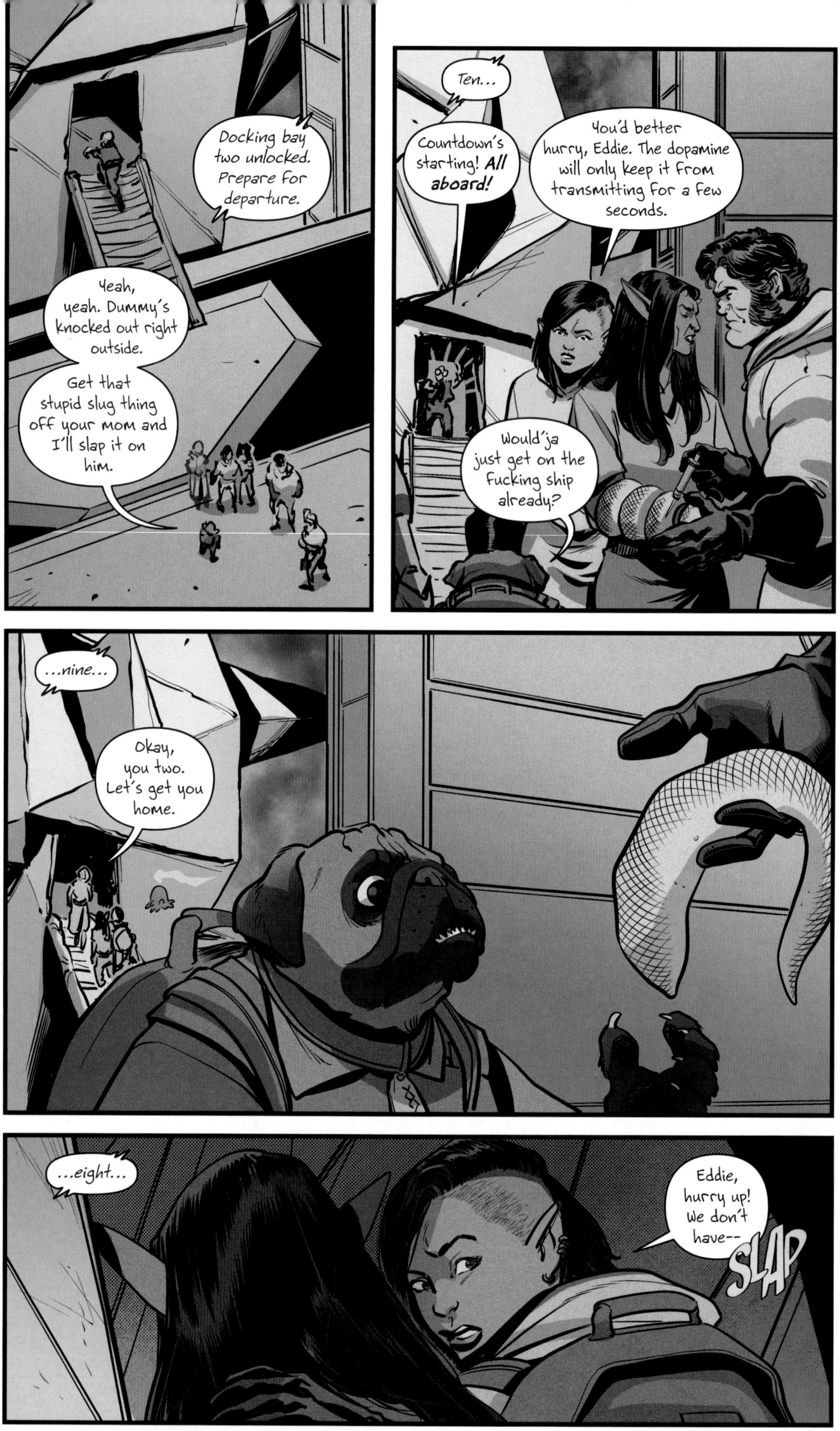
Docking bay two unlocked. Prepare for departure.
Yeah, yeah. Dummy's knocked out right outside.
Get that stupid slug thing off your mom and I'll slap it on him.
Ten...
Countdown's starting! All aboard!
You'd better hurry, Eddie. The dopamine will only keep it from transmitting for a few seconds.
Would'ja just get on the fucking ship already?
...nine...
Okay, you two. Let's get you home.
...eight...
Eddie, hurry up! We don't have--
SLAP

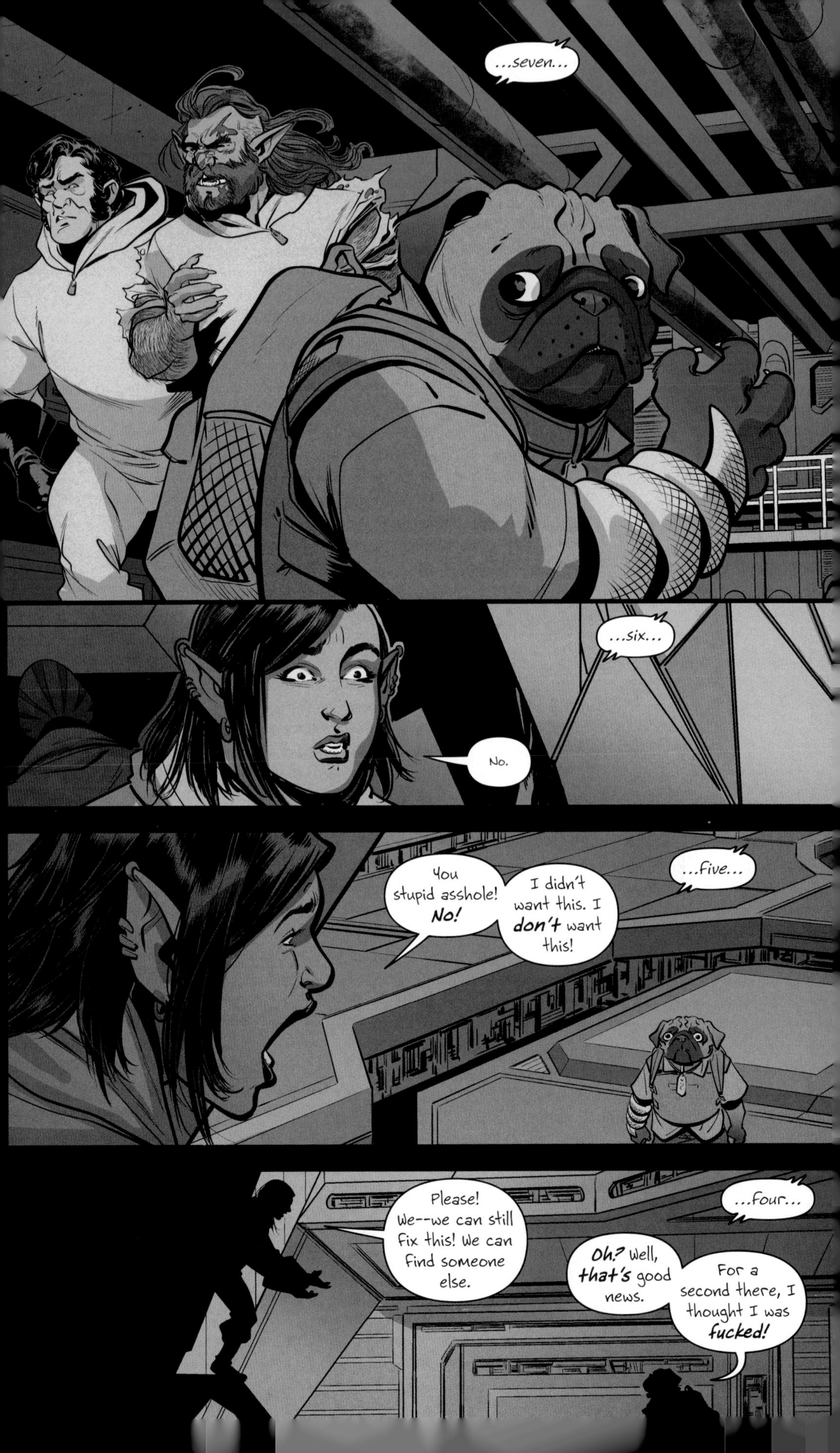

...seven...
...six...
No.
You stupid asshole! No!
I didn't want this. I don't want this!
...five...
Please! We--we can still fix this! We can find someone else.
...four...
Oh? Well, that's good news.
For a second there, I thought I was fucked!

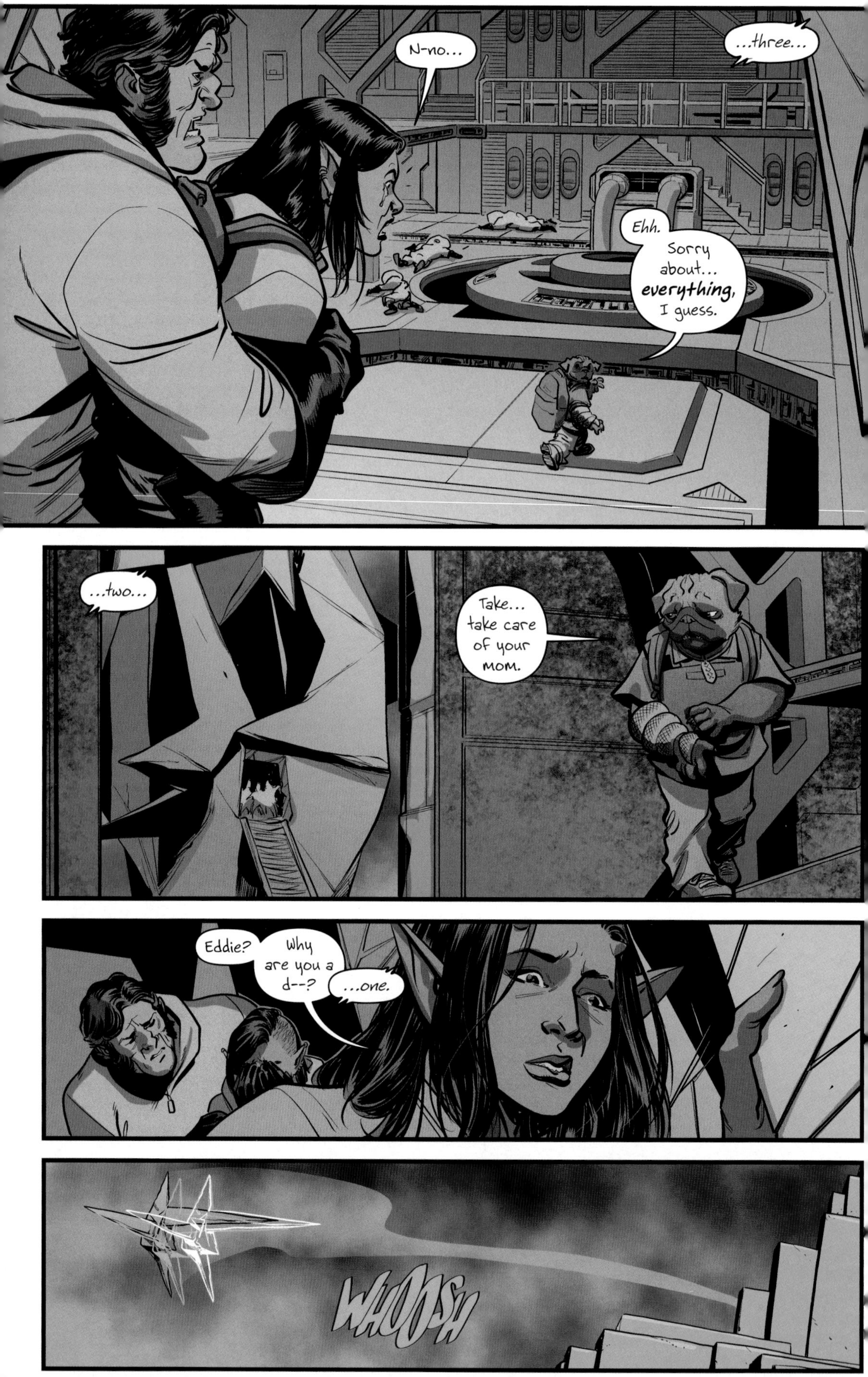
N-no...
...three...
Ehh.
Sorry about... **everything,** I guess.
...two...
Take... take care of your mom.
Eddie?
Why are you a d--?
...one.
WHOOSH

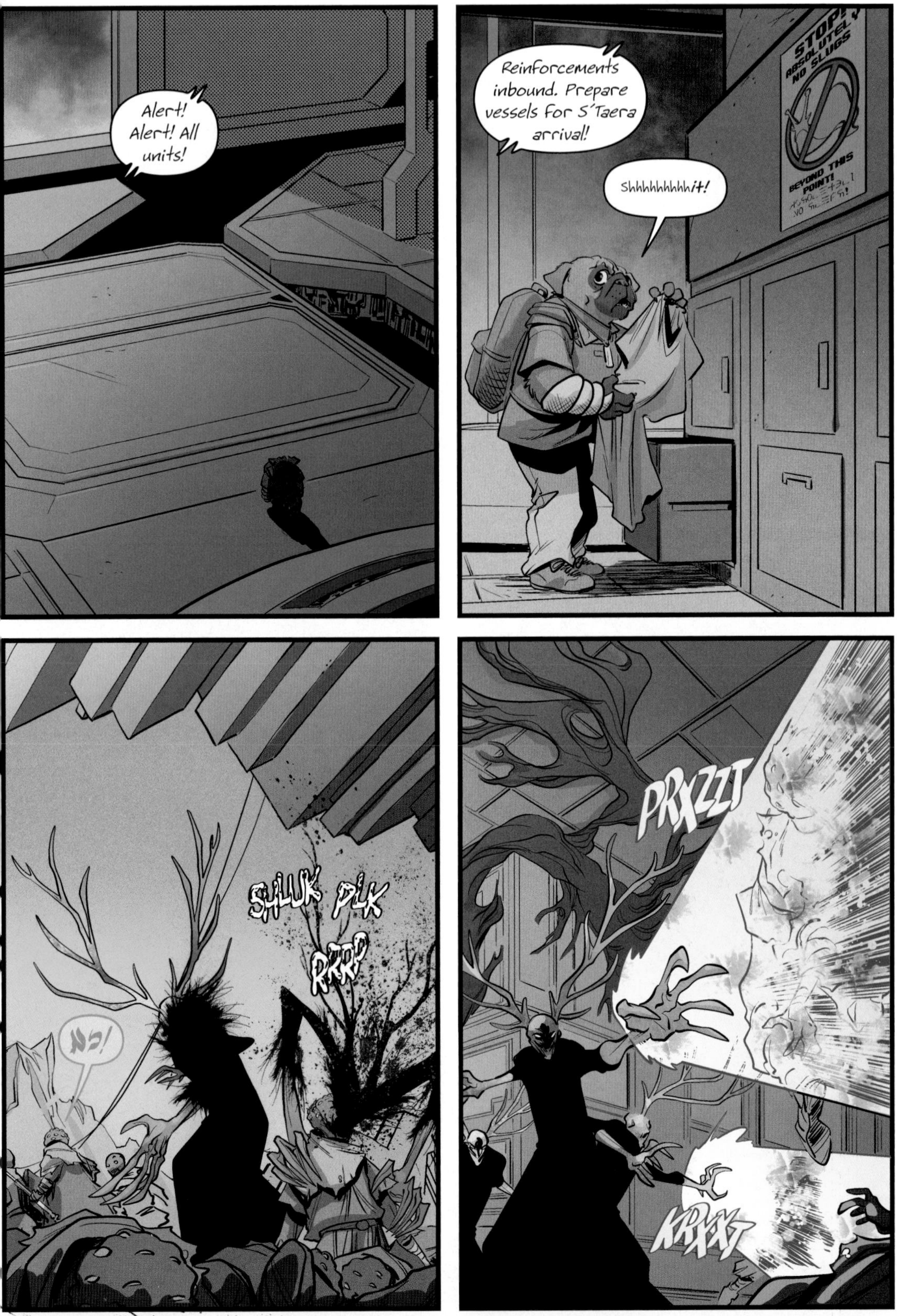
Alert! Alert! All units!
Reinforcements inbound. Prepare vessels for S'Taera arrival!
STOP!
ABSOLUTEL
NO SLUGS
BEYOND THIS POINT!
Shhhhhhhhhit!
SHLUK PLK
RRRP
PRXZZT
KRXXT

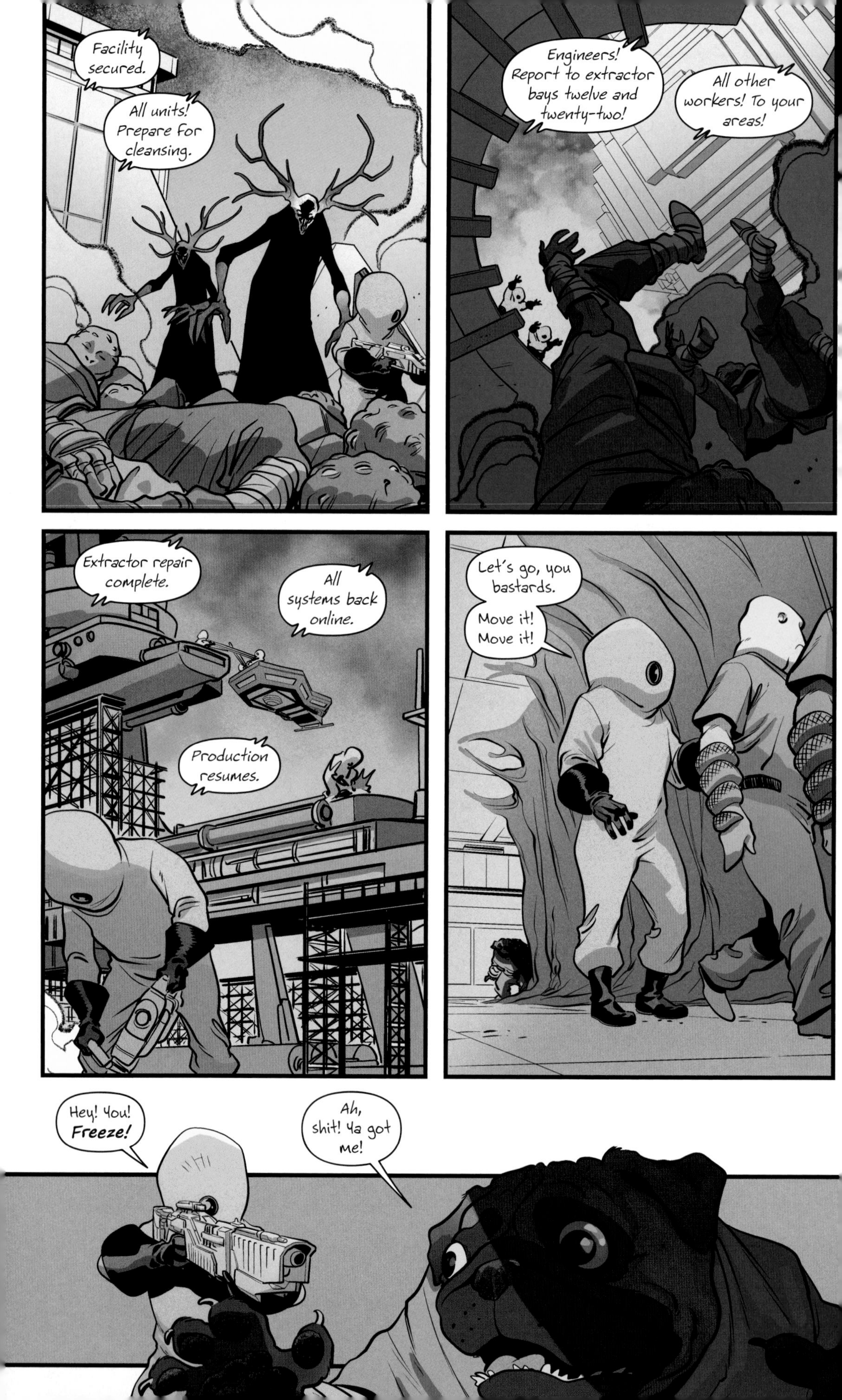
Facility secured.
All units! Prepare for cleansing.
Engineers! Report to extractor bays twelve and twenty-two!
All other workers! To your areas!
Extractor repair complete.
All systems back online.
Production resumes.
Let's go, you bastards.
Move it! Move it!
Hey! You! **Freeze!**
Ah, shit! Ya got me!

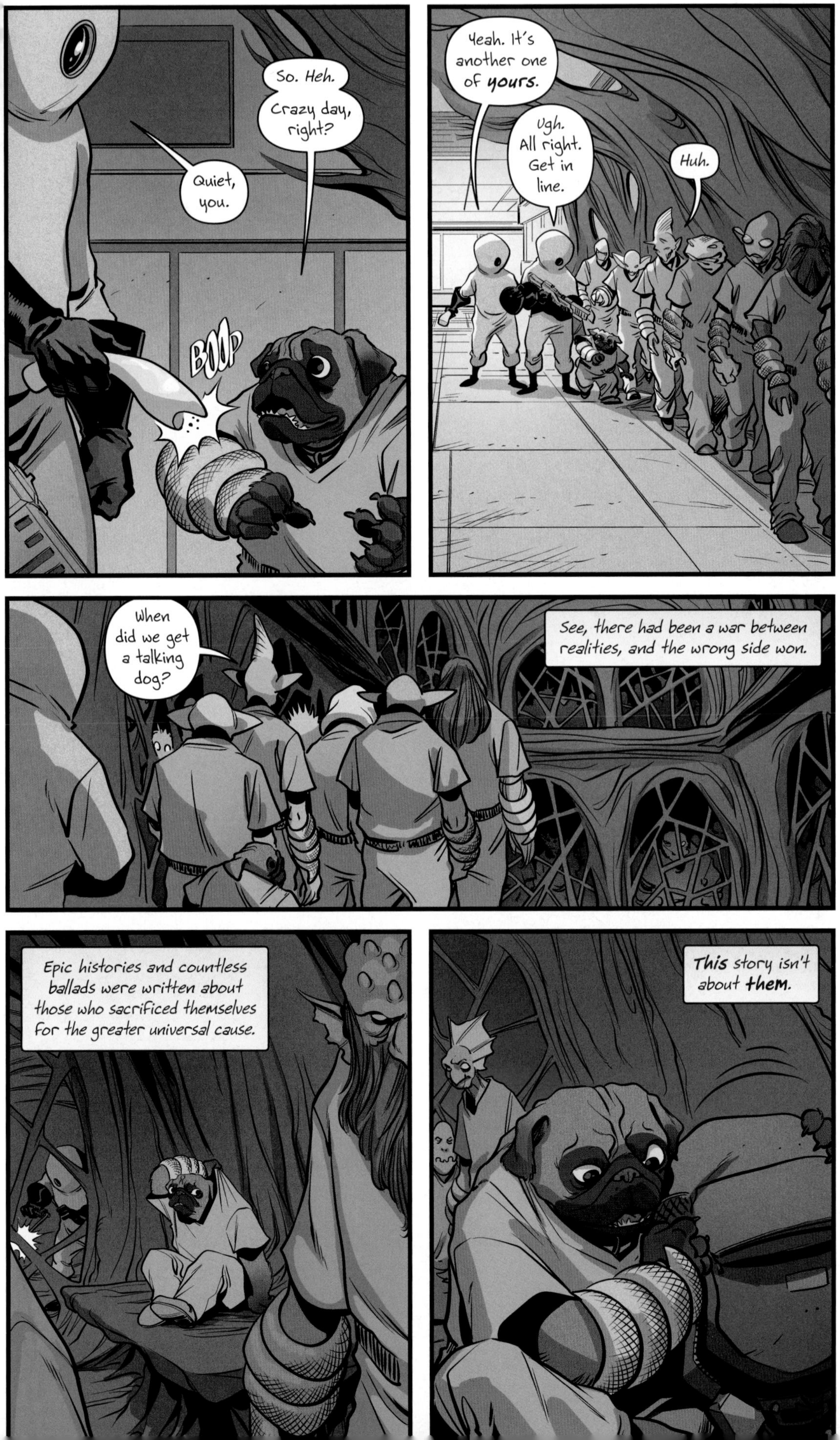
So. Heh.
Crazy day, right?
Quiet, you.
BOOP
Yeah. It's another one of **yours**.
Ugh. All right. Get in line.
Huh.
When did we get a talking dog?
See, there had been a war between realities, and the wrong side won.
Epic histories and countless ballads were written about those who sacrificed themselves for the greater universal cause.
This story isn't about **them**.

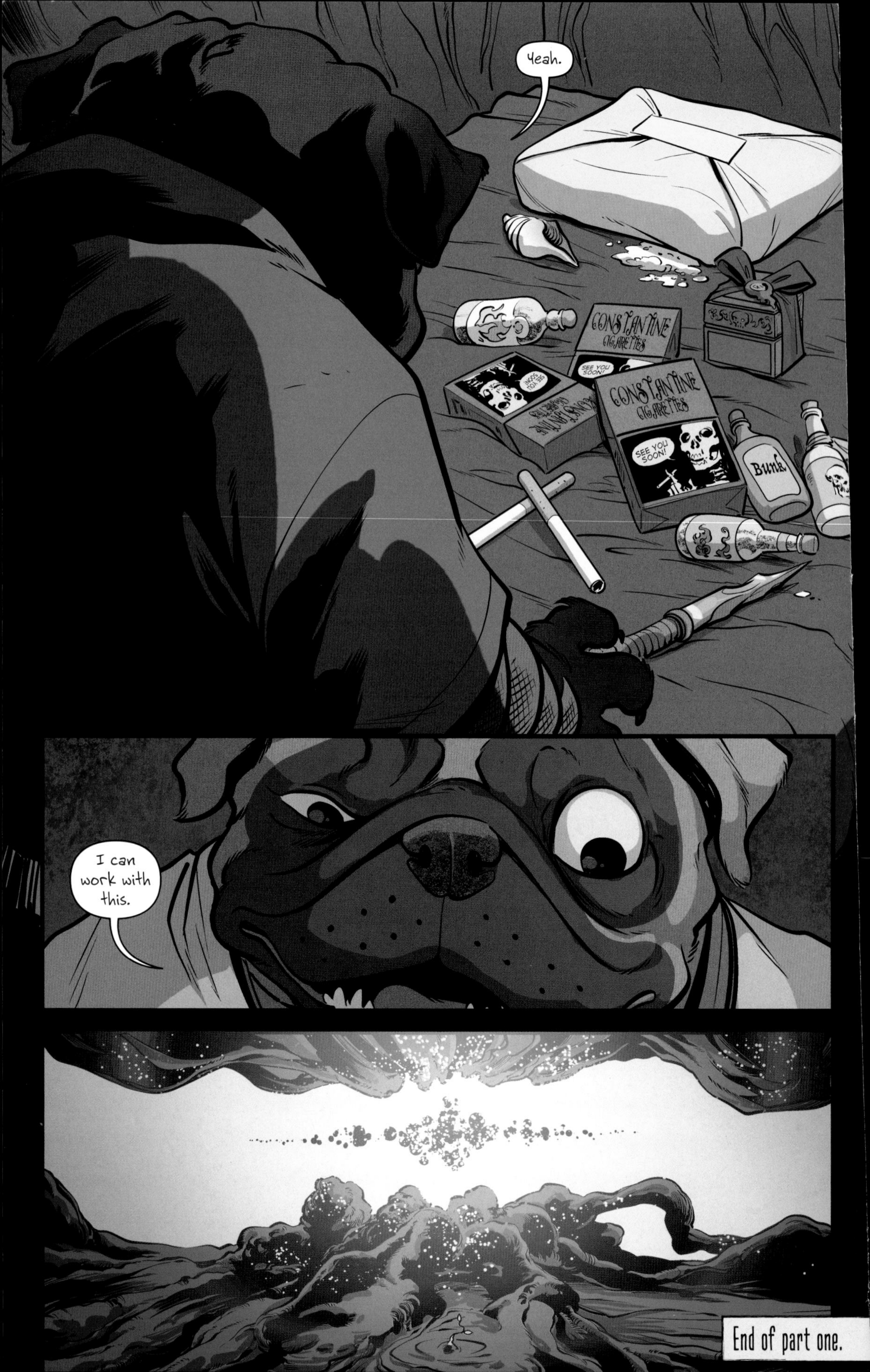
Yeah.
CONSTANTINE CIGARETTES
SEE YOU SOON!
CONSTANTINE CIGARETTES
SEE YOU SOON!
Bunk
I can work with this.
End of part one.

THE CREATORS

Rafer Roberts is the writer and co-creator of **Modern Fantasy**, published by Dark Horse Comics, and was the writer on **A&A: The Adventures of Archer & Armstrong** and **Harbinger: Renegades** for Valiant Comics. His self-published work includes the long running **Plastic Farm**, **Nightmare the Rat**, and the Tumblr famous **Thanos and Darkseid: Carpool Buddies of Doom.**

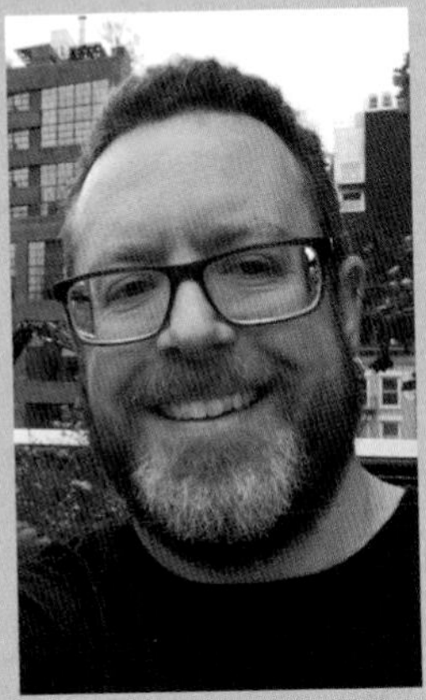

Mike Norton is the creator of the Eisner and Harvey award-winning webcomic **Battlepug** and the co-creator and artist of **Revival.** He has worked for Marvel, DC, Dark Horse and just about everybody else. He has a webcomic called **Lil' Donnie** about the worst president in US history. He lives in Chicago with his wife, two pugs, and a fridge full of beer.

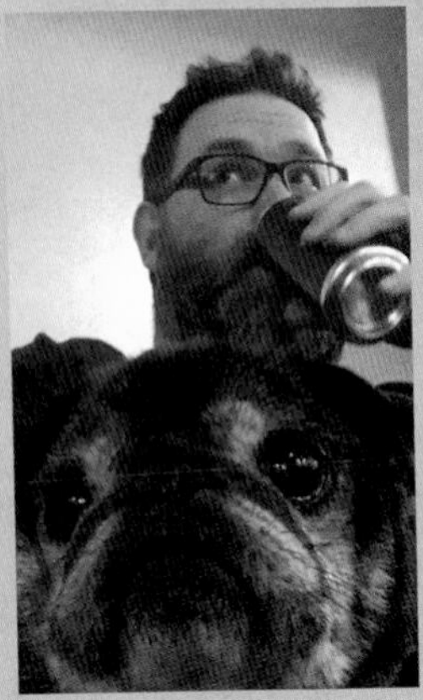

Marissa Louise is a colorist for DC, Dark Horse, Image, and others. She also does a twice monthly Curse of Strahd podcast called Bite Club, wherein she plays multiple loveable scamps.

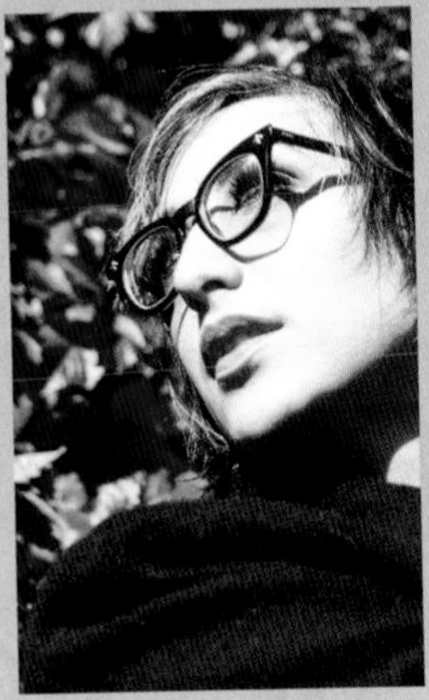

Christopher Crank (crank!) letters a bunch of books put out by Image, Dark Horse, Oni Press, Dynamite, and elsewhere. He also has a podcast with comic artist Mike Norton and members of Four Star Studios in Chicago (crankcast.com) and makes music. (sonomorti.bandcamp.com)

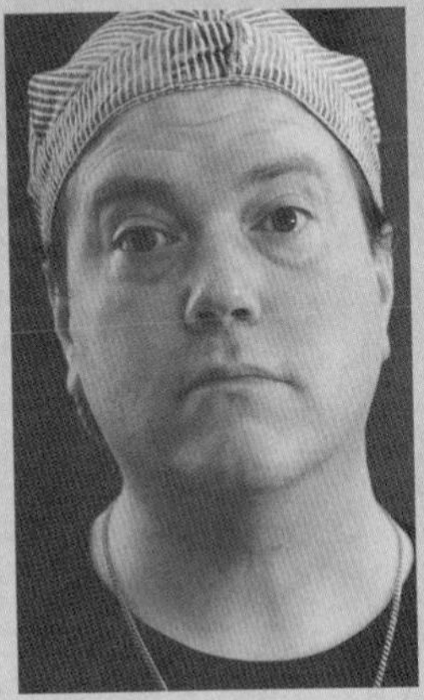

Addison Duke is an artist based in Chicago, IL. After graduating with a BFA in illustration from Academy of Art University, Addison began his professional career working as a Production Artist at Image Comics. Coloring work has included **Curse Words** (Image Comics), **Barbarella/Deja Thoris** (Dynamite Comics), **The Mall** (Vault Comics), as well as work for **Heavy Metal**

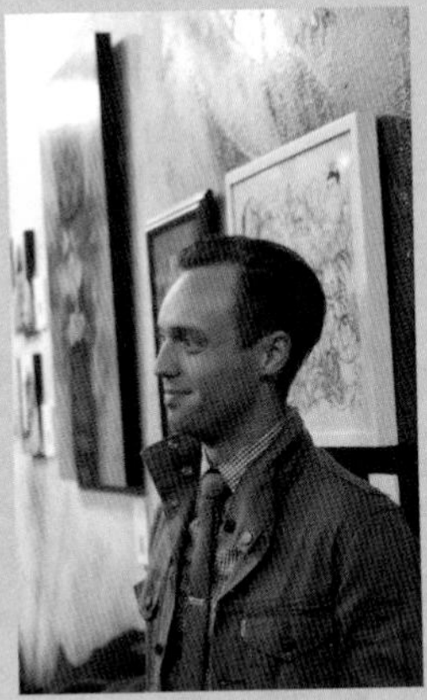

In addition to Grumble, Alejandro Arbona currently edits **Lazarus: Risen, Black Magick**, and **The Old Guard** for Image Comics, and recently edited **Ghost in the Shell: Global Neural Network** for Kodansha/Penguin Random House. He also wrote the non-fiction kids' books **Awesome Minds: Video Game Creators** and **Awesome Minds: Comic Book Creators.** Alejandro lives in New York City with a dog who only speaks Spanish.

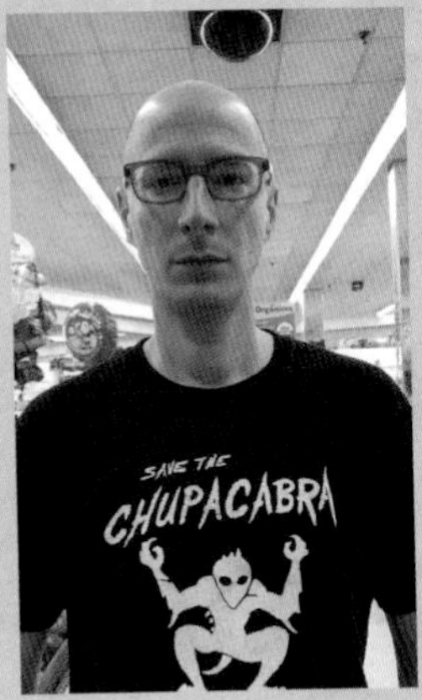
SAVE THE
CHUPACABRA

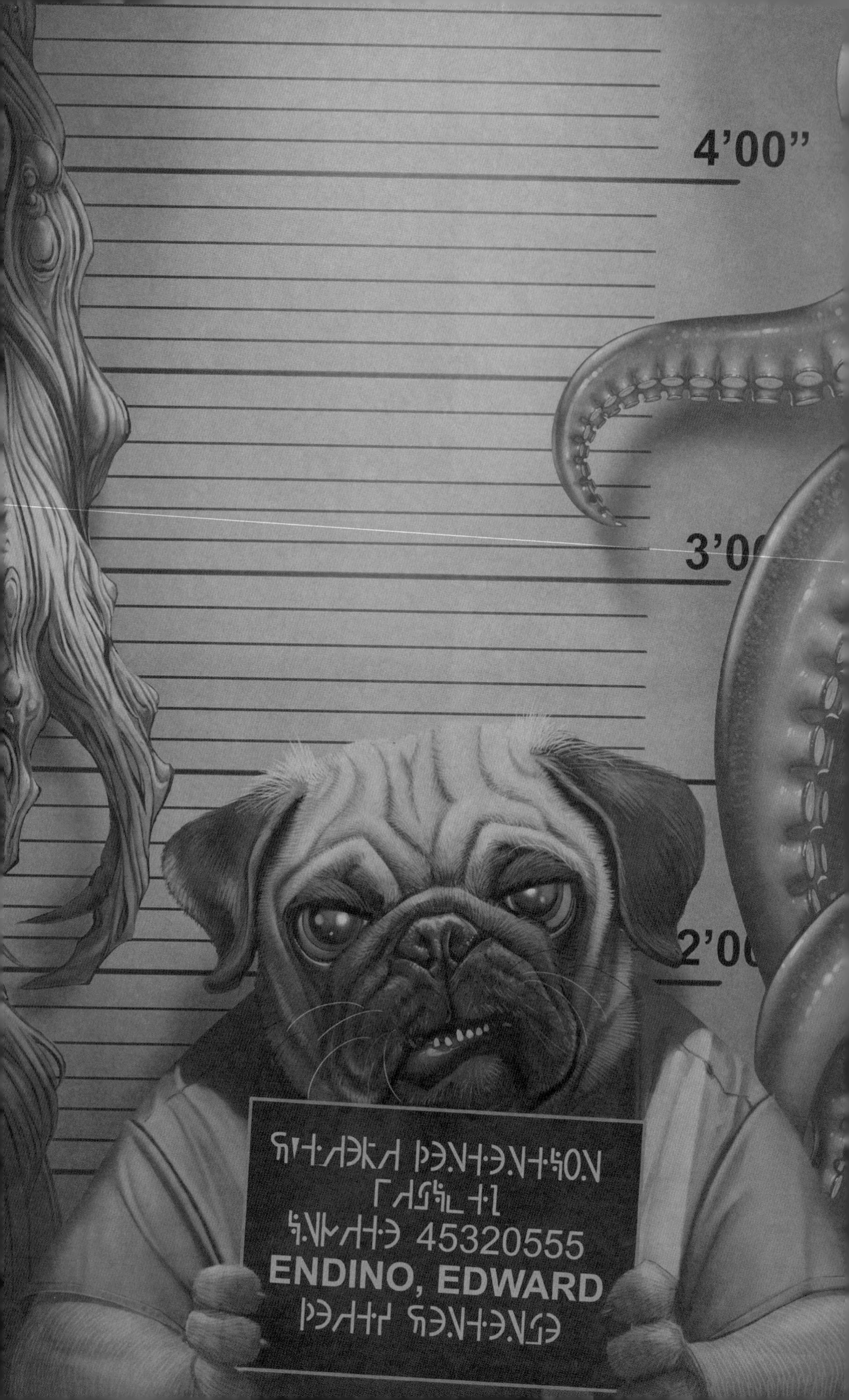

4'00"
3'00
2'00
45320555
ENDINO, EDWARD

LOOK FOR THESE OTHER ALBATROSS TITLES!

THE GOON VOLUME 1

THE GOON VOLUME 2

THE GOON VOLUME 3

THE LORDS OF MISERY

THE GOON: BUNCH OF OLD CRAP, AN OMNIBUS VOLUME 1

THE GOON: BUNCH OF OLD CRAP, AN OMNIBUS VOLUME 2

THE GOON: BUNCH OF OLD CRAP, AN OMNIBUS VOLUME 3

THE GOON: BUNCH OF OLD CRAP, AN OMNIBUS VOLUME 4

THE GOON: BUNCH OF OLD CRAP, AN OMNIBUS VOLUME 5

HILLBILLY VOLUME 1

HILLBILLY VOLUME 2

HILLBILLY VOLUME 3

HILLBILLY VOLUME 4

GALAKTIKON

GRUMBLE VOLUME 1

GRUMBLE VOLUME 2

GRUMBLE VOLUME 3

MEGAGHOST

'NAMWOLF

SPOOK HOUSE VOLUME 1

SPOOK HOUSE VOLUME 2

REBECCA SUGAR'S PUG DAVIS

- **THE GOON VOLUME 1** ISBN: 978-1-949889-92-5 $17.99
- **THE GOON VOLUME 2** ISBN: 978-1-949889-94-9 $17.99
- **THE GOON VOLUME 3** ISBN: 978-1-949889-02-4 $17.99
- **THE LORDS OF MISERY** ISBN: 978-1-949889-81-9 $7.99
- **THE GOON : BUNCH OF OLD CRAP, AN OMNIBUS VOLUME 1** ISBN: 978-0-9983792-9-6 $29.99
- **THE GOON : BUNCH OF OLD CRAP, AN OMNIBUS VOLUME 2** ISBN: 978-1-949889-93-2 $29.99
- **THE GOON : BUNCH OF OLD CRAP, AN OMNIBUS VOLUME 3** ISBN: 978-1-949889-95-6 $29.99
- **THE GOON : BUNCH OF OLD CRAP, AN OMNIBUS VOLUME 4** ISBN: 978-1-949889-97-0 $29.99
- **THE GOON : BUNCH OF OLD CRAP, AN OMNIBUS VOLUME 5** ISBN: 978-1-949889-03-1 $29.99
- **HILLBILLY VOLUME 1** ISBN: 978-0-9983792-0-3 $17.99
- **HILLBILLY VOLUME 2** ISBN: 978-0-9983792-3-4 $17.99
- **HILLBILLY VOLUME 3** ISBN: 978-0-9983792-4-1 $17.99
- **HILLBILLY VOLUME 4** ISBN: 978-0-9983792-8-9 $17.99
- **SPOOK HOUSE VOLUME 1** ISBN: 978-0-9983792-1-0 $17.99
- **SPOOK HOUSE VOLUME 2** ISBN: 978-0-9983792-7-2 $17.99
- **GRUMBLE VOLUME 1** ISBN: 978-1-949889-90-1 $17.99
- **GRUMBLE VOLUME 2** ISBN: 978-1-949889-82-6 $17.99
- **GRUMBLE VOLUME 3** ISBN: 978-1-949889-01-7 $17.99
- **GALAKTIKON** ISBN: 978-0-9983792-5-8 $17.99
- **MEGAGHOST** ISBN: 978-1-949889-99-4 $17.99
- **REBECCA SUGAR'S PUG DAVIS** ISBN: 978-1-949889-91-8 $17.99

ALBATROSSFUNNYBOOKS.COM

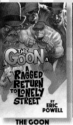

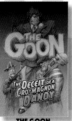

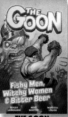

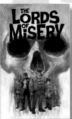

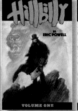

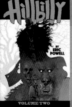

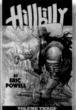

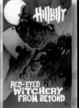

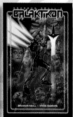

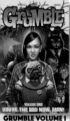

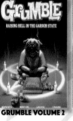

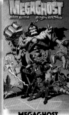

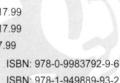

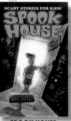

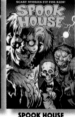

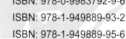

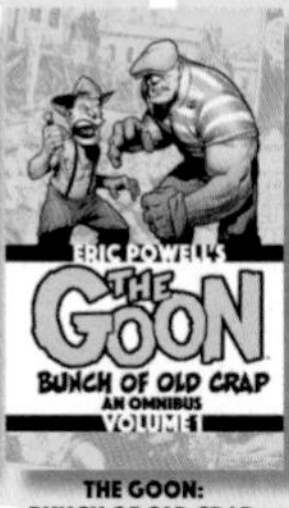

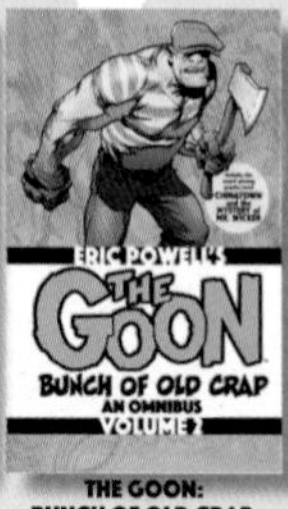

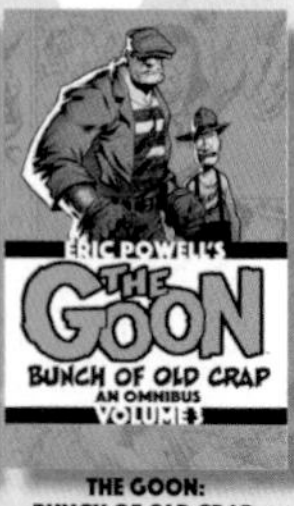

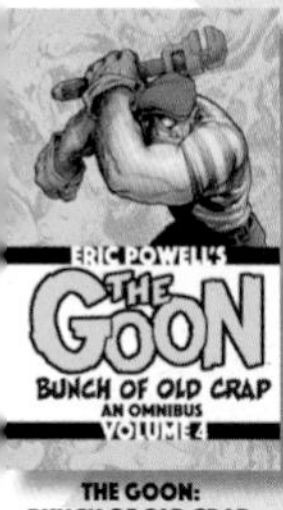

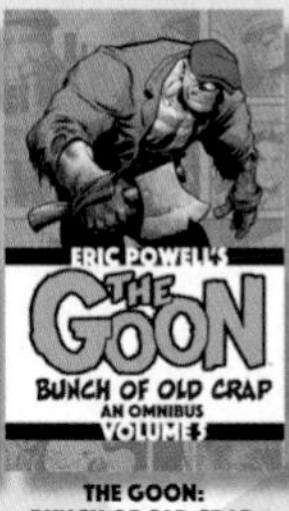

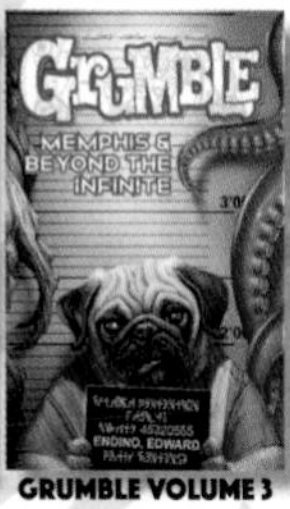

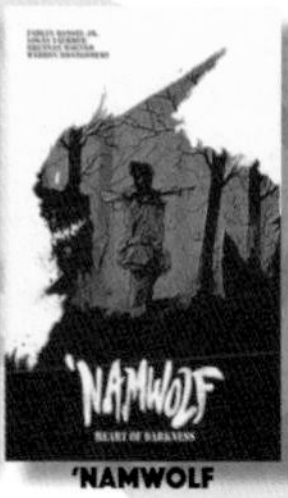

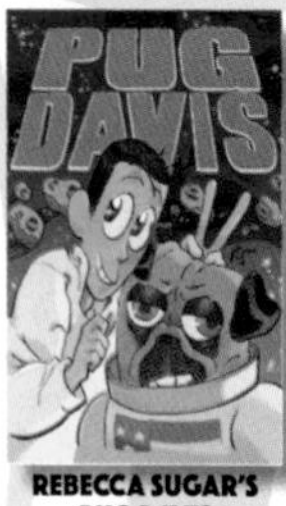

ALBATROSS

FUNNY BOOKS™

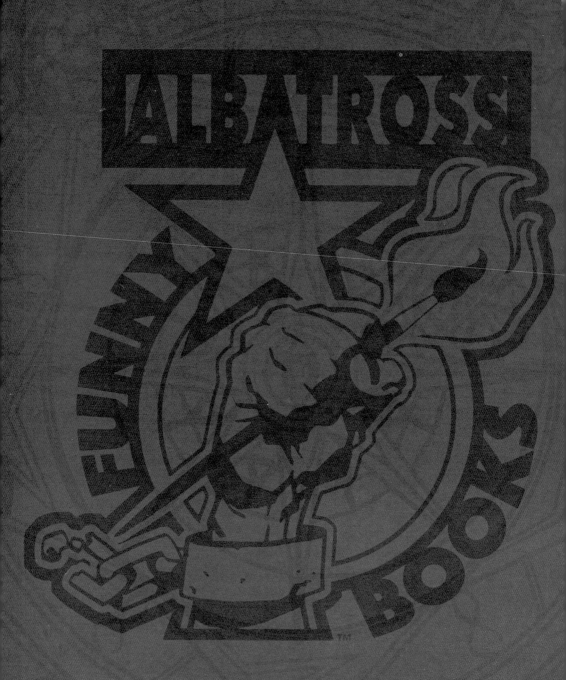